A Passion for Castles

A PASSION FOR CASTLES

THE STORY OF MACGIBBON AND ROSS AND THE CASTLES THEY SURVEYED

JANET BRENNAN-INGLIS

Foreword by David Walker

JOHN DONALD

PREVIOUS SPREAD.
Hatton House, Edinburgh,
from John Slezer's *Theatrum Scotiae*.

First published in Great Britain in 2022 by
John Donald, an imprint of Birlinn Ltd

This paperback edition published 2024

West Newington House
10 Newington Road
Edinburgh
EH9 1QS

ISBN: 978 0 85976 716 3

The author and publisher gratefully acknowledge the
support of the Society of Antiquaries of Scotland
towards the publication of this book.

British Library Cataloguing-in-Publication Data
A catalogue record for this book is available on
request from the British Library

Typeset by Mark Blackadder

Printed and bound in Britain by Bell & Bain Ltd, Glasgow

Contents

Acknowledgements

First and foremost, my grateful thanks go to Professor David Walker for his generosity in lending me his papers and sharing his exhaustive knowledge of MacGibbon and Ross, and much else besides. He has been the kindest of critics, most meticulous proofreader and the friendliest supporter I could have wished for.

For gallantly reading drafts, spotting errors and omissions and offering helpful advice: Richard Agnew, Dr John Brennan (to whom extra special thanks are due for his unstinting support for this project over six long years), Michael Davis, Dr Mavis Donner, Professor Michael Golombok, Dr Fiona McLean, Professor Lesley Milne and Ian Robertson. Any mistakes remaining are mine alone.

For general support and responding to requests for help: Ian Boyter, printer and author; Barbara Brown, genealogist; Jamie Crawford, author; Professor James Stevens Curl, historian and author; Agatha Ann Graves, historian; Carol-Ann Hildersley, Senior Manager of RIAS; Duncan McAra, librarian of the Order of St John; Alison MacDonald of Inch House Community Centre; John MacKenzie, photographer; Frances MacRae, archivist at the Dower House Corstorphine; Bob Marshall, digital artist; Dr Alastair Maxwell-Irving, historian; Dr David Mitchell, Director of Conservation at HES; Gregor Murray, Merchants Company of Edinburgh; Richard Paxman aka Arjayempee, photographer; Ian Riches of the NTS Archives; Ian Robertson, Deacon-Convener of the Trades of Edinburgh; Ken Smyth, artist; Ralph Sutherland, great grandson of Thomas Ross's cousin; Frances Sutton of Garron Communications; Dr David W. Walker, author and historian. The staff of the following institutions: Edinburgh City Libraries, in particular Alison Stoddart; Glasgow Museums and Collections, in particular Mary Anne Meyering; HES Archives, in particular Mindy Lynch; National Galleries Scotland; the National Library of Scotland, in particular Louise Speller; Merchiston School in Edinburgh; the Society of Antiquaries of Scotland, particularly Catherine Aitken and Adela Rauchova; the University of Dundee archives; the University of Glasgow Library. All have been generous with their time and resources, even when we have been unable to meet in person.

Finally, for welcoming me into their castle homes before and during the Covid pandemic: Sir Archibald and Lady Grant of Monymusk; Nicola and John Teal of Castle Leslie; Michael Savage of Harthill; Jamie Raine-Fraser of Wedderlie; Alan and Alison Gibbs of Hills Tower; Scott MacKay and Laura Hudson (and, previously, Peter and Lesley Kormylo) of Abbot's Tower; Tobias Parker and James Cavendish of Buittle.

Editorial Notes

Spelling

Many castle spellings are a nightmare of seemingly random variations: for example, Cumstoun, Cumston, Compstone and Campston; Fa'side, Faside, Falside, Fawside and Fawsyde. I have done my best to be consistent and followed MacGibbon and Ross's spellings when describing their surveys, but otherwise used the generally accepted modern spelling, if there is a difference. There will doubtless be instances when a spelling does not accord with the reader's 'correct' version, for which I apologise. Dismay at variations in spelling is not new. The Reverend Andrew Symson (1638–1712), in his *History of Galloway*, grumbles throughout at the lack of consistent spelling of local names. He was particularly critical of Timothy Pont's maps, in which he found 'the names of places are so very ill spell'd, that although I was very well acquainted with the bounds, yet it was a long time before I could understand the particular places designed in that' (p. 109).

Quotations from *The Castellated and Domestic Architecture of Scotland*

The text is liberally peppered with quotations from the five volumes of MacGibbon and Ross, *The Castellated and Domestic Architecture of Scotland* (1887–1892). These end with a cross-reference to the volume and page number, e.g. '(1: 190)'.

County names

Throughout the text I mainly use the historical (1890) Scottish county names, as used by MacGibbon and Ross, referencing modern council area names where helpful.

Abbreviations

HES	Historic Environment Scotland
NLS	National Library of Scotland
NTS	National Trust for Scotland
RCAHMS	Royal Commission on the Ancient and Historical Monuments of Scotland
RIAS	Royal Incorporation of Architects in Scotland
SPAB	Society for the Protection of Ancient Buildings

Picture Credits

The author and publisher are grateful to the following individuals and organisations for kind permission to reproduce the images listed.

Jo Cound / Drummond Castle Gardens: Drummond Castle and Gardens, Plate 28

Family Tree Magazine – county map of Scotland, Plate 5

Francis Frith Collection: Druminnor Castle, p. 162

Clare Hastings: Crotchet Castle by Osbert Lancaster, p. 133; Fantasy Castle by Osbert Lancaster, p. 218

Glasgow Museums and Collections: Haggs Castle 1855, p. 160; Cardarroch House, p. 135

Historic Environment Scotland (HES): Wester Kames, p. 10; Ashfield Grange, p. 22; Fresco by Jessie MacGibbon, p. 24; Thomas Ross at Trimontium, p. 36; Fordell House, p. 66; Grangepans House, p. 92; Flemington House, p. 99; Granton House, p. 109; Stonebyres Castle, p. 111; Wallyford House, p. 121; Cassencarie interior, p. 125; Midhope Castle interior, p. 137; Aiket Castle 1974, p. 152; Castle of Park, p. 163; Powrie Castle, p. 177; Kinneil Castle (both images), pp. 188 and 189; Lochmaben Castle shelter, p. 208. All of these images are available on the Canmore website: https://canmore.org.uk.

John MacKenzie / The Edinburgh Merchant Company: portrait of Charles MacGibbon, p. 14

Bob Marshall: Lochore Castle model, p. 186

National Galleries Scotland (NGS): Cormiston Towers, p. 13 (Gift of Mrs Ridell in memory of Peter Fletcher Riddell 1985); *Royal Volunteer Review, 7 August 1860* by Samuel Bough, Plate 2 (Presented by Charles T. Combe 1887); *A View of Tantallon Castle with the Bass Rock* by Alexander Nasmyth 1816, Plate 3 (Purchased with the assistance of the Art Fund 1994) (all Creative Commons CC by NC)

National Library of Scotland (NLS): detail of Pont map, p. 42; Stirling Castle by Slezer, p. 43; MacGibbon and Ross at work, p. 57; Haggs Castle by Miss Mildmay, p. 161; Hatton House, pp. ii (detail) and 123

National Trust for Scotland (NTS): Crathes Castle after the fire, p. 127

Richard Paxman: Crosbie Castle, p. 88; Aiket Castle in 2019, pp. 154–55

Royal Incorporation of Architects in Scotland (RIAS): Untitled castle, p. 18; Ardstinchar Castle, p. 114; Costumed Figures, Plate 1; Tantallon Castle by David MacGibbon, Plate 4; Edinburgh Castle with Bryce's Tower, Plate 29

Ken Smyth, artist: portraits of David MacGibbon and Thomas Ross, p. 2

Tate: *Edinburgh Castle: March of the Highlanders* by J.M.W. Turner c. 1834–5, Plate 30 (Bequeathed by R.H. Williamson 1938)

David Walker Junior: Cairnbulg Castle, Plate 20

Wikipedia Creative Commons – Almond Castle, p. 134 (Rob Burke CC BY-SA 2.0); Stirling Head, Plate 16 (Stefan Schaffer, Lich CC BY-SA 3.0)

All images not listed here are the author's own.

PART I

The Men

———

MacGibbon and Ross,
Architects and Scholars

David MacGibbon (1831–1902).

Thomas Ross (1839–1930).

Introduction

In the 1880s two busy Edinburgh architects embarked upon an enormously ambitious project. David MacGibbon and Thomas Ross began to survey, measure and sketch the castles of Scotland, travelling the length and breadth of the country on trains, bicycles and on foot, working at weekends when they could get away from their office. Neither was young and in the middle of the project MacGibbon's life was blighted by both family tragedy and the prospect of financial ruin, but together they produced five lengthy volumes of engagingly written text entitled *The Castellated and Domestic Architecture of Scotland,* illustrated with thousands of accurate sketches and plans. This magisterial work surveyed more than 700 of Scotland's castles and castle-like buildings, ranging from great mediaeval fortresses to little laird's houses with pepper-pot turrets. The combination of breadth and depth, the sweeping scale coupled with scholarly attention to detail, and the construction of a systematic approach to categorising the development of Scottish castellated architecture, along with passionate conservationist campaigning, had never before been attempted and has never yet been surpassed. The scale of their work is monumental; the 2,500 drawings, plans and sketches cover Scotland's castles in minute detail and have frequently been reproduced since their first publication. In addition, the volumes survey town houses, tolbooths, sundials, and some church buildings. It is for this survey that MacGibbon and Ross are best known today; the five volumes are still used by those who share their interest in castles.

The five volumes represent only a part of their scholarly literary output, however. 'While engaged upon their work on *The Castellated and Domestic Architecture of Scotland,* the authors were frequently brought in contact with the various ecclesiastical structures throughout the country, and they naturally availed themselves of such opportunities to make notes and sketches of these interesting edifices' (1: Preface). In 1896–97 the indefatigable pair went on to complete *The Ecclesiastical Architecture of Scotland: From the Earliest Christian Times to the Seventeenth Century* in three volumes. This was yet another large-scale project. MacGibbon and Ross estimated that 'In the 8 volumes already published about 1500 subjects have been described and illustrated by about 4270 figures, the latter consisting of measured plans, sections and elevations with general views and details.'[1] Additionally, both were regular contributors of articles to learned journals on Scottish architectural history and archaeology.

The two men were also working architects

with a successful practice that made its mark upon the cityscape of Victorian Edinburgh and beyond. Buildings such as the Maitland Hotel in Shandwick Place, the former Edinburgh Royal Maternity Hospital at 79 Lauriston Place, Morningside Free Church (now the Baptist Church) and the middle-class houses of Merchiston Gardens and Ravelston Terrace were designed by the MacGibbon and Ross practice. Moreover, both MacGibbon and Ross were immensely productive beyond their established work as architects and authors. David MacGibbon became Lt Colonel of the 2nd Battalion of the Queen's City of Edinburgh Rifle Brigade, as an excellent shot and swordsman. He was also a keen photographer and founding member of the Edinburgh Photographic Club and a widely travelled expert on French ecclesiastical architecture. He became President of the Edinburgh Architectural Association in 1880. Thomas Ross, with few of the birth advantages of MacGibbon, nevertheless achieved much in his long life in addition to his architectural partnership and writing collaboration with David MacGibbon. During the lifetime of David MacGibbon, Thomas Ross was at least partly in the shadow of his senior partner but later became one of the first commissioners of the Royal Commission on the Ancient and Historical Monuments of Scotland (RCAHMS), an active elder of St Giles' Cathedral in Edinburgh, Vice President of the Old Edinburgh Club, Vice President of the Society of Antiquaries of Scotland and a contributor to the National Art Survey of Scotland in the 1920s.

Both David MacGibbon and Thomas Ross had those qualities of inquisitive interest, enthusiasm, attention to detail, commitment, persistence and determination that carry scholars through fruitful research projects. In their architectural practice they were successful businessmen, but they were also passionate and romantic men; they campaigned with passion for heritage, a century

ahead of their time, and they were lured by the romance of castles, in the wake of the Romantic Movement of the eighteenth century. Their lives spanned the Victorian era and typified the earnest industry of the Victorian professional middle and upper classes. Both were awarded honorary doctorates late in life for their contributions to Scottish history: MacGibbon by the University of St Andrews in 1899 and Ross by the University of Edinburgh in 1910. These two men made a great contribution to the life of Victorian Scotland, yet the story of their lives has never been fully told. Their existence has been largely forgotten, save by the many Scottish castle enthusiasts who still regularly consult *The Castellated and Domestic Architecture of Scotland*.

Victorian Scotland

The lives of MacGibbon and Ross reflect many of the attributes we associate with the great figures of the Victorian period: confidence, industry and a pushing back of the boundaries of intellectual exploration and discovery. This was a time of larger-than-life achievements by inventors, engineers, scientists and polymaths. The Western world was in the middle of the second industrial revolution, on the cusp of the widespread use of motor cars, cameras, telegraphs, electric lighting, chromolithographic colour printing, films, cars, flight and X-rays. There were rich seams of literature reflecting Victorian lives; Thomas Ross, later in life, would relate anecdotes about encountering Charles Dickens, Robert Louis Stevenson, Thomas Carlyle and William Thackeray in Edinburgh. The Royal Scottish Academy of Painting, Sculpture and Architecture presided over a lively cultural world – although it never awarded full recognition to David MacGibbon and it only extended a hand to Thomas Ross in his old age.

Queen Victoria's reign (1837–1901) saw great

changes in Scotland. In addition to huge improvements in technology and communication in the middle of the century, rapid population growth meant that MacGibbon and Ross lived through a time of enormous social change. The expansion of the middle classes, in both numbers and wealth, created a high demand for goods and services. The population of Edinburgh almost doubled in both MacGibbon's and Ross's lifetimes. As architects, MacGibbon and Ross were well placed to capitalise on the need for more housing and for homes that displayed the status of their new and wealthy owners. Glendinning and MacKechnie point out that between 1850 and 1914 almost 1,000 new civic, public and religious buildings were constructed in Edinburgh.[2] The second half of the nineteenth century was a time when Scottish architectural landscapes were crowded with great names. The architecture of David Bryce, Walter Newall, David Rhind, Charles Wilson, Alexander Thomson, John Dick Peddie and Charles Kinnear, James Maitland Wardrop, Rowand Anderson, Peter MacGregor Chalmers, Hew Maitland Wardrop, Robert Lorimer, Charles Rennie Mackintosh and many others transformed the cities and towns of Scotland.

Important for the success of *The Castellated and Domestic Architecture of Scotland* was the expansion of print culture, which whetted the appetite of a growing and better-educated audience for information and entertainment. New technology meant more and cheaper books in print, although the price of MacGibbon and Ross's volumes was high. The fervour of historical romanticism whipped up by the novels of Sir Walter Scott at the beginning of the nineteenth century was still a part of popular culture throughout the Victorian period – Waverley Station, opened in Edinburgh in 1846, was named in tribute to Scott – and Scottish castles featured prominently in a number of the Waverley novels. *The Castellated and Domestic Architecture of Scotland* fulfilled a desire for more and better knowledge about these buildings and tapped into the public's taste for Gothic Revival architecture.

Further, the expansion of the railways opened up Scotland, making rural areas accessible to all and allowing MacGibbon and Ross to make excursions to remote castles across Scotland. The railway infrastructure, coupled with an increase in leisure time, also led to the rapid development of the tourism market. By the late eighteenth century, Scotland had already become a destination of choice for European and English cultural devotees, entranced by the romantic epic verses of the blind poet 'Ossian' and the works of Robert Burns and Sir Walter Scott. Then in 1846 Thomas Cook offered the first package holiday to Scotland – an 800-mile round trip of the land of Ossian, Scott and Burns, which was heavily subscribed. When Queen Victoria started to visit Scotland, and in 1855 finally completed the building of Balmoral as her holiday home, the attraction of the Scottish Highlands became irresistible. MacGibbon and Ross's works chimed with the public appetite for information, romance and Highland travel – although they would never have viewed their work in that light.

Edinburgh

In 1883 Alfred Domett, poet and former Prime Minister of New Zealand, visited Edinburgh. His diary entry for 3 May was gushingly enthusiastic:

> At Edinburgh for my first time! A wonderful place with all that a town should have, in compactness and completeness unmatched – a perfect ideal of a city! Romantic site of hill and vale – fine buildings and monuments mediaeval and modern; palace and castle; antiquated gloomy wynds and closes and lofty houses towering up like cliffs, dotted

with windows like loopholes; all teeming with associations, historical, poetical, scientific – national and individual – heroic, tragic, comic, quaint, terrible or humorous; all in their appropriate places, disposed like a scene in a theatre – all as it were within a space to be seen almost at a glance![3]

Earlier in the century, Queen Victoria had also been much impressed. On 3 September 1842 she wrote in her diary: 'There was that beautiful large town, all of stone (no mingled colours of brick to mar it), with the bold Castle on one side, and the Calton Hill on the other, with those high sharp hills of Arthur's Seat and Salisbury Crags towering above all, and making the finest, boldest background imaginable. Albert said he felt sure the Acropolis could not be finer; and I hear they sometimes call Edinburgh "the modern Athens".'[4]

The landscape of nineteenth-century Edinburgh, like many cities of that time, was a combination of confident public architecture and wretched slums, in this case in the Old Town, which housed the poor. The darker side of Edinburgh's buildings was demonstrated in 1861 by the 'Heave Awa' Disaster' when a tenement collapsed between Bailie Fyfe's Close and Paisley Close in the High Street, killing 35 people. The disaster shocked the city, with the terrible event being mentioned from all of Edinburgh's church pulpits the next Sunday. It led eventually to a report in 1865 on the city's sanitation which painted a picture of degradation and high death rates. The report was written by Dr Henry Littlejohn, a public health pioneer who was a close contemporary of MacGibbon and Ross. He attended both Perth Academy, where Ross was a pupil, and the Royal High School, where MacGibbon was a pupil, and would almost certainly have known them both. In 1867 the Edinburgh City Improvement Act, conceived in the wake of Littlejohn's report,

received the Royal assent and initiated the rebuilding of the Old Town. This was overseen by the architects David Cousin (City Superintendent of Works) and John Lessels, whose first apprentice had been David MacGibbon.

However, about the dark side of Edinburgh's civic architecture both MacGibbon and Ross were silent. In terms of their architectural practice, theirs was a world for celebratory public consumption – theatres, churches, monuments, hotels, schools and banks – and private homes for the well-off. In their research and historical writing, despite devoting 21 pages to the architecture of the Royal Mile, including the High Street, in *The Castellated and Domestic Architecture of Scotland* (4: 411–31), with detailed descriptions and sketches of the interiors and exteriors of various houses, they make no mention of the wretched and insanitary living conditions of many of their contemporary inhabitants. The Royal Mile housed both rich and poor; it seems almost wilful of MacGibbon and Ross to have ignored the plight of the latter.

MacGibbon and Ross, Conservationists

Despite its longevity as a working reference, *The Castellated and Domestic Architecture of Scotland*, like any survey, is merely a snapshot in time. Every building described by MacGibbon and Ross has changed over the past 130 years, even if only in relatively minor ways. We think of castles as solid and static, but in reality nothing stands still. MacGibbon and Ross understood the dynamic nature of the history of the buildings they surveyed and demonstrated this in their careful unpicking of the complex built history of such buildings as Glamis Castle and Inchcolm Abbey and in their

OPPOSITE. House of the Knights Hospitaller, Linlithgow, interior of hall, by Thomas Ross. The building was demolished in 1885.

NIGHTS OF
LITHGOW
78.

heartfelt campaigns to save those buildings they saw as under threat. From the very start of *The Castellated and Domestic Architecture of Scotland* they laid out their stall:

> It is greatly to be regretted that most of our ancient edifices are rapidly passing away, either from natural decay or other destructive causes. Even since our sketches were made, many have disappeared either in whole or in part. The neglect with which they are generally treated probably arises, to some extent, from their bearing on the architectural and natural history of Scotland not being sufficiently understood and appreciated. We are not without hope that this work may serve to direct the attention of proprietors and others to the value of our ancient domestic remains, and may thus help to preserve some of them from the decay and demolition which at present threaten speedily to overtake the greater number. Such a result would be most gratifying, not only to us, but to everyone interested in our national history. (1: vii)

Although *The Castellated and Domestic Architecture of Scotland* gave MacGibbon and Ross a platform from which to express their dismay and to campaign about buildings at risk, they were not always successful. The Town Residence of the Knights Hospitallers of St John of Jerusalem, a fifteenth-century town house situated on Linlithgow's High Street and described as 'the finest recorded medieval town house in Scotland',[5] was demolished in 1885 to make way for a new 'undigested Scots revival building',[6] i.e. St Michael's Hotel. 'This took place notwithstanding strong protests from the Antiquarian Society of Scotland and the Glasgow Architectural Association, and we understand that even the Town Council of Linlithgow were aroused by the Vandalism which threatened to sweep away from their good town this unique and important edifice. But all protests were in vain' (1: 508).

Another lost cause was the mansion house in Green Market, Dundee: 'This old mansion-house – one of the most remarkable specimens of a town residence left in Scotland – is about to be taken down. Having braved the storms of three centuries, it has to submit to the rage for so-called modern improvements, which has done so much to destroy the interest of our old towns. This house, with care, might have lasted for centuries to come. It stands in a fine open site, in no way obstructing the traffic, and is the most interesting private house in the town' (5: 68).

MacGibbon and Ross despaired about the destruction in Scottish town centres:

> The ancient buildings of Aberdeen are, like most of our Scottish towns, rapidly disappearing, so that probably before the century finishes most of the towns in Scotland will be possessed of no more interest to the historian and antiquary than the cities of America and Australia which have sprung up during the present generation. Some of them have already achieved this distinction. Perth, which was once famous for its churches and houses, has been swept bare; hardly anything remains in Dumfries or Ayr; and Glasgow, which half a century ago was rich in ancient remains, has lost nearly everything. (5: 77)

Hyperbole, perhaps, but mostly truthful. Sadly, wholesale losses of historic buildings continued in Dumfries, Ayr and Glasgow and most other Scottish towns and cities throughout the twentieth century. MacGibbon and Ross would be terribly saddened.

The campaigns to save the Knights Hospitaller building in Linlithgow in 1885 had been preceded by the setting up of the Society for the Protection of Ancient Buildings (SPAB) by William Morris in 1877. SPAB's manifesto was a purist plea 'to resist all tampering with either the fabric or ornament of the building as it stands; if it has become inconvenient for its present use, to raise another building rather than alter or enlarge the old one; in fine to treat our ancient buildings as monuments of a bygone art, created by bygone manners, that modern art cannot meddle with without destroying.'[7] The context of this ideological entrenchment was Morris's anger at English and Welsh 'restorations' which replaced mediaeval features with Victorian Gothic Revival rebuilding, such as St Albans Cathedral and, in Paris, Viollet-le-Duc's alterations of Notre Dame and La Sainte Chapelle. Despite their conservationist stance, MacGibbon and Ross were admirers of Viollet-le-Duc and were not hardliners in the purist mould of William Morris and John Ruskin, who argued against the very idea of intervention and restoration for historic buildings.

Thomas Ross wrote an impassioned essay, undated, on the subject of restoration.[8] Speaking of the ecclesiastical and castellated buildings of Europe, he highlighted the fraught nature of the debate:

The word Restoration as applied to these buildings is used with various shades of meaning. It is sometimes a term of contempt and sometimes a term of praise with various shades between depending very much on the temperament of the individual. These regard it as preservation of the building and those as the destruction of its interest and beauty. So sharp is this conflict of opinion that many prudent men eschew the word and speak of *preservation* and *repair* when their object is Restoration.

He went on to attack Ruskin's views very directly, advocating the installation of protecting roofs over ruined buildings to avoid 'lingering decay'. Throughout the text of *The Castellated and Domestic Architecture of Scotland*, MacGibbon and Ross make very clear their views on conservation and they used the books to voice their campaigns for the saving and restoration of many specific buildings.

MacGibbon and Ross, the Architects' Practice

Business partnerships are often short-lived. The stress of negotiating roles, balancing relationships and managing financial risk alongside running a profitable business and attracting clients with a partner is too demanding for most in the long term. Partnerships founder on a combination of these factors and sometimes on incompatible personalities. The highly successful Scottish architectural partnership of Burn and Bryce (1844–49) was formally dissolved shortly before 11 July 1850 when Burn wrote to the publisher John Blackwood: 'I have closed my partnership with Bryce it being utterly impossible to go on with him.'[9] It had lasted less than six years. The partnership of Charles Rennie Mackintosh and John Keppie was dissolved in unhappy circumstances in 1914, as were a number of other architectural partnerships.

It is to the credit of both David MacGibbon and Thomas Ross that their creative and business partnership lasted successfully for 30 years, until the death of David MacGibbon. David had already had ten years of working with Thomas before he offered the partnership in 1872, so by then they had had ample time to assess the quality of their relationship and their potential fit as business partners. They were very different in style and personality. Thomas was 'a fine simple old-time Scottish gentleman . . . his sense of humour was unfailing'.[10]

ABOVE. Wester Kames Tower, Bute, before the restoration by Robert Weir Schultz.

OPPOSITE. Wester Kames Tower after restoration.

He was someone who inspired great affection in others. There is little evidence on which to assess David's personality. His obituaries were fewer and more factual; from this, coupled with the fact that he did not manage to break into the country house market as an architect and that he repeatedly failed to gain election to the Royal Scottish Academy, one might infer that he was perhaps not quite as engaging and personable a character as his partner. But David was a very competent architect and an astute businessman, able to take bold commercial decisions and fearless in his ambitious investments – until the Glasgow City Bank crash, that is. He was said to have 'lived and travelled fairly extrava-gantly, being remembered, even in his later years, as a stylish dresser with a taste for richly patterned waistcoats'.[11]

What makes a good architect? Architects need much more than competent draughtsmanship, certainly. Good communication skills are essential, along with business sense, creative artistry and an eye for design and detail. Success involves an element of risk and a degree of luck. A good architect has to be an efficient project manager with excellent social skills and an ability to be persuasive, tactful, authoritative and at least to appear to be willing to listen to the demands of clients. In order to be a partner, especially a junior partner, Thomas

would have to keep his ego in check but still be quietly assertive enough to command respect from his partner and from clients. He managed both demands very well.

It is particularly surprising that the MacGibbon and Ross practice never broke into the castellated country house / castle restoration market: 'Their fame as authors brought in a flood of commissions, some of the greatest promise, which for one reason or another either did not go ahead or were handed on to others to finish.'[12] During the second half of the nineteenth century around 50 Scottish castles and castellated mansions were significantly remodelled and extended and several were restored from ruins or dereliction. When MacGibbon and Ross visited Barcaldine Castle in Perthshire, they reported 'It is now a roofless ruin, and all signs of decoration and comfort have entirely vanished' (3: 620). It was completely restored in 1897 and MacGibbon and Ross may have expected to gain the commission. However, the work was overseen by Alexander Buttar, an architect within the surveying department of the legal practice of Condie & Co. in Perth. Kilcoy Castle, a large tower in Ross and Cromarty, was restored from a roofless ruin and extended by Alexander Ross of Ross and Macbeth in 1890. Both of these projects were major reconstructions of buildings that had been surveyed as ruins by MacGibbon and Ross; other such projects commissioned after publication of *The Castellated and Domestic Architecture of Scotland* and before the death of David MacGibbon include Bavelaw, Borthwick, Cairnbulg, Cessnock, Dalcross, Earlshall, Isle Tower, Sanquhar Castle (never finished after the death of the 3rd Marquess of Bute) and Wester Kames Tower.

Yet no restorations of ruinous castles were overseen by the architectural offices of MacGibbon and Ross. They carried out renovations and made additions to Inch House in 1891 and extended Venlaw Castle (built in 1782 and thus a modern castellated

mansion rather than a 'real' castle) in 1900, when David MacGibbon was too ill to be effectively in charge. Carberry Tower was partially rebuilt and extended by the MacGibbon and Ross practice in 1911, after MacGibbon had died. Also in 1911 plans were commissioned for the restoration of Duart Castle, but the actual work was carried out by Sir John Burnet. MacGibbon and Ross's younger and better known contemporary, Robert Lorimer, whose father's help was acknowledged in the preface to Volume 1 of *The Castellated and Domestic Architecture of Scotland* 'for information in connection with Kellie Castle', seized opportunities to work on castles and country houses, such as Earlshall and Ellary Castle. It is likely that he received commissions because of his skilful social networking (he was friendly with the wealthy Glasgow ship owner William Burrell, among other powerful people), and his engaging personal qualities, although his commissions fell off in later years.

Although MacGibbon and Ross had the highest reputation as architectural historians, as architects their reputation may not have matched the expectations of clients in the castle and country house market. Much of the work the practice carried out for the Merchant Company and other clients consisted of piecemeal alterations and additions. The quality of the buildings they designed from scratch was sometimes great, but overall uneven. The early work of David MacGibbon on the Theatre Royal and on the banks was very good, but the execution of Cormiston Towers in Biggar would probably not have attracted potential clients, being rather clumsy and top-heavy in design. The work MacGibbon and Ross carried out on Inch House near Edinburgh was described damningly in the *Buildings of Scotland* as 'without consistency or outstanding quality'.[13]

Ask any group of architects what the biggest problem is in their work and they will most likely answer 'clients'. There is a space between deference

Cormiston Towers, Biggar, designed by David MacGibbon and photographed by J. McGhie.
The building is now demolished.

and persuasion where client expectations are both excited and managed. Perhaps MacGibbon and Ross's somewhat disappointing performance in terms of prestigious commissions was also due to a lack of will or imagination in filling that space. Or perhaps they just preferred to prioritise energy into their antiquarian research and use the commercial practice for making money out of buildings by whichever means was the easiest.

Although MacGibbon and Ross contributed much to the buildings of Victorian Edinburgh, there is a clear demarcation between MacGibbon and Ross the commercial architects and MacGib-bon and Ross the architectural historians: 'it is as historians that they will always be most affection-ately remembered, no longer young, and tired by the week's work, but still gamely setting out together for the railway stations on Friday evenings equipped with bicycles, weekend bags, maps and drawing boards to get in two full days of measur-ing and sketching before the office reopened again on Monday morning'.[14] Their moving personal stories show the challenges they faced and the hard work and dedication that went into *The Castellated and Domestic Architecture of Scotland* and *The Ecclesiastical Architecture of Scotland*.

I

The Life of David MacGibbon

(1831–1902)

———

Forebears

Like Robert Adam a century before him, David MacGibbon made his entry into a career in architecture from a position of privilege and wealth. And, like William Adam, father of the Adam brothers, David's father Charles made his money from the building trade. Charles MacGibbon (1800–1867) came from a line of builders and was a very successful entrepreneur and a prominent figure in Edinburgh. Charles's father, David (David MacGibbon's grandfather), had founded the successful family building business, David MacGibbon and Son, which built large parts of Edinburgh's New Town in the early nineteenth century, including the north side of London Street and the southern part of Bellevue Crescent. Grandfather David had been a member of the Dean of Guild Court[1] in the 1820s and was an Extraordinary Council Deacon representing the Wrights (joiners) 1824–25. Charles was Dean of Guild in 1861–64 and an Edinburgh Town Councillor 1865–67, convening the Streets and Buildings Committee and sitting on several other council committees. The family business had interests not only in Scotland but also in Wales, where they owned slate quarries, and in Ireland, where Charles was responsible for the building work at Brownlow Hall under the architect William Henry Playfair from 1833 to 1836. On the strength of that work he also gained the contract, worth £8,550 (about £1 million at current rates), for Crom Castle in Ireland, whose architect was Edward Blore.[2] Much of the work on these two enormous houses was carried out concurrently; mustering a reliable workforce, across the Irish Sea, must have involved considerable resources and powers of organisation.

The family lived at 33 East Claremont Street, on the edge of Edinburgh's New Town, half a mile from the centre of the city. In 1830 Charles married Miss Rachel Ritchie, the daughter of another prosperous Edinburgh builder, who resided at 50 India Street, in the parish church of St Cuthbert. In 1838 Charles MacGibbon was admitted as an ordinary member of The Society for the Encouragement of the Useful Arts in Scotland ('useful', that is, as opposed to fine arts – i.e. science, technology, engineering and manufacture), which met twice monthly in the prestigious premises of the Royal Scottish Academy, dedicated to 'the promotion of invention and enterprise'. The following year the society was re-named the Royal Scottish Society

OPPOSITE. Portrait of Charles MacGibbon, father of David MacGibbon.

of Arts and in 1841 was given a Royal Charter. The men admitted at the same time as Charles MacGibbon, who listed his profession as 'builder', paint a fascinating picture of the cross-section of contemporary Edinburgh society – academics, gentry, professionals and skilled craftsmen – who attended the meetings of the Society. They gave their professions as, variously: a Bengal civil servant, a teacher of mathematics, a bookbinder, a merchant, a civil engineer, the deputy inspector-general of hospitals, a painter, an assistant-clerk of Session and a glass-merchant.[3] Later that year His Grace the Duke of Roxburghe was also admitted as an ordinary member, which must have boosted the social profile.

Charles MacGibbon's portrait by an unknown artist hangs on the stairwell of the Merchant's Hall of the Company of Merchants in Edinburgh, donated by his granddaughter Rachel in 1926. Apparently painted posthumously in 1870, the portrait depicts him in 1852–53 as Master of the Merchant Company, a position of considerable influence in the City of Edinburgh. A slightly portly man in late middle age with mutton chop whiskers, he is seated on a red leather chair, wearing a double-breasted silk jacket and cravat, the very essence of respectability.

The Early Years

David MacGibbon was born on 2 April 1831 in St Cuthbert's Parish, Edinburgh, Charles and Rachel's only child. Charles's brother John married Rachel's sister Agnes, making a very close-knit family. Charles and his brother John, who lived in Dundas Street, worked together as close associates in the family building business. John and Agnes MacGibbon had six children, younger cousins for David.[4] At the age of seven, David was sent to boarding school in Lanarkshire, firstly in Kirkmichael. He then attended Stanmore Academy in Lanark, a

boarding school for boys built by Robert and William Lithgow. After Stanmore Academy, David came home to Edinburgh and was sent to the prestigious Royal High School. King George IV had contributed £500 to the fund for a new building, which, as a royal foundation, 'had conferred for ages incalculable benefits on the community'.[5] The building which David attended was erected between 1826 and 1829 as part of Edinburgh's Greek revival Acropolis on Calton Hill. It was designed by Thomas Hamilton, who modelled the portico of the Great Hall on the Hephaisteion at Athens – a most fitting school building for a boy interested in architecture.

School days at the Royal High School, 20 minutes' walk from home, gave David a classical education and a secure foundation in Edinburgh society with a ready network of friends from influential families. The Royal High School was the alma mater of architects Robert Adam, James Fergusson, William Burn and David Bryce. Among other famous alumni were Walter Scott and Alexander Graham Bell, the latter a friend of Thomas Ross. The school had an international reputation, and in the nineteenth century took in many boarders from England and Ireland and overseas. Greek, the basis of the early curriculum, ceased to be a compulsory subject in 1836, and the time allotted to its study was reduced in 1839, just before David attended, as mathematics became recognised as a worthy subject. The curriculum was gradually broadened to include French (1834), German (1845) and science (1848). David would learn fencing at school, where after-hours gymnastics and fencing had been introduced in 1843.[6] He became an accomplished swordsman and, as an excellent shot, a member of the exclusive Scottish Twenty Club. After the Royal High School, in 1846 David went on to the University of Edinburgh, where 'the local gentry and merchant elite often sent their sons for a year or two of classics and

The Royal High School, Edinburgh, in 1829, the school attended by David MacGibbon before he studied at the University of Edinburgh.

philosophy to polish off their general education'.[7] David did not graduate. Graduation was unnecessary in those days for an upper-class young man with the security of a job for life ahead of him. Indeed, 'formal graduation in arts had become rare; it involved extra fees, and in the 1830s there were only half a dozen graduations a year'.[8] Although the Senate tried to encourage graduation by introducing the Bachelor of Arts degree in 1842, just before David started, even by the 1860s the situation had not changed.

In 1849 David left the University of Edinburgh and that year produced some sketches and watercolours of Scottish ancient buildings, showing a developing talent for draughtsmanship.

Until the summer of 1851 he received training in Edinburgh as an apprentice to John Lessels, who had been trained by William Burn and had started a new architectural practice in St Vincent Street. Lessels managed the commissions to reconstruct Cleish Castle in 1846 and, during David's apprenticeship, to design the massive porte-cochère for Stobo Castle. He was also a keen photographer and watercolourist, both interests shared by David. David MacGibbon later wrote fondly of Lessels that 'his ability, together with his perfect honesty and fearless impartiality, had gradually raised him, in spite of many adverse circumstances, to a high position among his fellow citizens . . . his modesty prevented his full merits as an architect from being recognised and appreciated'.[9]

In 1851, after spending some time on an architectural sketching tour in north-east England, David migrated south to London, where he was

Craigneil Castle by David MacGibbon, probably 1849.

The Grand Tour

David was immensely privileged to have his education extended by the experience of the Grand Tour in his early twenties. This coming-of-age ritual of the wealthy young had been a rite of passage since the mid seventeenth century. As Sanderson remarked of Robert Adam's Grand Tour, 'It was the chance of a lifetime to enlarge his artistic experience, to see at first hand the remains of the ancient world . . . and to gain a whole new, authoritarian dimension for the Adam firm's already considerable reputation at home.'[12] Like Robert Adam, David avidly seized the opportunity to gain a rich first-hand understanding of classical architecture. In the summers of 1851 and 1852 he had already travelled on sketching trips in north-east England and also in Coblenz and Frankfurt in Germany. Then in April 1855 he set off on a tour of Europe, mostly in the company of his friend from William Burn's office, Richard Norman Shaw, and latterly with John Thomas Christopher. Over a period of a year he visited at least 40 towns and cities in France, Italy, Germany, Belgium and Bohemia, producing prodigious quantities of sketches of buildings of classical antiquity, the Middle Ages and the Renaissance. He and Christopher exchanged tracings so that each had a full record of what the other had seen. David also painted and sketched locals in picturesque costume.

The Young Architect

After returning from his tour of Europe, David started in practice as an architect in 1856. Although he was to meet with serious setbacks in later years, David MacGibbon began his working life with every advantage. At first, he worked in his father's office in East Claremont Street, until in 1858, at the age of 27, he opened his own office in 89 George Street. With good family contacts and

accepted into the lively Piccadilly office of William Burn to work with several other up-and-coming young architects. David could hardly have had a more thorough and comprehensive training for his articles in architecture. Burn was by then a grand old man of architecture with 30 years' experience – he was said to have been directly influenced by Sir Walter Scott.[10] He ran an office with an impressive output which covered a range of styles and types of public and private buildings.[11]

youthful enthusiasm David was successful in gaining significant commissions for banks, theatres and hotels within the first few years.

In 1860 David succeeded Archibald Scott as the principal architect to the National Bank of Scotland, which had hitherto adopted a make-do and adapt policy to its branch offices. David's instructions appear to have been to give the bank a strongly nationalist image which would markedly differentiate it from the palazzi which John Dick Peddie was building for the Royal Bank and David Rhind for the Commercial Bank. Modelled on the Scots Baronial style of William Burn's country houses, these branch buildings had a dramatic impact on the high streets of the towns where they were situated. They set the tone for many of Peddie and Rhind's later branch offices. Some of David MacGibbon's branches have since been demolished or radically altered, but those at Falkirk and Forfar survive. However, by 1874 he was no longer architect to the bank; it is not known why he lost the commission.

David also became architect to the Edinburgh Merchant Company, where his father had been Master in 1852, replacing David Rhind. The work involved the estate development and feuing business of the George Watson's Hospital estates at Merchiston and Colinton, along with other large estates in Edinburgh and Bathgate. 'Thus MacGibbon, and in time Ross, became responsible for the layout of enormous areas of Edinburgh, even though the architectural control they exercised over them was often slight.'[13] By 1862 David MacGibbon's practice had enlarged beyond his own capabilities. He needed additional help and he saw potential in the young and unpolished architect Thomas Ross, whose background and personality were very different from his own, but who shared a passion for Scottish historical buildings and had skills, knowledge and enthusiasm to offer. He engaged Thomas as his assistant, taking him

into partnership ten years later. In 1862 the first of two theatre commissions came his way: the Alhambra in Nicolson Street, which had a 1,500-seat auditorium with blue and gold ornamentation in the proscenium and gallery fronts, and a 'night sky' ceiling decorated with stars and lit by crystal chandeliers. The second commission, in 1865, was for the New Theatre Royal in Broughton Street and was even more sumptuous and elaborate in its design: 'The fronts of the lower boxes had alto relievos of cupids, that of the dress circle was diapered with acanthus leaves and capped by a cable moulding . . . Richer still was the treatment of the spiral-columned, scrolled and diapered proscenium, which had bowed boxes, the upper tier being carried on life-size figures flanking the lower, and a deep soffit with the Royal arms as its centerpiece.'[14] Both theatres have long since gone, but the drawings for the Theatre Royal remain and show a flamboyant side of David's talent that was little further developed. As can be seen in the illustration overleaf, the exterior was also impressively ornate, with an Italian Renaissance façade.

This was architecture at its most celebratory. Not all of the practice's commissions were so exciting, however. Low-cost tenements in Lothian Road and Grindlay Street took up much of David's time; the MacGibbon and Ross practice was essentially a commercial one, rather than one with a focus on designing elegant buildings. In 1867 the Leith magnate Don R. MacGregor commissioned David to upgrade his Royal Hotel buildings on Princes Street, which established him briefly as a hotel specialist. Within less than ten years, however, the hotel was almost completely rebuilt by W. Hamilton Beattie. The Osborne Hotel, at the junction of Princes Street and Hope Street (demolished in the 1930s to make way for Binns department store) was radically remodelled by the MacGibbon and Ross practice in 1874. In 1869 the Edinburgh builders William and Duncan MacGregor commissioned

The Theatre Royal, Broughton Street, Edinburgh, 1865, designed by David MacGibbon.
It has since been demolished.

a number of housing developments including two large terraces overlooking Bruntsfield Links, still a very desirable Edinburgh location. Business was thriving.

In 1860 David had inherited from his maternal grandfather's estate three valuable houses in Randolph Cliff, a Georgian terrace near Edinburgh city centre with spectacular views over the Water of Leith and the Dean Valley to Fife. The following year he provided a meeting room and library for the Architectural Institute of Scotland in his offices in George Street, carving out for himself a prominent role in the architectural community. He also wrote the architectural entries for *Chambers Encyclopaedia* from 1859 to 1869. David quickly became well established, being clever, talented and ambitious to make his mark upon the Edinburgh architectural world. He applied to be an Associate of the Royal Scottish Academy, the body which set the standard for the arts of painting, sculpture and architecture in Scotland. The most promising artists were elected as Associates in the hope and expectation that they would in time become full Academicians, the apogee of attainment in the world of Scottish arts. Five times he applied; five times he was rejected, even with all of his skills, qualities and advantages. The disappointment at each setback must have been enormously dispiriting and painful, but David was dogged and determined. In spite of the rejections, or perhaps in further pursuit of his goal, he nonetheless in 1880 organised a major exhibition for the Royal Scottish Academy, as the newly elected President of the Edinburgh Architectural Association.

Marriage, Family and Career

In 1865 David married Jessie Vannan Rintoul, the 19-year-old daughter of a wealthy Glasgow merchant, Peter Rintoul of Bothwell Bank. They had five children in the first nine years after their wedding: Jessie (1867), Rachel (1869), Isabella (1870), William Peter (1872) and Alfred Lightly (Fred) (1874). David's father Charles MacGibbon settled the estate of Laggan at Ballantrae on him at the time of his marriage. In addition, Jessie brought a substantial settlement to the marriage, which was put in the hands of trustees.

David MacGibbon has already been compared to Robert Adam in terms of his good fortune at birth, his assured position in the architectural world and his privileged education. Like Robert Adam, David also became a risk-taker.[15] The MacGibbons at first lived comfortably in Edgehill Villa in the Dean Village, near to Edinburgh's New Town. On the edge of their extensive grounds David developed a terrace of houses: Ravelston Terrace. To finance this, and other speculative building, he raised a £20,000 bond on the Laggan estate – over £2 million at today's rates. From the mid 1870s,

Laggan, Ballantrae, David and Jessie MacGibbon's first home.

Ashfield Grange, Grange Loan, Edinburgh: the MacGibbon family home from 1875, now demolished.

David speculated in property development, building much of Learmonth Terrace in the West End of Edinburgh, although the elevations are to John Chesser's design. He purchased houses at 92 George Street and at 131 Princes Street for remodelling as offices, raising further hefty loans. Although the scale of David's investments was enormous and risky, his business was prospering and in 1874–75 he was sufficiently confident to design and build a much larger and grander house for his family at Grange Loan in Edinburgh. However, 'with his indebtedness now at least £37,250, and probably much more, two very large houses with extensive gardens to keep up and a diminishing rental from Laggan as a result of the agricultural depression of 1873 onwards, MacGibbon must have been severely overstretched in servicing his bonds'.[16]

Disaster and Tragedy

Then in 1878 disaster struck: a massive financial calamity that David MacGibbon was very lucky to survive without bankruptcy, though it was no fault of his own. The City of Glasgow Bank (CGB) crashed, due to a combination of highly risky trading in a small number of overseas assets and fraudulent accounting. Liabilities were found to exceed assets by £5.2 million (about £500 million today). The manager and six of the directors were arrested, tried at the High Court in Edinburgh and imprisoned. The collapse of CGB caused a short-lived panic in financial markets, especially among Scottish banks. Although the crash did not cause a major banking crisis in the UK, and most of the Scottish banks recovered quickly, it did have a large impact on the economy of the west of Scotland, with over 500 bankruptcies directly attributable to CGB's liquidation.[17] Shareholders of CGB were exposed to unlimited liability. As a result, the full weight of the crash fell on the 1,819 shareholders of the bank. At the end of the liquidation process only 129 shareholders and 125 shareholder trustees remained solvent. David was caught up in the crash, not as a result of his own poor investment, but that of his late Uncle John, who had held shares in the City of Glasgow Bank. David's younger cousins, John and James MacGibbon, had inherited shares worth £750 each. The first call by creditors came in at 500%, which meant finding £3,750 each (approximately £435,000 at today's rates). The MacGibbon family slate quarries in Wales were sold to finance this, but when a further call came in at 2,250%, or £16,875 each, David began to sell his own property. Both his homes at Laggan and

Ashfield Grange were sold, in 1881 and 1882, in a remarkably selfless gesture of family solidarity. Jessie's marriage settlement saved the George Street office and eventually bought them another family home in Learmonth Terrace. The family and the practice were thus plunged into years of financial uncertainty. Nevertheless, David ploughed on with business as usual in his professional life, although he turned his back on property speculation from then on.

Much worse was to come for the MacGibbon family. While on their summer holiday at their country residence of Tomdhu in the Highland village of Kincraig in 1884, a tragic event occurred. On 30 July *The Scotsman* printed a fatal accident report from Kingussie:

> Yesterday afternoon, about four o'clock, a melancholy accident happened to a boy and girl, son and daughter of Mr MacGibbon, Edinburgh, who were in search of swallows' eggs in a sandbank to the east of the Parish Manse. The children were accompanied by a man-servant, and had a ladder placed against the bank. The boy, who was about thirteen years of age, was on the ladder when, without any warning, the whole face of the embankment gave way, burying the party in the fallen dunes. The little girl fortunately had her head above the sand, but the boy was covered up, there being about ten tons of sand above him. As soon as the alarm could be given a number of people gathered to give assistance; but fully twenty minutes had elapsed before the body was recovered. He was quite dead.[18]

Behind this brief newspaper report is the reality of a family bereaved by the sudden and shocking death of a child, the beloved older son, William Peter. One can only imagine the grief of David

Alleluia: for the Lord God Omnipotent reigneth.

and Jessie and their three daughters, Isabella, Jessie and Rachel and surviving son, Fred. Rachel was the little girl who had her head above the sand and survived, but her lungs were damaged and she was left with permanent hearing loss. Her younger sister, Isabella, already had hearing loss.

Fred was now the precious only son. It is telling that he was sent to school for only one year, to Edinburgh Academy in 1890, and surely no coincidence that his father was commissioned that year to build new laboratories in the Academy school grounds. For the rest of his education Fred was privately tutored. He shared his father's antiquarian interests and most probably helped with *The Castellated and Domestic Architecture of Scotland* from 1891 to 1893. He became an accomplished draughtsman, his precocious studies of Iona being published in *The Builder* in April 1893. Fred lived at home until his father's death in 1902, then left his mother and sisters in Learmonth Terrace for a bachelor flat in India Street, where his grandmother had lived, 15 minutes' walk away. When Fred married Alice Christian Sainsbury in 1906, he moved to Lynedoch Place, nearer to his mother and to the city centre.

After William Peter's death in 1884, the Learmonth Terrace house was closed up and the family spent a great deal of time in the French Riviera over the following months to aid Rachel's recovery, leaving Thomas Ross in charge of the Edinburgh office. During their time in France, David produced *The Architecture of Provence and the Riviera* in 1888. The volume is almost 500 pages long, with 284 detailed sketches of Roman arches and amphitheatres and mediaeval churches and cloisters, all backed with clear and careful explanatory text and prefaced by a lengthy history of the mediaeval social and political infrastructure of the region. This

mammoth task was achieved midway between Volumes 1 and 2 of *The Castellated and Domestic Architecture of Scotland*. David sketched buildings throughout Provence in Arles, Vallon, Frejus, Avignon, Monaco and Menton. He absorbed himself in the work of sketching and interpretation during the months after the funeral of his elder son. To have achieved so much so quickly at the best of times would be a splendid achievement; to have done so in the teeth of tragedy is quite astonishing.

David's last significant publication was *The Five Great Churches of Galloway*, published by the Ayrshire and Galloway Archaeological Association in 1899.[19] From 1897 David had been in poor health with a heart condition and in 1899 was unable to attend the ceremony when the University of St Andrews conferred on him the honorary degree of Doctor of Laws. In 1901 he had to resign from the Merchant Company on medical advice, being unfit to attend meetings. He died on 20 February 1902, aged 70, leaving moveable estate of £22,688; this was a very substantial sum at the time, although his total wealth was much less than it had been when he inherited from his father. He is buried in the north-west section of the nineteenth-century northern extension to Dean Cemetery in western Edinburgh. His gravestone is small and modest and has been moved back to rest against the much larger gravestone of his wife Jessie.

David's wife Jessie survived him until 1926. Four of her five children had predeceased her: William Peter died in 1884; Fred, who had followed his father into a career in architecture and succeeded him in the MacGibbon and Ross practice, died of diabetes in 1915; daughters Jessie and Isabella, both of whom were artists, died in 1918 and 1924. Jessie was an accomplished painter; her elegant Arts and Crafts fresco of three angels can be seen in the apse of the tiny Hoselaw Chapel in the Borders. Rachel MacGibbon died in 1931 at the age of 62; like her sisters, she had never married.

OPPOSITE. Fresco by Jessie MacGibbon, Hoselaw Chapel, Kelso, Scottish Borders.

PETRVS·HAY·
AEDIFICIVM·FXS=
TRVXIT·AN: 1575

2

The Life of Thomas Ross

(1839–1930)

———

Unlike his partner David MacGibbon, the only child of very wealthy parents, Thomas Ross – Tom, to his father – was one of 12 children, the son of Thomas Ross (1809–1884), a prosperous tenant farmer, and his wife Ann Murray (1812–1883). He was born on 24 November 1839 in the parish of Errol, the fourth child, between two sisters, Margaret and Helen. The family home was Wardheads Farm, in the fertile agricultural countryside of Carse of Gowrie in Perthshire. It was owned by the Drummonds of Megginch Castle. In about 1844, when the lease ran out, the family moved to Bachilton, a 700-acre farm close by. Megginch Castle must have been well known to Thomas, as it was very close to the farm where he lived. Did this connection prompt an early interest in castellated architecture?

Perthshire is a castle-rich county and within a few miles of Wardheads Farm are Evelick Castle, Fingask Castle, Kinnaird Castle, Balhousie Castle, Pitheavlis Castle and Huntingtower Castle. Evidence of prehistory, too, is also all around: within five miles are several stone circles, brochs, cairns and hill forts. In addition to his research into castles, Thomas became a keen archaeologist and an authority on early history in his later years.

Forebears

Thomas Ross Snr was not just a tenant farmer. He was educated and ambitious, and used his farming knowledge and skills to increase his income and provide for his large family. Despite having had to lose lengthy chunks of school attendance every year to help out at harvest on his father's farm, he recorded that,

> (A)s time wore on I was advanced to go to the schools in Perth. For one year I attended arithmetic, writing and drawing etc. The second year and third I attended the Perth Academy and was for both years regularly Second Dux . . . After this I was for a good part of three seasons in the Tax Office in Perth under Mr. Blair, Surveyor and Collector there and I got a great part of my learning as to business, almost daily handling money, and carrying it to the Bank, etc.

OPPOSITE. Megginch Castle, Perthshire, sketched by Thomas Ross in 1879. The castle was close to the farm where he lived as a child and may have sparked his interest in castellated architecture.

which I have found through life most bene-
ficial. After this I came home and stuck close
to work at Elliothead until I went to Oil
Mill.[1]

Thomas Snr never knew his mother: 'My dear
Mother who departed this life very shortly after I
was born and of whom I can only state what every
friend has over and over again told me: she was a
woman of deep and heartfelt piety having been
brought up by pious and God-fearing parents, and
after her marriage enjoyed the blessing of a Home
where the worship of God was daily observed.'
His father re-married and had a second family of
two boys and a girl. The older son, Peter, was
clearly favoured over Thomas – the cause of some
resentment and a desire for one-upmanship:

As soon as Peter was able to manage my
Father took the Farm of Kingdom in the
Carse of Gowrie for my second brother
Peter while I still lived at Oil Mill, a married
man and two dear girls. I did not like the
idea of my younger brother having a
holding twice as large as mine and more.
Although the Mill had paid me, the machin-
ery of the Mill was fast getting quite done
and unworkable so I was at once on the
lookout for another and larger farm and,
strange enough, the farm of Wardheads on
the Megginch Estate adjoining Peter's farm
came into the market. I with my Father-in-
law, Mr Murray, and another friend crossed
the Tay and looked over it. I offered and
was accepted which was a surprise to every
friend I had. My Father not excepted.[2]

From then on Thomas Snr embarked upon a series
of ambitious moves to better his position, perhaps
propelled by a chip on his shoulder at his father's
unfair treatment. He became a Public Salesman

(auctioneer) and, as a result of work he successfully
completed for Captain Hay, was offered the position of Land Steward for the Estate of Leys and
subsequently for the Estates of Mugdrum, Carpow
and Randerston. When the lease for Wardheads
was due up, the factor encouraged him to bid for
the lease of Bachilton Farm, at 700 acres one of
the largest arable farms in Perthshire. He farmed
the land successfully for many years, but in 1883
wrote to his son Thomas 'the past ten bad and
miserable seasons have been most ruinous and
eaten up all profits made before but here we are
plodding on still expecting every year would turn
the tide but the latter end is to all appearance worse
than the beginning'.

The letter of 1883, written not long before his
death at the age of 75, enclosed two 'memoranda'
detailing his family and his early life and struggles
as a farmer, which his son Thomas had requested.
It also contained complaints about spectacular tight-
fistedness and some ruinous profligacy on the part
of various family members. Thomas Snr painted
a picture of constant change in his rural community: 'there is not now occupying any of these
farms, a length of ten or twelve miles, one single
solitary farmer, not even the son of any of those I
can remember as the Tenants all along that distance.
Taking the River Earn and all up to the Hill of
Moncrieff, Duplin, etc. of these farms many have
changed Tenants, four, five or even six tenants.' At
the end of his letter is a mundane domestic
postscript: 'A bag of potatoes sent today by rail.'

The railway had come to the village of Errol
when Thomas Jnr was eight years old, the station
only a couple of miles from Wardheads Farm.
Later, Thomas would tell the story of how 'the
scholars of Errol got a holiday when the first
railway engine steamed from Dundee into the
village'.[3] Errol station was halfway on the line
between Perth and Dundee, so Thomas and his
family would have been able to travel directly from

the local village to those cities and onwards to Glasgow, Stirling and Edinburgh relatively easily. He must have been drawn to the excitement of those metropolises, away from the sleepy Perthshire countryside.

A Career in Architecture

The majority of Victorian architects came from a background of privilege, like David MacGibbon, with fathers who were either themselves architects or from the landed or professional classes. Indeed, both David MacGibbon and Thomas Ross had sons who became successful architects in their turn. The professions had – and still have – a corporate solidarity which brings access to power and to influential patrons. Thomas Ross, a farmer's son, was not an obvious candidate for the professional life, but he did have an uncle by marriage – David Salmond, Aunt Isabella's husband – who was an architect in Dundee and may have given encouragement to his wife's nephew. When the parish school at Errol in Perthshire was visited by a travelling drawing master, it was noticed that Thomas displayed an early talent for drawing. Perhaps a schoolteacher or family member suggested to him the possibility of a career in architecture and as a result, after secondary schooling at Perth Academy, he was fortunate to gain a position as an apprentice in the office of Alexander Kirkland in 1856. Kirkland was a prominent Glasgow architect and had been responsible for the developments of Bothwell Street, Bothwell Circus, St Vincent Crescent, Minerva Street and Corunna Street. However, at the end of 1861 Kirkland withdrew from his Glasgow practice, perhaps as a result of a lawsuit, and moved to London to practise as a civil engineer.

As a result of Kirkland's move to London, in 1861 Thomas transferred to the much busier office of Charles Wilson and worked there as an assistant.

Charles Wilson had been responsible for the design of the Glasgow Royal Asylum for Lunatics and for building Lews Castle in Stornoway and was at that time completing the great campanile of the Free Church College on Woodlands Hill in Glasgow. In Wilson's office, Thomas met his hero, Alexander 'Greek' Thomson, visionary architect of many of Glasgow's public buildings, including St Vincent Street United Presbyterian Church and the Egyptian Halls on Union Street. Thomas would also have met John Thomas Rochead (1814–1878), a former apprentice of David Bryce. Rochead had been successful in several architectural competitions, including the Stirling Wallace Monument competition, and subsequently offered his own measured-drawing prize. Thomas won the Rochead prize for a set of drawings of Glasgow Cathedral while working in the practice of Charles Wilson. Perhaps he was inspired by the elegant drawings of the soaring interior of Glasgow Cathedral published by R.W. Billings in *The Baronial and Ecclesiastical Antiquities of Scotland*.

Billings would have been a source of awed admiration for any early career architect of the time, although later, in *The Castellated and Domestic Architecture of Scotland*, MacGibbon and Ross forthrightly criticised the text of Billings's books. Thomas may not have had access to the Grand Tour, but he was able, with his prize money, to set off on a study trip to Yorkshire, where he visited the great mediaeval abbeys of Fountains and Selby and Ripon Cathedral, producing sketches of them.

Charles Wilson was already in failing health by 1861, when Thomas joined his firm. By 1862 Wilson was no longer effectively in charge of his office. That year, Thomas transferred to David MacGibbon's office in Edinburgh. His credentials as a Rochead prizewinner and his experience in two of Glasgow's most prominent architectural offices made him a good prospect for David MacGibbon. From Thomas's viewpoint, the offer

of an assistant's job from a highly successful up-and-coming Edinburgh architect, a Fellow of the Society of Antiquaries of Scotland with a reputation as an enthusiastic antiquarian, was a wonderful opportunity.

Glasgow and Edinburgh have always been rival cities with very different characters. Glasgow was then, as now, much bigger and more populous. It was a city that had benefited from advances in industrial technology, capitalised upon by members of the merchant class who had earlier made their fortunes in the slave and tobacco trades. Its architectural development was exciting, but the buildings were window dressing for an essentially industrial and commercial city. Edinburgh was not only the city of law, printing and publishing and banking, it was also, by contrast to Glasgow, the centre of history and culture, epitomised by the massive monument on Princes Street to Scotland's historical novelist, Sir Walter Scott, and the Royal Scottish Academy building at the foot of the Mound. The visitor to Edinburgh, arriving at Waverley Station, would see at a glance the imposing architectural landscape of central Edinburgh: the Scott Monument, the Castle, the Royal Scottish Academy, the distinctive crown steeple of St Giles' Cathedral peeping up behind the turreted tenements and shops of Cockburn Street, David Bryce's magnificent Bank of Scotland building and the Greek revivalist monuments on Calton Hill, under which sat Robert Adam's imposing Bridewell Prison (mentioned in Queen Victoria's diary but demolished 1884), his only use of the castle style for a public building. Edinburgh had a much larger professional class per head of population than Glasgow; but although David MacGibbon was an Edinburgh resident through and through, he had 'more of the manner of a wealthy Glasgow merchant than an Edinburgh professional man'.[4]

Thomas Ross might just qualify as that powerful icon of social mobility, the 'lad o' pairts' – a quasi-mythical term for a talented young Scot who is able to transcend his origins through cleverness, hard work and access to an open educational system. Although there was some degree of social mobility, it was relatively unusual in the mid nineteenth century for a boy to rise from rural obscurity to the professional heights achieved by Thomas. We should not underestimate his determination, hard work and ability.

When Thomas was a young man just out of his teens in 1859, three significant books of ideas were published: *On Liberty* by John Stuart Mill, *On the Origin of Species* by Charles Darwin and *Self-Help* by Samuel Smiles. The first two remain the best known, but it was the last that sold by far the most in its time, at over a quarter of a million copies in the nineteenth century – including a copy bought by Charles Darwin. Smiles was a Lowland Scots Calvinist who set out to tell people, in the first modern behavioural improvement guide, that the two things needed for success in life are morality and hard work. Smiles argued that individuals were responsible for their own future through hard work, energy, perseverance, thrift, prudence and self-reliance. Perhaps Thomas had a copy of *Self-Help*; he was exactly the kind of young man that the anti-establishment and rather subversive Smiles aimed his book at. Given the book's celebrity it is very likely that he would at least have been exposed to its ideas.

Thomas was present at the Edinburgh Royal Volunteer Review in 1860, the defining social event of the year, when only 21 years old. Despite the alliance between Britain and France during the Crimean War of 1854–56, a renewed fear of invasion by the French caused much concern about Britain's defensive capability. This surged dramat-

OPPOSITE. The Lady Chapel in Glasgow Cathedral, sketch by Robert Billings, 1847.

ically in April 1859 following the outbreak of war between France and Austria, with a growing newspaper scare campaign supporting the creation of a volunteer military corps. The Government quickly realised that the establishment of a volunteer force would not only satisfy the public advocates of the movement and reduce the clamour of the press, but would also cost the state very little and possibly prove to be of short-term benefit. On 12 May 1859 the War Office sanctioned the formation of the Volunteer Corps, which grew quickly. On 23 June 1860 Queen Victoria reviewed the Volunteer Rifle Corps in Hyde Park and on 7 August she went to Edinburgh and inspected the regiments of 22,000 Scottish volunteers, presented in an impressive parade of loyalty. Thomas Ross is listed on the Muster Roll of the programme of volunteers under the Edinburgh City 1st Brigade, 1st Battalion of Artillery.[5] Being a volunteer brought opportunities for useful social contacts and positioned him as a patriotic player in the defence of the country. Thomas's future employer and partner, David MacGibbon, was also present at the Edinburgh Review, as Captain of the 14th Company of Edinburgh City Rifles.

Thomas inspired affection in all those who knew him. He had a tremendous appetite for work and was always encouraging to others. 'His time, learning, professional skill, even his architectural books and drawings were at the disposal of those who sought them. Nothing impressed his friends more than his generous enthusiasm for the work of others.'[6] Thomas had a great personal friend in Alexander (Alick) Graham Bell, who was a distant relation, and, like David MacGibbon, a pupil at the Royal High School.

Thomas was not only interested in Scottish history, but also his own genealogy. At the time of his mother's death in 1883 he had asked his father to write down an account of family history, which he did, in great detail – and just in time, for Thomas

Ross Snr died within the year. A few years later, in 1888, Thomas wrote to his father's sister, Aunt Isabella, asking for details of his family. She was then 84 years old, but she also replied to him at some length, particularly about the genealogy of the Ross family, with an impressive attempt to link the family's Ross forebears, via Culloden, to the Clan Ross of Ross-shire. In the 1960s Thomas's daughter, Ella, when she was 95, wrote her memories of her maternal grandfather, James MacLaren. There is thus considerably more documentary evidence about the personal, professional and family life of Thomas Ross than of his partner, David MacGibbon.

Marriage and Family

In 1869 Thomas married Mary MacLaren (born 1838) in Edinburgh. They started married life in Thomas's flat at 14 East Claremont Street, close to the former home and offices of David's father, Charles MacGibbon. Thomas and Mary were married in the house of her father, James MacLaren, at 10 Hamilton Place, Stockbridge, Edinburgh. James (born c.1809) ran a school next door at number 12, and it was there that Thomas and Mary's children were educated, by their grandfather and Uncle James, before the boys were sent on to the Edinburgh Academy, five minutes' walk from home, and the girls to a private girls' school. Thomas and Mary had two daughters, Johanna Caird (Anna) (1872) and Elizabeth Hume (Ella) (1871), and two sons, one of whom also became an architect (James MacLaren Ross, 1878–1944) and the other (Thomas Arthur Ross 1875–1941) a distinguished doctor. The two sons died in the 1940s, but the daughters lived until the 1960s, both unmarried.

When Ella was 95 her account of the history of her maternal grandfather was published. In the 1880s James Maclaren, 'for long a widower' (his wife Elizabeth MacLaren, née Barnet, died in 1863 aged 53), 'was beginning to grow old, and his house was not so comfortable as it once was . . . so my parents decided to leave their flat in East Claremont Street and come, bag and baggage, to ten Hamilton Place and look for a house to take their own family and my grandfather and Uncle James which they eventually did. My grandfather died in my father's house.'[7] The house which they found was in Saxe Coburg Place, a short walk from Hamilton Place, an elegant terrace within the village of Stockbridge, but also close to the centre of Edinburgh. It was designed and built by Adam Ogilvie Turnbull between 1828 and 1834. The Ross family had moved there by 1885 and Thomas, Mary and their two daughters lived there for the rest of their lives.

Like his father, James MacLaren Ross was a high-achieving student. He studied at the Edinburgh College of Art and the Architectural Association, where he won the Essay Medal in 1900, his essay being published as 'The Life and Work of Sir William Chambers' in 'AA Notes' in 1901. He won the Design Medal in 1902 and was appointed the Association's librarian. James established a good domestic practice with commissions as far away as Vancouver, Canada, but this was interrupted by war service as a lieutenant in the Royal Engineers, during which he was awarded the Military Cross at Cambrai in 1915. The same year, James married Cecilia Mary Neill, a jeweller's daughter, at St Giles' Cathedral, where Thomas was an elder. During the Second World War, James's architectural practice worked on air raid shelters, factories and the restoration of business premises damaged by enemy action. He died, aged 65, in 1944.

Thomas's other son, Thomas Arthur Ross (1875–1941), had a distinguished career as a doctor of psychiatry, serving on BMA committees, writing medical textbooks and becoming a Fellow of the

Royal Colleges of Physicians in both Edinburgh and London. In 1919 he was appointed the first medical director of the Cassel Hospital for Functional Nervous Disorders at Swaylands, Kent. In 1927 Thomas Arthur Ross wrote to his cousin, John Sutherland, who had emigrated to New Zealand and had got in touch unexpectedly to ask advice about how his daughter Helen could gain a position as a nurse in London. After giving some helpful advice about nursing Thomas Arthur went on to say:

You will like to know something of me. My parents are still alive and vigorous. Their address is 14 Saxe Coburg Place, Edinburgh. The old man is very famous. He is the authority in Scotland on all antiquities and was made an L.L.D. of the University of Edinburgh. I shall send him your letter. My sisters are unmarried and live with them. James is an architect in London, married but with no children.

Now for myself. I have been lucky with this world in goods but have otherwise had some bad blows too. My wife died in 1917: I had two children, a boy and a girl. The boy died last November aged 23. He was a splendid person and a very dear friend of mine. He was a Medical student and a very good one and was just about to qualify. I miss him more than I can say. I think everyone who knew him loved him. The girl is 20 she is very sweet to me but I do not see a great deal of her, as she is a student at Oxford. What she is going to make of it I do not know. She is clever and attractive. So I live mostly alone, but I have some very good dear friends and I often go to London to medical meetings: I can get to the places I want there in an hour and a half. I often go up when the days [sic] work is done. This hospital is a special one for nervous people a thing I have specialized in more or less from the beginning. I do hope this letter will be of some use to you.[8]

The tragic death of a promising young son and grandson would have hit Thomas Arthur and his parents hard. Twelve years later, in 1939, Thomas Arthur married again, this time to a woman who had become something of a celebrity. Norah Cecil Hasluck, widow of the wealthy sugar broker Julius Joseph Runge, had been a Member of Parliament with an interesting political career until 1935, when she lost her seat within a couple of weeks of the death of her husband. She lived until the age of 93, but Thomas Arthur died only a couple of years after marrying her, at the age of 66. His daughter Jean, who had been at Oxford, became a doctor, working first at Maudsley Hospital and then at Swaylands Hospital like her father. She married Theodore V.S. Durrant. 'She had immense charm; one was instantly aware that she had extraordinary intelligence.'[9]

After MacGibbon

Thomas Ross had been a faithful and hard-working partner in the MacGibbon and Ross firm and enthusiastic co-author of the architectural history books; he probably contributed more than his fair share to the joint ventures. But he was always the junior partner, in fact if not in name. David MacGibbon brought the money, the connections, the commissions and the experience of wide overseas travel to the partnership. He also had the advantage of seniority, being almost nine years the elder. Thomas Ross brought skilled draughtsmanship, erudition, a willingness to work hard, and ambition coupled with an accommodating nature. It was only after the death of David MacGibbon in 1902 that Thomas shone in his own right, as a

historian and member of the Edinburgh antiquarian establishment. For the first few years after David's death he continued in partnership with Fred MacGibbon, David's son, who had been articled to the practice at the same time as Thomas's son James in 1894. James had moved to London in 1899 in order to gain wider experience and Fred had moved to the Edinburgh office of Robert Rowand Anderson, a particular friend of his father, to complete his articles between 1896 and 1899. In 1914 the MacGibbon and Ross practice, which had been in decline for some years, effectively ceased to exist when Fred had to resign because of ill health caused by diabetes. He died the next year, aged only 40, ironically at the MacGibbon country residence of Tomdhu in Kincraig, where his older brother William Peter had died in a tragic accident 30 years earlier. Fred was survived by two young sons, touchingly named David and Thomas, a two-year-old daughter, Helen, and his English wife, Alice, who took the children to live in England after her husband's death.

In 1902 Thomas was appointed by the Board of Trustees of Iona Cathedral jointly with John Honeyman – who had been a colleague of David MacGibbon in William Burn's London office half a century previously – to carry out the restoration of the choir and transepts. Thomas's was the greater contribution, as Honeyman's sight had failed; his role must by then have been primarily his knowledge of the building that he had surveyed with Mackintosh and McNair's help in the 1890s.

In 1906 the Earl of Leven left £40,000 for the rebuilding of the nave of Holyrood Abbey as a chapel for the Knights of the Thistle, specifying Thomas Ross as architect. However, Professor Lethaby advised that the surviving walls were not strong enough to support a new vault and roof, and St Giles' was chosen instead for the chapel.[10] King Edward VII appointed Thomas to the Board of Trustees responsible for overseeing the construction.

The trustees appointed Robert Lorimer as the architect and he was knighted by George V for his work on the chapel in 1911. There is a fine line drawing by Thomas Ross entitled 'Proposed Chapel of Knights of the Thistle, St Giles' Cathedral' in the Edinburgh Libraries Collection (item 12102) dated 1905. There are similarities to the Lorimer plan; it is not known whether Thomas sketched this in anticipation of being invited to draw up plans.

In 1908 Thomas Ross was appointed a founder member of the Royal Commission on the Ancient and Historic Monuments of Scotland (RCAHMS), and threw himself into its activities with great enthusiasm, writing detailed and lengthy reports for them. His report on Ardrossan Castle ran to six and a half foolscap pages (MS 686). Two years later the Commission appointed Fred MacGibbon their architect, at a salary of £200 per annum for three-quarters of his time, a measure of the degree to which the MacGibbon and Ross practice had declined. The early twentieth century was a period when many architectural practices in Scotland were short of work due to economic constraints and a lack of credit facilities. The effects were compounded by the 'People's Budgets' of 1909 and 1910, which introduced unprecedented taxes on the lands and incomes of Britain's wealthy to fund new social welfare programmes. Thomas also edited, along with Robert Rowand Anderson and William T. Oldrieve, *Examples of Scottish Architecture from the 12th to the 17th Century: A Series of Reproductions from the National Art Survey Drawings*, published in four volumes by Waterston between 1921 and 1933.

During the First World War, when suspicions about enemy spying were high, Thomas, aged 76, was involved in a slightly comic episode:

EDINBURGH ARTIST FINED AT CUPAR.
Thomas Ross, architect, 6 Coburg Place Edinburgh, appeared before Sheriff Armour Hannay at Cupar yesterday, charged with having made a sketch at Burntisland tidal harbour, the Firth of Forth and the vessels lying in the harbour. The Fiscal said accused was a very respectable man, and there was no suggestion that he had made the sketch with any ulterior motive. He seemed to have a great fancy for sketching old castles.[11]

Thomas had been sketching Rossend Castle, with the harbour in the foreground, and although he claimed in court that his sketch was not an architectural drawing, he asked that it be returned to him, 'as some of the details were of value to the Royal Society for the Preservation of Ancient Monuments [sic]'. The Sheriff said that 'he had seen that the German aviators flying over the Gulf of Finland had been much aided by sketches which the Kaiser had made when on a visit to the Czar'. However, after imposing a fine of five shillings, he directed that the sketch should be returned to the accused.

Thomas became Vice President of the Old Edinburgh Club in 1916. That summer he led two heavily subscribed members' visits, to Ravelston House and Gardens and to Craigcrook Castle and Gardens. Both are described and illustrated in Volume 4 of the *Book of the Old Edinburgh Club* and were also extensively surveyed for *The Castellated and Domestic Architecture of Scotland*.

In 1918 the Royal Scottish Academy elected Thomas Honorary Academician and Professor of Antiquities. He was continually busy with research, visiting archaeological digs across the country and writing up his findings. Between 1889 and 1918 he authored 11 articles for the Proceedings of the Society of Antiquaries of Scotland, reporting on excavations in Argyllshire, Perthshire and Dunbartonshire, and describing sculptures, statues and paintings of interest. He took a physically active role on sites of interest:

ABOVE. Thomas Ross visiting the Roman fort excavations at Newstead ('Trimontium') near Melrose in 1906.

OPPOSITE. The statue of Edward VII outside the Palace of Holyroodhouse, Edinburgh. Thomas Ross campaigned vigorously against the erection of the high wall behind the monument, without success.

From the end of February till the end of August 1901 I visited Inchtuthil almost every Saturday, or sent an assistant (Mr. G.W. Tod) for the purpose of taking measurements of the work as disclosed by the workmen, and before they restored the ground to its natural condition by filling in the excavated soil.[12]

One of Thomas's last commissions was working on 3–11 Abbey Strand, the building at the foot of the Canongate just outside the precincts of the Palace of Holyrood. He restored the original roofline with a dormered attic in 1916. At this time, plans were being made to erect a monument to Edward VII outside the Palace. In Thomas's papers, in shaky handwriting which descends into near-illegibility as the writer becomes increasingly agitated, is a letter, presumably intended for *The Scotsman*, about the view from Abbey Strand being spoiled by the wall of the monument:

we are to get a high wall which will entirely block the view so long enjoyed as one of the charms of the house . . . This is the compensation to be given for the loss of a view of exquisite beauty extending for some hundreds of feet. This dismal lane between high walls will be nothing less than a public nuisance. Then there are the useless high pillars and iron gates encumbering a street already too narrow. . . . A model of this part of the memorial was erected on the ground when representation from the Royal S.A. the Cockburn Society, the Architects Association, the Old E.C. and others met on the spot when these gentlemen (who may be regarded as well qualified to judge on a matter of this kind) sent in a Report disapproving of the model, but in the face of this protest the project is to be persisted in. One would like to know if this report was ever placed before their Majesties the K&Q as one cannot suppose that they would be indifferent to the opinions of the citizens of Edinburgh elicited in this way.[13]

It seems he lost the argument, however, as the high wall around the monument was constructed, despite his passionate protests, and still stands.

In July 1927 Mary Ross, Thomas's wife of more than 50 years, died. Three years later Thomas died at the grand age of 91, on 4 December 1930. His moveable estate amounted to £7,639. He is buried in Comely Bank Cemetery in north Edinburgh. The tributes paid to Thomas Ross after his death are fulsome in the extreme. It is obvious that he was held in the highest regard by friends and colleagues and that he was a man of remarkable personal and professional qualities:

> Dr Ross was in no sense a man of narrow or of limited interests. He had a wide knowledge of English History, Literature, and Poetry, and, in particular, his acquaintance with the works of Sir Walter Scott and with old Scottish ballads was intimate and deep. Personally he was a man of the finest and the most lovable character, who endeared himself to all who knew him.[14]

On the Sunday after Thomas's death a lengthy and effusive tribute was paid to him from the pulpit in St Giles' Cathedral, where he had been an elder of the kirk and whose services he had attended both morning and evening every Sunday:

> He was such a great Christian, and such a gallant gentleman; so gracious, courteous and considerate; so much a pattern of gentle manners and of simple unaffected dignity. His great age, which nevertheless he bore so lightly, his genial smile and imperturbable demeanour, carried a sense of repose and benediction as he moved among us. Never have I met a man with a mind more at peace with itself and with all the world, and this because his mind was at peace with God. His friends were of all ages and all classes, and he had no enemy – how could he have, he who never spoke ill of any man, and who seemed to live only to encourage, help and bless?[15]

A brief phrase from *The Scotsman*'s lengthy obituary seems to sum up Thomas Ross's character nicely: 'he radiated sunshine wherever he went'.

PART 2

The Books

———

MacGibbon and Ross and
The Castellated and Domestic
Architecture of Scotland

3

The Predecessors

———

One of the most important and complete books on Scottish architecture that has ever been compiled. Its value to the architect, the archaeologist, and the student of styles is at once apparent . . . constituting a monument of patient research, capable draughtsmanship, and of well sustained effort, which do the authors infinite credit.

The Scotsman, 25 July 1892

The Castellated and Domestic Architecture of Scotland, published between 1887 and 1892, was well received as a ground-breaking contribution to the literature on Scottish architecture. It did not arise out of a vacuum. MacGibbon and Ross stand in a long line of dedicated enthusiasts, from the sixteenth to the nineteenth century, who have shared their knowledge and experience of Scottish architecture and landscape in print. Some published picturesque travelogues of their adventurous journeys to remote and beautiful areas of Scotland. Others were inspired by an interest in antiquities; antiquarianism was well established during the Scottish Enlightenment and MacGibbon and Ross were working in a tradition where scholarly interest in the past was an admirable trait in an educated gentleman. MacGibbon and Ross were well aware of the work of their predecessors and they make regular references to earlier publications. In their extensive entry on Glamis Castle (2: 113), for example, they mention the work of Slezer, Defoe, Gray, Pennant and Grose as they try to make sense of the history of the castle's complex architecture.

Standing on the Shoulders of Giants? From Pont to Billings

The earliest and most comprehensive survey of the castles and great houses of Scotland was carried out by the mapmaker Timothy Pont at the end of the sixteenth century. Pont mapped the whole of Scotland in extraordinary detail. His tiny drawings of castles and mansions in the manuscript maps give us a picture of the complexity and scale of the architecture of Scottish buildings up until the end of the sixteenth century. Charles McKean's theory of first, second, third and fourth ranks of Scottish 'chateaux',[1] a challenge to the theory of four periods proposed by MacGibbon and Ross, is informed by Pont's exquisitely detailed drawings.[2]

Detail of map of Stirling Castle and environs by Timothy Pont, showing his typically tiny, meticulous drawings.

MacGibbon and Ross briefly mention what they call 'Robert Gordon's Atlas, published by Joan Blaeu in Amsterdam in 1654' (5: 558). This contains the maps of Timothy Pont, accompanied by written contributions from Robert Gordon of Straloch and Robert Sibbald. 'The maps of Scotland in the great atlas (many of them drawn by himself . . .) with the topographical descriptions which accompany them, are amongst the most valuable contributions ever made by an individual to the physical history of his country'[3] (5: 558). They also reference Pont's 'admirable' *County History of Cunninghame* when discussing the history of Kilburnie Castle (1: 393).

One of the earliest travelogues was by William Lithgow (1582–1645), also known as 'Lugless Willie', following a dispute over a romantic involvement which resulted in his ears being chopped off. His most famous book, *The Totall Discourse of the Rare Adventures and Painful Peregrinations of Long Nineteen Years' Travel from Scotland to the Most Famous Kingdoms in Europe, Asia and Africa* was first published in London in 1632. David MacGibbon would have known of Lithgow, since he was the founder of Stanmore Academy, where David was educated in Lanark.[4]

Captain John Slezer published his comprehensive *Theatrum Scotiae* in 1693. This work contains a series of engravings of views of castles, abbeys, towns, and seats of the nobility he encountered whilst travelling throughout Scotland in his capacity as Captain of the Artillery Company. It was one of the first illustrated travelogue accounts of a journey through Scotland intended to educate and entertain. The text was written by Robert Sibbald, Geographer Royal for Scotland, as a series of 'chorographies' which praise the places described and their noble owners. MacGibbon and Ross refer to the *Theatrum Scotiae* in their entries on Glamis, Stirling and Bothwell. David MacGibbon's drawing of Stirling Castle (1: 469) is explicitly partly conjectural and based on Slezer's views (1: 470).[5]

Richard Pococke, an English churchman who was Bishop of Ossary and Meath in Ireland, made three tours of Scotland – in 1747, 1750 and 1760 – and his accounts are written in the form of letters,

Stirling Castle, by John Slezer, 1693.

illustrated with drawings of ecclesiastical buildings and a few castles, although they were not published until 1887. MacGibbon and Ross heard about his work and refer to it in their entry on Repentance Tower: 'In the travels of Bishop Pococke, about to be published for the first time by the Scottish Historical Society, our attention has been kindly drawn by the editor, Mr D. William Kemp, to the following remarks on the Tower . . .' (2: 61).

Picturesque Antiquities of Scotland, etched by Adam de Cardonnel, was published in four parts from 1788 to 1793. De Cardonnel described mainly ecclesiastical buildings, but he also sketched and described many castles in his gazetteer. He was elected a fellow of the Society of Antiquaries of Scotland under the presidency of the Earl of Bute in December 1780; he also served as Curator from 1782 to 1784. When Captain Francis Grose visited Scotland, Cardonnel did all he could to assist his fellow antiquary with notes from his extensive collections, besides accompanying him on various archaeological expeditions, help which Grose gratefully acknowledged in the introduction to his *Antiquities*

of Scotland. This two-volume work gave details of 89 castles and was well known to MacGibbon and Ross.

Others who sketched and wrote about Scotland's buildings before MacGibbon and Ross include Daniel Defoe, Thomas Pennant, John Clerk of Eldin, Paul Sandby, the Rev. Charles Cordiner, William Daniell, Boswell and Johnson and J.M.W. Turner, who produced illustrations for Walter Scott's *Provincial Antiquities and Picturesque Scenery of Scotland.* As the eighteenth and nineteenth centuries went on, more and more was added to the literature on Scotland's landscapes and architecture. As Jamie Crawford reports, 'In the 1760s there were just seven books describing tours of Scotland. By the 1820s there were 53.'[6]

The nearest contemporary author of Scottish architectural history to MacGibbon and Ross was Robert William Billings who, about 1840, had been commissioned by William Burn to produce *The Baronial and Ecclesiastical Antiquities of Scotland.* When the publication was first published by Blackwood and Sons, as a 60-part volume priced two shillings and sixpence per part, the authors named on the pictorial title page were Billings and Burn. When Burn withdrew his capital from the project, Billings and Blackwood bought out his £1,000 share and Burn's name was removed from the title page. This was then published in four volumes between 1845 and 1862 and contained 240 illustrations, with explanatory text. Commercially, Billings's work was a success as it became the source book for every Scottish architectural practice undertaking work in the baronial idiom until *The Castellated and Domestic Architecture of Scotland* began to appear from 1887 onwards.[7] MacGibbon and Ross refer to Billings's work as 'an important contribution and his beautiful drawings are a charming record of the edifices he illustrates. But the absence of plans is a serious drawback' (1: v). In Volume 2 they robustly challenge the ideas contained in *The Baronial and Ecclesiastical Antiquities of Scotland* with regard to the French influence on the sixteenth-century architecture of Scotland. They quote from Billings's views on Tolquhon: 'Firm and massive as a Scottish fortalice required to be in those troubled days [1586], it grotesquely associates with its rude strength the fantastic ornaments of a more fanciful and civilised people, and stands a type of what the French must have produced among the gentlemen of the age – the rugged nature of the Scot decorated with the style and manners of the mercurial Frenchman' (2: 14). MacGibbon and Ross firmly rebut this: 'This is no doubt a fine, though fanciful piece of writing, but whether applicable to the Scottish gentleman of the period or not, the comparison between the imaginary grotesque gentleman and his castle is unfortunately founded on an entirely erroneous view of the conditions of Scottish Architecture at the end of the sixteenth century. The fact is that this idea is the offspring of the writer's imagination, and is absolutely without any proof whatever' (2: 14).

A contemporary of Billings was James Fergus-son, a distinguished and prolific Scottish architectural historian – and alumnus of the Royal High School – who also wrote and illustrated several volumes, including *A History of Architecture in All Countries from the Earliest Times to the Present Day*. But Fergusson's worldwide focus meant that Scottish architecture was given little space, as MacGibbon and Ross noted disapprovingly: 'it is evident that he has not regarded it as an important element in the general history of the art' (1: vi). It was left to MacGibbon and Ross to remedy the gap.

In 1901 the architect Rowand Anderson, a personal friend of both MacGibbon and of Ross, wrote 'an appreciation' in the preface of a new edition of Billings's *Baronial and Ecclesiastical Antiquities of Scotland*, published by Oliver and Boyd 'at an affordable price'. He stated: 'The high standard of artistic and accurate draughtsmanship, and careful selection of examples, at once placed this work in the front rank of Architectural publications, and from this position it has not yet been displaced.'[8] Anderson had reviewed the works of five previous authors in this appreciation, pointing out that before Billings the quality of draughtsmanship in published architectural drawings and sketches was consistently poor; he dismissed Adam de Cardonnel's etchings as 'all of them equally bad and inaccurate. The views in Cordiner's volumes are no better.'[9] It is surprising that he does not mention the subsequent work of MacGibbon and Ross, especially given his friendship with them. But since this was a commercial publication and a rival work to *The Castellated and Domestic Architecture of Scotland* perhaps it would not have been politic to do so. Or it may because Anderson had himself planned to produce a rival publication on the development of Scottish mediaeval architecture, in conjunction with the Swedish architectural illustrator, Axel Haig, although the project was eventually shelved for financial reasons.[10]

Billings certainly brought an unprecedented combination of skill and artistry to his architectural sketches, although Charles McKean found that 'The drawings were almost too perfect. He and his exceptional engraver, Le Keux, knowingly dramatised the buildings by overemphasising height, exaggerating perspective and by highlighting important details using sun and shade in parts of the building where sun could not reach.'[11] McKean has a point; note that the carefully positioned person in Billings's drawing of the Lady Chapel in Glasgow Cathedral (page 30) makes the rib vaulting appear even higher and grander than it is.

The descriptions of the buildings that Billings sketched were written by John Hill Burton, Historiographer Royal. His style is in stark contrast to that of MacGibbon and Ross. Burton expresses himself in the Walter Scott mould of Scottish writing style: florid, discursive, heavy with adjectives and lengthy, multi-clause sentences. MacGibbon and Ross are brisk, straightforward and businesslike. These are the first two sentences in their entry on Craigmillar Castle: 'The castle of Craigmillar, near Edinburgh, contains one of the finest examples of the keep enlarged with other buildings of a later date. This keep probably belongs to the latter part of the fourteenth century' (1: 190). Contrast Burton's first two sentences on the same building:

Nearly every stranger visiting Edinburgh, as well as every inhabitant of the town, must have seen this old fortified mansion, if not on a near approach and inspection, at least in observing how its brown ruins dignify the summit of a long slope of wooded eminence rising out of the great valley between Arthur Seat and the Pentland Hills. It may be a disputed matter whether a castellated edifice is seen to its greatest advantage starting straight from the edge of a precipice, or forming in itself the only abrupt elevation, and crowning, like Craigmillar, a gentle but dignified ascent.[12]

Billings's drawings, too, are elaborate, often incorporating figures and greenery in elegant compositions of landscape settings that can still be seen framed on the walls of country houses and castles throughout Scotland.[13] The sketches of MacGibbon and Ross are functional and straightforward, although attractive nonetheless. In what seems like a broadside at Billings they said: 'Our sketches are not intended to imitate or rival the beautiful and artistic etchings of some of our Scottish edifices which have from time to time been published, but simply to represent ARCHITECTURE in what appeared to us the most intelligible and effective manner' (1: vi, emphasis as in original text). Users of Plain English ahead of its time, MacGibbon and Ross did, however, resort to poetic metaphor on occasion, particularly when moved by distress at the poor condition of a building. Of the sad state of Ferniehirst Castle they say, 'Although yet entire, the ivy has it in its deadly embrace' (2: 157).

They were, to an extent, 'standing on the shoulders of giants' in their survey; they built upon the knowledge of previous generations and were always careful to reference other authors and to give thanks to those who helped them. But much as one may admire the determination and contributions of their predecessors, it is clear that MacGibbon and Ross were themselves giants, standing head and shoulders above all others.

The Lure of Ruins

MacGibbon and Ross had identified a gap in the published works on architectural history and theory, and in this they were in tune with the zeit-

Balvenie Castle, Morayshire, by MacGibbon and Ross.

geist. There had been a large appetite for historical works about Scotland throughout the Romantic period, and ruins inspired a particular fascination. Although MacGibbon and Ross frequently lament the ruinous state of the castles they visited and put forward proposals for restoration, they must have been drawn to the seductive charm of the ruined castles they surveyed. The paintings of artists such as Turner, Nasmyth and McCulloch mythologised ancient castles and fed into the romantic narrative promoted by Sir Walter Scott, the poet 'Ossian' and the Wordsworths. Even Charles Dickens, not normally associated with romanticism, extolled and almost fetishised the beauty of the ruined Coliseum in his *Letters from Italy* in 1846: 'It is the most impressive, the most stately, the most solemn, grand, majestic, mournful sight, conceivable. Never, in its bloodiest prime, can the sight of the gigantic Coliseum, full and running over with the lustiest life, have moved one heart, as it must move

Balvenie Castle, by Billings, 1852. His romantic sketch of Balvenie contrasts with
the more prosaic depiction by MacGibbon and Ross shown opposite.

all who look upon it now, a ruin. GOD be thanked: a ruin!'[14]

Although MacGibbon and Ross were working in the shadow of the Romantic Era of the first half of the nineteenth century, Victorian industrious pragmatism had begun to replace it. Compare the safe, domestic depiction of Tantallon Castle by David MacGibbon (Plate 3) with the dramatic vision of a fortress under siege from a raging sea by Alexander Nasmyth in 1816 (Plate 4), or the intensely romantic drawings of Billings with the more workaday sketches of MacGibbon and Ross.

Thomas Ross wrote an essay defending the restoration of ruined buildings (see Appendix) and claiming not to be enamoured of ruins. He would not have approved of Sir William Forbes of Pitsligo partly demolishing Colinton Castle in 1800, to make a picturesque ruin in the grounds of his new mansion, on the advice of the painter Alexander Nasmyth.

4

Surveying the Castellated Architecture of Scotland

Wide-ranging and sometimes brilliant as the legacy of their adventurous antiquarian predecessors was, there were several major ways in which the survey by MacGibbon and Ross differed from those which came before it. One was the sheer scale of their undertaking; not only did they travel the length and breadth of Scotland, including the remote islands, they took in a far greater number of buildings than any previous survey, apart from Timothy Pont's sixteenth-century annotated cartography. They were pioneers in providing plans and measurements of the buildings they surveyed; this had almost never been done in Scotland before and never systematically. Slezer had provided a floor plan of Thirlestane, and Billings had a plan of Terpersie – his only one, which MacGibbon and Ross noted as evidence of a major lack in Billings's surveys. The measurements MacGibbon and Ross took were reflected in the quality and accuracy of their copious sketches. In the five volumes the entries average more than three drawings, plans and sketches per building surveyed, although the range varies widely.

The theoretical underpinning of their work again made them pioneers in the field; they did not merely describe their buildings in detail, they also placed them contextually by period and type according to a systematic theory which they developed, partly in the hope of exciting greater interest in Scotland's castles: '. . . it may be doubted whether the attention of the public has yet been fully awakened to the more important bearings of these ancient structures on the history of our land, and we trust that what we have got to tell about them may have some influence in arousing a deeper and more intelligent interest in the venerable remains of our castles and domestic edifices than they have hitherto excited' (3: 2).

Essentially, MacGibbon and Ross were scholars, fascinated by the whole gamut of Scottish architecture, and willing to put in the research needed to describe and categorise it. Their survey contains several essays on various aspects of historic buildings and a number of interesting asides. In Volume 5 they reprint the contract for building Partick Castle, 'which throws a very considerable light on the method of proceeding adopted in building a mansion-house early in the seventeenth century' (5: 5). In Volume 3, in their entry on Anstruther Manse, they say: 'The history of the construction of the manse cannot be given better than in the words of its builder, Mr. James Melville, minister of Anstruther' (3: 560). They provide an entertaining quote from his 1591 diary of the construction, of which this is only a small part:

This was vndertakin and begoun at Witson-
day in an, 1590, bot wald neuer haiff bein
peryted giff the bountifull hand of my God
haid nocht maid me to tak the wark in hand
myself, and furnished stranglie to my
consideratioun all things neidfull, sa that
neuer ouk past but all sort of workmen was
weill payit, never a dayes intermission fra
the beginning to the compleitting, and
never a soar finger during the hail labour.
(3: 561)

MacGibbon and Ross's focus on the *social* aspects
of the buildings is unusual; they almost always
mention the current and/or past owner of each
building and often add anecdotes about the house
and the people connected with it – without harping
on sycophantically about genealogy, as some castle
authors are prone to do. On Fernielee, for example:
'It adds an interest to this house, situated in the
midst of Ettrick Forest, to know that in it Miss
Alison Rutherford, afterwards Mrs. Cockburn,
wrote her popular version of the "Flowers of the
Forest"' (2: 520). In their entry on Finlarig Castle
in Perthshire they tell a gruesome story. 'Close to
the castle on the north is a stone tank with overflow drain, evidently intended for storing water;
but the local memories of the tender mercies of
the Campbells have invested it with a more terrible
office. The tank is regarded as the scaffold within
which the victim kneeled, and the overflow as the
hollow in which he placed his neck for the convenience of the headsman!' (3: 585).

Finally, their vigorous campaigning sets them
apart from the mere chroniclers of antiquarian
buildings – MacGibbon and Ross were passionate
not only about the past but also about the future
of Scottish castellated architecture. Their text is
peppered with exhortations to look after the built
heritage of Scotland's castles, and sorrowful
descriptions of neglected buildings at risk. Again,

they were pioneers, promoting the idea of conservation before it was taken seriously. Indeed, they
were the first true building conservationists in Scotland, campaigning tirelessly against deliberate
decay and proposed demolitions. They feared
demolition and they were right to do so.

What prompted MacGibbon and Ross to
produce *The Castellated and Domestic Architecture of
Scotland*? In 1880, when David MacGibbon was
President of the Edinburgh Architectural Association, he had delivered presidential lectures on
early Scottish art and architecture which were
followed up by papers on Scottish castles and
houses in May of 1883 and 1884. Thomas Ross
had helped; both men had been sketching in the
course of their travels on business since the mid
1860s. The lectures were well received and
MacGibbon was encouraged to publish them. The
groundwork of the great project had been laid,
but it did not leap out, fully formed. The ambitions
of MacGibbon and Ross developed and changed
as they worked at their history, their theory and
their surveys.

They were both enthralled by castles and
ancient Scottish buildings and their primary stated
reason was to put forward a developmental theory
of Scottish architecture: 'The object of this treatise
is to endeavour to trace the historical sequence of
the various phases of Architecture which have
prevailed in the old castles and houses of Scotland,
and to try to define and explain the different styles
of building adopted at different periods from the
twelfth century till the revival of classic architecture
in modern times' (1: introduction).

Scope and Organisation

In dealing with this important series of
buildings our chief object has been to trace
the development of the Architecture and
to determine the stages of progress or

'Periods' into which it naturally divides itself. In order to render the historic sequence clear and distinct, and also to follow the steps by which the designs of one period passed into those of the period that followed it, it is essential that the plans of the buildings be fully taken into account. We have therefore devoted much care to the accurate representation of these important elements in the design. (1: vi)

MacGibbon and Ross organised their five volumes by four 'periods' which divided the history of the castle in Scotland over five centuries: first period (1200–1300); second period (1300–1400); third period (1400–1542) and fourth period (1542–1700). Their theory was linear and chronological – but, after all, what other approach could a pair of Victorian historians have taken? The days of psycho-history, cultural relativism and postmodernism, with a critical view of narrative chronology as simplistic and sometimes even misleading, had yet to arrive. As Miles Glendinning and Aonghus MacKechnie point out in the Introduction to *Scotland's Castle Culture*, 'MacGibbon and Ross, living in an age of high empire as well as continuing Improvement felt it a historian's patriotic duty to … propagate the concept of a pre-union Scotland fettered by war, and condemn Jacobitism and Highlanders as primitive and disruptive.'[1] But, to do them justice, although it is possible to find the occasional example in their five volumes, MacGibbon and Ross were not tub-thumping imperialists and were not, as has been claimed, seduced by the defensive features of the buildings to the exclusion of all else. They were meticulous scholars who strove hard to understand the buildings they surveyed and took care to place them in a social context. They do mention defensive features when describing the minority of their castles that were military fortresses, but for most of the buildings they survey there is little or no talk of defence.

One can chart their ideas and ambitions developing as they progress through the five volumes. In the preface of Volume 1, completed in October 1886 and published in 1887, they were relatively modest in their appraisal of the scope of *The Castellated and Domestic Architecture of Scotland:* 'It may be thought that the number of buildings illustrated is unnecessarily large. But it is, after all, only a small proportion of the still surviving examples of Scottish Domestic Architecture and there really is almost no repetition. In most of the keeps and towers there is doubtless a great similarity in general design, but it will be found that each furnishes some points of variety which give it a special interest' (1: vii). They had surveyed only 98 Scottish castles, towers and keeps in Volume 1, although they first described 34 French and English castles in their 60-page introduction – a 20,000-word essay on the early development of castles in France and England, in which they repeatedly highlight the increasing emphasis on comfort, ornament and domesticity in the buildings of the fifteenth and sixteenth centuries. Volume 1 dealt with the first three of their historical periods and the plan was to address the fourth period (1542–1700) in Volume 2. Accordingly, Volume 2 describes 147 towers and other buildings from that period.

By the end of Volume 2, also published in 1887, they seemed satisfied that they had come to the end of the task they had originally set themselves. 'We have now completed our survey of Scottish Castellated and Domestic Architecture up to the time when Scotland, like the other countries of Europe, yielded up her native style and adopted that of the Revival of Classic Art' (2: 567). But then, in a contradictory postscript a few pages later, they suggest, 'it would be very desirable if a reliable guide were prepared, – a kind of *catalogue raisonné* of ALL the Castellated and Domestic Buildings of Scotland. It would be to us a labour of love to engage in such a work, and provided a general interest were aroused in the subject, and the assistance of local architects and other competent advisors were volunteered, probably the thing might be accomplished' (2: 595).

To that end, they provided a list of 696 castles, 107 of which they already had notes and plans for, but had omitted from volumes one and two for want of space, and 589 about which they said they would be 'happy to receive information' (2: 596); thus they turned the future of the survey into a kind of community endeavour. The response was good and, to their immense credit, before the days of easy mass communication, they managed to galvanise dozens of architects and other men to help with surveying the castles described in Volumes 3, 4 and 5.

Of those on the list that they did not manage to describe, about half were already completely gone or mere piles of stones by the late nineteenth century and would not have been worth surveying. A significant number do not seem to have existed at all; this is especially the case in Argyll and Dumfries and one wonders whether they consulted some rogue reference books for those areas which threw around fanciful names. The rest of the castles and houses represent a mixture of occupied laird's houses, most of which have later additions, and a very small number of really significant buildings that they must have been sorry to miss. These include the former episcopal palace of Fetternear, Slains Castles (old and new), Dumbarton Castle, Blair Castle in Perthshire and Orchardton Tower, Scotland's only round tower house. In the end, however, they had to call a halt and finalise the last volume – their 'labour of love' complete.

Volume 3, published in 1889, starts over again, adding in 117 more buildings of the first, second and third periods. In the fourth period, 'Each series of buildings is taken topographically, in the same order as formerly – i.e., beginning in the west, we move by the south-west along the south of Scotland, then take the central districts, and finally those further north' (3: 372). Volume 3 begins with a largely non-military history of Scotland and its architecture, stressing again the increasing domesticity and comfort as time passed: 'Such piles as Craigmillar, Edzell, Crichton &c., show . . . how the simple keep of the days of distress in the fourteenth century became enlarged into the spacious and sumptuous mansion of the days of abundance at a later date' (3: 22).

Volume 4 continues the descriptions of fourth period houses, adding a further 155.

When the third volume of this work was issued it was believed that one more volume would suffice to contain an account of all the remaining castellated and domestic structures of Scotland still unpublished. But the response given to the invitation for information and assistance to enable the authors of these edifices has been so cordial, and has so much exceeded their expectation, that it has been found necessary to add another volume to the intended number of four. It is hoped, however, that this addition will not be unacceptable to those interested in the subject, as has thereby been rendered possible to include many more subjects than could otherwise have been done, and thus, it is believed, *to omit no building in the country within the selected sphere containing architectural features of any consequence.* (4: preface, italics added)

Is their confidence justified? Well, they are almost correct here, as they certainly surveyed the majority of significant castellated buildings in Scotland – but they missed out about half of the buildings that they identified at the end of Volume 2 as being worthy of inclusion in the proposed *catalogue raisonné* and also a large number of buildings which were not mentioned at all in their lists. In Dumfries and Galloway alone there are an estimated 50 buildings still in existence which might reasonably have featured in *The Castellated and Domestic Architecture of Scotland* but were not surveyed by MacGibbon and Ross.[2] Geoffrey Stell proposes about 1,200 as a 'reasonable working hypothesis'[3] for the numbers of towers and castles extant in Scotland, which gives MacGibbon and Ross a shortfall of 400–500. However, they could only survey the buildings that they knew about, and before the transformative days of the internet many were simply unknown to them.

The fifth volume completes the section on Houses in Towns, started in Volume 4, and adds in tolbooths, town halls, 'Churches and Monuments of the Scottish style' and sundials, in addition to the 700 plus castles surveyed. At the end there is a 50-page essay on Early Scottish Masters of Works, Master Masons and Architects, which traces the history of the designers and builders of the royal palaces and other significant secular and ecclesiastical buildings, using both primary and secondary sources. Volume 5 also contains the supplement of 63 castles and houses 'information regarding which was obtained too late to allow of their being inserted in their proper places in the foregoing series'. Finally, their *catalogue raisonné* was complete, with more than 700 castles and houses surveyed, giving the impression of a project completed with enormous energy and at almost breathless speed. Indeed, *The Castellated and Domestic Architecture of Scotland* is much more than a *catalogue raisonné*, with its essays, analysis, illustrations and anecdotes. It is not only a work of reference but a rattling good read.

Within the second, third and fourth periods, MacGibbon and Ross assigned the buildings surveyed to various architectural types. The first period (1200–1300) contains only 15 entries and no sub-divisions. The second period (1300–1400) is divided into 'simple keeps', L plans and fragmentary remains. In the second period are 13 simple keeps, in the third period 47 and in the fourth period 65. The third period adds courtyard plans and special plans. And in the fourth period are added Z plans, T plans, E plans, exceptional plans and altered and fragmentary structures. This may all seem very complex, but the reality is probably very much more so. For example, Barholm Castle is included in the fourth period under the list of L Plans, but we now know, from an archaeological survey carried out between 2001 and 2005 and from observation over several years of living in the building and discussing the structure with archaeologists and architectural historians, that it almost certainly started out as a simple fifteenth-century two-storey tower with an external entrance at first-floor level and an internal stair within the walls between the first and second storeys. To this was added a stair tower, one further storey and a caphouse, probably at the end of the sixteenth century. Barholm is a small tower and a relatively straightforward building to which nothing was added or changed after the sixteenth century. How many of the L plans, Z plans and E plans were not thus planned at all, but took on their alphabetical shape as a result of add-ons in subsequent centuries? MacGibbon and Ross were, of course, well aware of the developing nature of towers and castles and frequently describe changes made over the centuries; it would be a mistake to condemn them for a simplistic view of architectural history. But they undoubtedly did miss things; their surveys were very often based on viewing the buildings for the first time and since they were always short of time, they were not often able to build up the degree of knowledge and understanding that comes from repeated visits.

Indeed, the complexity gave MacGibbon and Ross problems, as so many of the buildings they

Aboyne Castle, Aberdeenshire, at the turn of the twentieth century, as remodelled by George Truefitt.

surveyed had a history of changes and additions, some of it quite impenetrable to the observer. See, for example their entry on Aboyne: 'The structure has been so much and so frequently altered and added to that its original plan cannot now be determined' (4: 375). And it has been so much altered again and greatly reduced in the twentieth century that, although conforming roughly to what is expected of a tower house (tall and imposing, with turrets, a cap house and crow step gables), its history is now architecturally almost unintelligible. MacGibbon and Ross assigned it to the fourth period.

The range of building types, sizes and conditions they surveyed was immense and truly comprehensive: mere 'rickles o' stanes' left from some great building, vast mediaeval fortresses still standing, tiny laird's houses in town centres, sumptuous palaces, baronialised mansions, towers left as tall stumps that were once part of a range of buildings, clifftop castles, ancient island forts and comfortable country houses and buildings that have been so much added to over the years that their original core is barely recognisable. There were even a few castles that could easily illustrate a fairy tale, such as Craigievar in Aberdeenshire and Caerlaverock in Dumfriesshire, and some that are now movie stars in their own right, such as Doune Castle, location of *Game of Thrones, Outlander* and *Monty Python and the Holy Grail,* Dunnottar and Blackness Castles, locations of *Hamlet* and Drummond and Crichton Castles, locations of *Rob Roy.*

Some entries are very brief. Corsindae Castle in Aberdeenshire (4: 80), a large late-fifteenth-century tower house with additions in the seventeenth, eighteenth and nineteenth centuries, for example, gets only three lines and no sketch, so

one might assume it was not visited by MacGibbon and Ross. Yet it is one of those listed in the back of Volume 2 for which they said they already had plans and notes. There are no notes, plans or sketches for Corsindae in the NLS collection, however. Other entries are extensive in both text and the number of sketches, and for very understandable reasons. There is so much to say about Edinburgh Castle that it easily merits the 19 pages which include 17 illustrations and plans in Volume 1. The average length of an entry is three pages accompanied by a plan and two sketches, but with wide variations. There was clearly an element of serendipity in their choices, to do with both convenience and luck.

MacGibbon and Ross saw patterns among the buildings they surveyed, but there is also a randomness about the details of Scottish architecture which gives rise to endless speculation as to the reasons for particular styles and additions. Each building they surveyed was unique, many with mysterious features that seem to defy logical explanations. Sometimes logic is simply defied by whim. Nevertheless, their aim was to harmonise the history of these buildings into a coherent chronological typology. They planned to do much more than a largely descriptive survey with drawings, such as Adam de Cardonnel, Francis Grose and Robert William Billings had done before them; theirs was a conceptual theory.

> Although many excellent and well-known illustrations of our baronial and domestic architecture have been published, there is no systematic treatise on their architectural history. It is scarcely even recognised that the architecture of our castles and houses has a definite historical sequence. The interest of these buildings would therefore be very largely increased if their various styles and epochs, with the characteristics of each, can be distinctly defined. One would then know what points to specially examine, and what to look for, in order to be able to place each building, or portion of a building, in its appropriate niche, and to compare the various examples with each other, and with the corresponding buildings of other countries. Besides, nothing can be more interesting and instructive than to follow the records of our national history contained in these old castles, and to note the manners and customs of our ancestors at different epochs as reflected in them. (1: 1)

Were they successful? In a virtuoso performance, they took the nation's complex castellated architectural heritage and firmly imposed a structure upon it in a way that had never before been attempted and that reflected the Victorian ideal of order. Of course their conclusions, and the ideas that led to them, have been challenged by various scholars, as interest in and knowledge of castellology has developed over the past century. But MacGibbon and Ross's concept of a sequential approach to interpreting buildings, although apparently blindingly obvious, was pioneering. It is unsurprising that their legacy has lasted so long.

Difficulties, Logistics and Errors

In the Preface to Volume 1 MacGibbon and Ross acknowledge 'the cordial and generous reception we have almost invariably received from the proprietors and occupants of the houses we have visited in pursuit of our subject, and the free permission which has been accorded to us to make such measurements and drawings as we required'

OPPOSITE. Aboyne Castle in 2013.

(1: ix–x). There were a few exceptions – e.g. Castle Fraser and Monymusk Castle in Aberdeenshire; for illustration of the latter they had to use an eighteenth-century watercolour (5: 329).[4] It was particularly unfortunate that they could not visit Monymusk, as otherwise they would have seen the relationship between it and Crathes and perhaps been able to draw conclusions about the phased building of Crathes. Much of their work in building up a picture of the development of Scottish architecture depended on being able to make comparisons between castles, in a way that their predecessors did not attempt.

The logistics of reaching the buildings were challenging. Bishop Pococke, Boswell and Johnson and Dorothy Wordsworth all complained in their accounts about the poor state of the roads over which they had to travel in Scotland; most rural roads would be not much improved by the time MacGibbon and Ross set out, although they at least had the railways for covering both long and short distances in some comfort. However, in their entry on Maybole Castle they muse on small provincial towns: 'Such centres were in those days, when roads were bad and travelling dangerous, much more numerous than now, when travelling is easy and rapid' (3: 498). Perhaps they were referring to the railways, or perhaps we inevitably tend to compare our own time as more progressive and favourable than the past. Contrast the difficulties MacGibbon and Ross faced travelling by steam train and then bicycle or pony and trap,[5] or on foot along untarred roads, with the conditions for castle visitors today: most will travel in a car equipped to cope with all that the Scottish weather can supply, along roads that are mostly tarred, well maintained and well signposted, with satellite navigation or internet maps of the entire country to guide drivers to their destinations. Today, a quick internet search will usually bring up images of even the most remote and ruinous tower, along with an Ordnance Survey map reference and postcode. And on arrival at the target castles the visitor can whip out a digital camera or mobile phone with a sharp zoom and quickly take dozens of photographs to download, peruse and manipulate in the comfort of home. Aerial photographs can be taken with the latest drone technology, providing an opportunity to get up close to parts of buildings that were completely inaccessible to MacGibbon and Ross. They complained: 'In our various excursions we have spent many a weary day in the fruitless search for castles and houses, which the Gazetteers and Maps[6] declared to exist, but which have long ago disappeared' (2: 595 Postscript).

One cannot help but feel sorry for MacGibbon and Ross, trailing around in vain, looking for vanished buildings, with time pressures upon them and works of reference unreliable. Their work was tough and demanding and they worked late into the evening when they could; their entry for Muness Castle reads, 'As a striking illustration of its high latitude, we may mention that in the month of June, during the midnight hours, we had sufficient natural light to enable us to make our plans and sketches' (2: 256). Carrick House in Orkney they 'sketched from a passing steamboat!' (5: 97).

Thomas Ross's obituary stated that they devoted almost every Saturday to visiting their buildings. 'Far into the evening, while light lasted, they were to be seen "By some auld howlet-haunted biggin' / Or kirk deserted by its riggin."'[7] One wonders what their wives, Jessie and Mary, thought of the travelling their husbands undertook – did they heave a sigh of relief as David and Thomas left for yet another weekend away, or were they disgruntled at their status as 'castle widows'? They may even have accompanied their husbands from time to time, but there is no record of their involvement.

MacGibbon and Ross at work, surveying Inverkeithing Mercat Cross.
Ross is at the top of the ladder and MacGibbon is taking notes.

Some of the visits were made while travelling on other business, but most were weekend work undertaken by train and bicycle, usually setting out on a Friday evening equipped with weekend bags, drawing boards and provisions brought to Waverley Station by their daughters; sometimes they travelled together, sometimes separately, depending on what had to be done.[8]

Although both men were photographers, the illustrations were generally measured and drawn on the spot. Their sketches, although mostly faithful reproductions, were sometimes speculative. For example, Methven 'has been much added to and altered; but the original entrance doorway was probably in the position and of the style shown in the Sketch' (4: 278). The sketch of MacLellan's Castle was also speculative, as was one of the Stirling Castle drawings.

Often in the text they give the distance of the buildings from the nearest railway station, an indication of the importance of accessibility for them. 'Hermitage Castle is situated about four miles from Riccarton Junction,[9] amongst the wild uplands and morasses of Liddesdale' (1: 523), or Druminnor Castle in Aberdeenshire: 'The house is pleasantly situated on the banks of the burn of Kearn, in the parish of Auchindoir, and about three miles south from the Kennethmont Station of the North of Scotland Railway' (2: 291). Fortunately for them, Myres Castle 'is situated within a few minutes' walk from Auchtermuchty Railway Station and about two miles from Falkland Palace' (5: 330), so on that visit they could visit two significant buildings on one trip. They must have walked to the castles from the station, unless there was a pony and trap for hire, or someone who could pick them up – a local architect, perhaps?

Once arrived at their target building, the physical demands of surveying the property were sometimes arduous. As can be seen from the sketch on page 57, long ladders might be needed. When they surveyed MacLellan's House in Kirkcudbright 'The view from the south-east (fig. 610) was made with considerable difficulty with the aid of the plans, and by sketching here and there any part which was visible, and climbing where necessary to get a sight of the details' (2: 149).

Like all of us, MacGibbon and Ross made mistakes from time to time. Occasionally references are missing, or in the wrong place. When researching an article about the castles of Galloway I was puzzled that they did not mention Carsluith

(Carsleuth) Castle in the final index, since it is readily accessible from the coast road and close to two others that they describe. I also had a nagging feeling that I had seen their description of it somewhere. Eventually, I came across the sketches and description in Volume 3, page 513; Carsluith had simply been missed from the main index – and Carsleuth Castle has been placed in Kincardineshire instead of Kirkcudbrightshire in the topographical index in Volume 5. As I worked through every building in the book, matching each to the volume and page number from the indexes, I found a couple of dozen or so that had either been missed or wrongly allocated – or in some cases double allocated, as Dunvegan appears in both Inverness-shire and Argyll, Barochan Castle in Renfrewshire and Dumbartonshire, and Fatlips in Lanark and Roxburgh. However, mistakes of spelling or grammar are nowhere to be found. In Volume 3 only, there is an errata page after the preface, listing eight very minor errors in the text.

The tolbooths and sundials are not indexed individually, presumably to save additional time and effort. In the context of the many hundreds of entries and the boring slog that is involved in indexing (it is not known whether they did this themselves or whether they had help), the indexes themselves, both topographical and alphabetical, are a splendid achievement. Mistakes occurred not only in the indexing, but also in the descriptions, as Charles McKean pointed out: 'Sometimes, undoubtedly hard pressed for time, they recorded a wrong orientation, or a tower in the wrong place. Their hasty reconnaissance of the Palace of Pitsligo, Buchan, for example, concluded erroneously that it was but a tower surrounded by labourers' dwellings. Perhaps their train was due.'[10] This semi-facetious remark highlights again the difficulties MacGibbon and Ross faced when surveying their castles in haste. The majority of the errors and omissions occur mainly in volumes three, four and five, once the scope of their mission had been enlarged and external helpers engaged.[11]

The Helpers

Although MacGibbon and Ross completed the majority of their surveys themselves, they did have some assistance, as the great project developed. It is always a tricky business, acknowledging thanks in a publication to those who have helped. Will anyone be inadvertently missed out and thus offended? How best to differentiate between the occasional helper and those who gave significant amounts of time and support? At the beginning of Volume 1, long before their rallying cry for help at the end of Volume 2, MacGibbon and Ross acknowledge and thank a number of distinguished men for their help in providing plans, drawings and information. These include David Bryce's nephew, John Bryce, for plans of Drum Castle and Earl Patrick's Palace in Kirkwall; Dr Skene, Historiographer Royal of Scotland, for plans of Castle Fraser and Cluny Castle; the Earl of Cawdor, for plans of Cawdor Castle; and the Hon. H.C. Maxwell Stuart for plans of Traquair House. Altogether 16 men are thanked specifically, 'and many architectural friends for their aid and encouragement in our labours'. In the beginning of Volume 3 MacGibbon and Ross expand their list considerably and give 'special thanks' to a list of 49 men who rendered 'important aid'. They go on to pick out 11 of these whom the authors 'desire particularly to acknowledge their obligations'.

Among the 11 were Walter F. Lyon, an architect and antiquary who assisted with sketches for Otterston Castle, the Manse and the House in St Mary's Wynd in Stirling, the Kinghorn Tolbooth, Cupar-Fife Church, Fourmerkland Tower, Meggernie Castle, Newbyres Tower, Pitcullo Tower, before it became engulfed in ivy, and the plan of Dairsie Castle. William Railton, a Kilmarnock architect

and antiquary, also provided measurements and sketches, of Auchenharvie, Busbie, Clonbeith, Craigie and Stair Castles in Ayrshire, Kildonan Castle on Arran and Cathcart Castle in Renfrewshire. Not mentioned in the preface is William Galloway, who 'was a fine draughtsman and a careful excavator, and his long friendship with Sir Henry Dryden is a measure of the respect in which he was held by a man whose own standards were exacting. That respect was also held by David MacGibbon and Thomas Ross, who used many of Galloway's drawings in their two [sic] great volumes on Scottish architecture.'[12]

In the Preface to Volume 4, which serves both Volumes 4 and 5 – published in the same year, 1892 – again the authors extend a general thank you 'to all those numerous contributors who have so kindly aided them in their labours by supplying illustrations or information'. Thirteen men are thanked by name, several of whom had already been acknowledged in previous volumes. Extended thanks are offered to Thomas Saunders Robertson 'for furnishing sketches and descriptions of many of the structures contained in these volumes' and to Dr Dickson of Register House, who helped with the article on Masters of Work, Master Masons and Architects, which appears at the end of Volume 5.

MacGibbon and Ross were scrupulous about crediting illustrations; throughout the text of volumes three, four and five are acknowledgements and thanks for plans, sketches and information.[13] Contributors also appear in the index to Volume 5, with a list of the places their sketches appear. The Supplement at the end of Volume 5 gives details of 64 buildings 'information regarding which was obtained too late to allow of their being inserted in their proper places in the foregoing series' (5: 215). Almost all of these surveys and their illustrations are at least partially credited to others; although it is likely that MacGibbon and

Ross did not personally visit most of the supplemental buildings, these only represent a small percentage of the total.

The Sources

In addition to the help they received from individuals and consulting and referencing some of the surveys and travelogue accounts already mentioned, 'The authors began by preparing a list of ancient buildings arranged according to counties. This they complied from Sir John Sinclair's *Statistical Account* and from innumerable books dealing with history.'[14] *The Statistical Account* was a remarkable work of great social significance and a wonderful example of Enlightenment idealism at work. Sir John Sinclair of Ulbster, MP for Caithness, conceived a plan to ask parish ministers of the Church of Scotland all over Scotland to reply to a set of 160 planned questions dealing with local subjects including the geography, climate, natural resources, buildings, landowners and social customs of each of 938 parishes. The returns were published in a series of 21 volumes between 1791 and 1799 and they contain rich source material for historians and researchers about the minutiae of late eighteenth-century life. The 'New' or 'Second' *Statistical Account* was published in 1832 and included maps and contributions from other local figures such as schoolmasters and doctors. It reflected the changes that had taken place in Scotland during the agricultural and industrial revolutions. MacGibbon and Ross had access to both *Statistical Accounts*, in which they had a very useful resource to inform their research.

MacGibbon and Ross also used local history books such as *A History of Peeblesshire* (1864) by William Chambers, *A History of the Counties of Ayr and Wigton* by J. Paterson (1863–66), William Maitland's *History of Edinburgh* (1753) and the 'Books of the Works' of Edinburgh and Stirling castles.

The Society of Antiquaries of Scotland had been founded in 1780; there were articles of interest to MacGibbon and Ross in the volumes of the Proceedings and in the proceedings and transactions of other antiquarian societies such as the Literary and Antiquarian Society of Perth (founded 1827), the Montrose Natural History and Antiquarian Society (1836), Dumfriesshire and Galloway Natural History and Antiquarian Society (1862), Ayrshire and Wigtownshire Archaeological Association (1877), and the Scottish Burgh Records Society (1868). And in order to augment their introductory essay on French and English castles in Volume 1: 'The authors have freely availed themselves of the interesting works of Viollet-le-Duc and De Caumont on the Architecture of France, and of the equally interesting and very careful and comprehensive volumes of G. T. Clark and John Henry Parker on the Castles and Domestic Architecture of England' (1: 2).

One book that MacGibbon and Ross, surprisingly, did not acknowledge is *Castles of Aberdeenshire: Historical and Descriptive Notices* by Sir Andrew Leith Hay, first published in 1849 and updated and republished in 1887. In it, 45 castles are described, with pen and ink illustrations of 40 of them. Another local castles historian who is not mentioned was John Dickson, author of *The Ruined Castles of Midlothian* (1894).

The Illustrations, Printing and Publishing

MacGibbon and Ross were both accomplished draughtsmen, and both produced a plethora of fine and detailed measured drawings which give a plain and accurate picture of what existed at the time.

The Castellated and Domestic Architecture of Scotland is one of the last great volumes of architectural history that did not use photography and is thus instantly recognisable as Victorian. The

Craigcrook Castle, Edinburgh, by MacGibbon and Ross.

authors' contemporary John William Small, who had worked for Rowand Anderson and had set up an independent practice as architect and interior and furniture designer at George Street in Edinburgh, was ahead of MacGibbon and Ross in using photographs. In 1883 he published *Castles and Mansions of the Lothians, illustrated in one hundred and three views.* The 103 illustrations were high-

quality photographic plates. By the turn of the twentieth century photographic plates in illustrated books had become commonplace and indeed were expected by the modern reader. Despite the fact that photographic illustrations were possible at the time, MacGibbon and Ross decided to stick with traditional drawn sketches for *The Castellated and Domestic Architecture of Scotland* – fortunately for us, as without their careful measured drawings the books would lose much of their charm and interest. Both men were keen photographers. A few photographs are tucked between the sheets of sketches in the Ross Collection in the National Library of Scotland Collection – e.g. of Carberry Tower. The Edinburgh City Library holds a 'Capital Collection' of Thomas Ross's images, mainly watercolour sketches of castles and churches. Among them are 44 photographs taken by him of details of stonework in St Giles' Cathedral. The Canmore collection of HES also holds a large number of photographs of architectural details of Edinburgh Castle, signed by Thomas Ross. David MacGibbon was also a photographer; ironically, he was overtaken by the shift to photographic illustrations when he started to put together a book of his son Fred's sketches, together with those that he himself had made on his extensive tours of Europe 40 years earlier. Although trial proofs were made, the book never appeared, probably because photography had begun to replace drawn material in high-class book production.[15]

During the 1890s, the first commercially successful photo-engraving process that was compatible with ordinary letterpress printing was developed by Frederick Ives, so that halftone blocks could be printed along with blocks of text in books, periodicals and newspapers. His process quite quickly came into widespread use, largely replacing the hand-engraved blocks that had previously served to provide illustrations. MacGibbon and Ross's illustrations are so perfectly reproduced from the originals that it is clear that some form of early photographic process must have been used.

The Publisher

All of the works of MacGibbon and Ross were published by David Douglas (1823–1916) of 15 Castle St, Edinburgh. He was Editor of the *North British Review* (1863–69). He was made a Fellow of the Society of Antiquaries of Scotland in 1861 and in 1866 was elected a Fellow of the Royal Society of Edinburgh. Douglas, like Thomas Ross, was from a rural background and did not have a university education. He came from the remote Wigtownshire village of Whithorn, starting at age 15 as a printer's apprentice in the publishing house of Blackwood and Sons. He set up for himself in 1847, when only 24 years old, and published a relatively small but carefully curated collection of literature and non-fiction with an intellectual and historical focus. His most famous publications, apart from the works of MacGibbon and Ross, were the full text of Sir Walter Scott's *Journal* and a collection of his *Letters*, both of which Douglas edited and annotated himself, and a series of reprints of American novels, including those of Henry James. At the back of each volume of *The Castellated and Domestic Architecture of Scotland* and *The Ecclesiastical Architecture of Scotland* are advertisements for Douglas's Scottish history books. With commercial nous he further tapped into the Victorian appetite for Scottish history with enticing titles such as *Celtic Scotland, A History of Ancient Alban* and *Scotland under her Early Kings*. David Douglas's books were not cheap; *The Castellated and Domestic Architecture of Scotland* was priced at 42 shillings, or two guineas, per volume, equivalent to about £250 at current prices. This was not a book aimed at the mass market; indeed, it was one of the most expensive of the books advertised by David Douglas, whose prices per volume started at three shillings and sixpence. Few individuals now would even consider buying a new five-volume set of books, no matter how enticing, that cost £1,250. Today the relative cost of fine books is very much cheaper.

By the middle of the twentieth century, when the wave of tower house restorations was beginning and would-be restorers were trying to find information on Scottish castles ripe for rebuilding, *The Castellated and Domestic Architecture of Scotland* had become rare, very expensive and only available through specialist antiquarian booksellers or reference libraries. Nigel Tranter's five volumes on *The Fortified House in Scotland*, published in the 1960s, were easier to find, cheaper to purchase and some compensation for those seeking information on towers to restore. Tranter encouraged a number of restorers and successfully matched several towers with new owners who subsequently rebuilt them from ruins. He lamented the difficulty of finding copies of MacGibbon and Ross: 'It is to the nation's loss that their great work has now become so hard to obtain.'[16]

In 1971 and 1977 James Thin's Mercat Press published a well-produced facsimile edition of *The Castellated and Domestic Architecture of Scotland*, making the complete set available for under £100 and thus accessible – although still expensive at that time – for those without a generous antiquarian book budget. These reprints can now be found second hand, with some rarity value. Also the five volumes are available in photographic reproduction in paperback at a reasonable price, although the print quality is not great. But even better, thanks to the Internet Archive, *The Castellated and Domestic Architecture of Scotland* is absolutely free to download in its entirety or read online and is fully, if not entirely reliably, searchable.

The Archive Material

Many original drawings, sketches and notes by MacGibbon and Ross are available in the National Library of Scotland (MS 686–672, *The Ross Collection*), contained within 44 large document boxes. It is a real thrill to open one of these boxes, brought up from the depths of the library on George IV Bridge in Edinburgh, and to handle the drawings

that David MacGibbon and Thomas Ross made on their field trips, and read their original notes and letters. Some drawings are very large and beautifully detailed; others are small sketches. Rough field sketches of buildings, signed and dated, show only the outline of a building and its prominent features – windows, doors, moulding, etc.; when these are looked at side by side with the publication end product one can see how skilfully both MacGibbon and Ross used hatching and cross hatching to create texture, depth and the illusion of form and light in the finished drawings. As well as castle sketches, there are rubbings of stones and sundials, the occasional photograph and plans drawn by other architects, including a plan of Bachilton Farm Steading, with a note by Thomas Ross: 'my Father tenant of Bachilton for about forty years'.

The written material, some typed, some handwritten, includes many letters, lectures, notes, articles and both draft and final versions of the text of the five volumes. This is a rich resource that was donated to the nation by Thomas Ross's family after his death. One notebook of Thomas Ross's, full of annotated sketches, has a picture of Dunstaffnage Castle printed on the back cover; one imagines a son or daughter giving it to him as a small gift. Sadly, a number of items are missing from the collection of David MacGibbon's sketches held in the library of the Royal Incorporation of Architects in Scotland (RIAS), and the archive is thus incomplete. The Edinburgh City Library holds the Thomas Ross collection of 120 watercolour paintings, spanning over 30 years, now digitised and available online. Dundee University Archive has a collection of letters written to Thomas Ross in the late 1880s by his aunt, Isabella Salmond, and his father, Thomas Ross, giving details of family history (MS 87–88). The University of Aberdeen archives hold a small collection of Thomas Ross's essays and drawings.

What is a Castle? The Historiography

The title of MacGibbon and Ross's great work is *The Castellated and **Domestic** Architecture of Scotland*. Despite this, the focus of readers is usually on the castellated buildings that are surveyed. The question of what is and what is not a castle can be a thorny one. MacGibbon and Ross use architectural terminology interchangeably, with 'castle' as a convenient shorthand to refer to what they also call houses, keeps, towers, buildings, fortalices, edifices, villas, manors and mansions. Often a building will be called House in the topographical index (e.g. Fowlis Easter) and Castle in the main Volume 5 index and vice versa. MacGibbon and Ross's focus was on what they called 'native' Scottish architecture, including what is sometimes termed vernacular, although this was not a term used by them.

Many buildings now called 'Castle X' started out as plain X and acquired the appellation of castle sometime in the eighteenth and nineteenth centuries, when the legacy of Walter Scott, coupled with the enthusiasm of Queen Victoria, alerted opportunistic house owners to the added value, in terms of status if nothing else, of redefining their house as a castle – for example, Earlshall and Gogar. Queen Victoria's new castle, Balmoral, set the tone for a generation of baronial mansions which could become castles simply by labelling them such – what Ian Grimble calls the 'accident of nomenclature'.[17]

If MacGibbon and Ross were relaxed about castle terminology, however, the historian Charles McKean was not. His book, *The Scottish Chateau* (2001), was named to direct attention away from the 'fortress' view of Scotland's castles. McKean argued that MacGibbon and Ross were 'victims of their time' and that they 'believed the buildings they were studying were mostly castles in which defensiveness had been the primary consideration'.[18]

the ubiquitous 'heritage' presentation of Scottish Renaissance country seats as military objects, supported by countless publications on 'Scottish castles' that mingle genuine fortresses promiscuously with sometimes very minor country seats, diminishes rather than enhances their interest. For the focus upon defence distorts an understanding of how they worked as self-sustaining country houses functioning at the centre of their estates, as the centres of the regional economy or as the centres of regional power, culture and hospitality. Their classification as castles isolates them from the contemporary poetic, musical, artistic and literary cultures of the country which, in many cases were stimulated by them.[19]

There may be something of the straw man presented here. This is an underestimation of the sophisticated level of understanding of Scottish architectural history of both MacGibbon and Ross and many of their successors. In their survey of Cawdor Castle they demonstrate how well they understood the dramatic appeal of buildings:

Notwithstanding the well-known antiquity of the Thanedom of Cawdor, the existing castle is of comparatively modern date . . . The grim central keep, with its massive walls, crowned with battlements and turrets towering above the extended accommodation which, as at Craigmaillar, has been from time to time erected against the enclosing walls; the internal courtyards; the deep defensive moat, still crossed by its drawbridge; the gateway, protected by its iron-grated gate and loopholed walls, and surmounted with its belfry – are all features which combine to impress the beholder with a lively sense of the power and grandeur of an ancient mediaeval fortress. But most of these features, striking as they are, represent the traditions rather than the reality of an ancient fortalice. (2: 314–15)

Schomberg Scott (1976) put it well when he wrote about towers:

In Scotland such seventeenth century houses as these are almost always styled castles. In so far as this implies a military stronghold or a garrison it must be strictly regarded as a courtesy title. Functionally they are first and foremost complete and sophisticated dwellings. Within there was always that comfort and elegance which has enabled them to maintain their original purpose down to the present time almost without change . . . By the second half of the sixteenth century the external accoutrements of war of earlier times have all been modified and adapted to serve the needs of architectural design, but their military ancestry remains clear and conveys to the spectator the unequivocal message: 'Here is the seat of authority. Nemo me impune lacessit.'[20]

The power of the word was highlighted by Nicholas Fairbairn, the Scottish solicitor-general and politician who bought and restored Fordell Castle in the 1960s. He complained that the word 'castle' had been used to smear him politically and – somewhat disingenuously – that he did not win the Central Edinburgh parliamentary seat in the 1964 General Election because of its misuse in the 'politics of envy': 'With Socialist envy, the Labour campaign in Central Edinburgh was personal. They used the word "castle", which means a fortified residence, to impute to me grandeur, riches, exclusion, and all the legendary wickedness of the baron towards his vassals. I lived in luxury they alleged; the voters all lived in slums. I was a wicked, privileged oppressor . . . Little did they know the slum which I had bought and taken over.'[21]

When MacGibbon and Ross surveyed Fordell Castle it was in use as a summerhouse in the beautiful gardens of Fordell House, an eighteenth-century country house built to replace Fordell Castle as a residence for the Henderson family. Fordell House was demolished in 1963. By the time Nicholas Fairbairn bought the castle, for 'not much more than the price of a good overcoat',[22] it had become almost derelict, a 'slum', and was ripe for restoration as a comfortable home. Fordell Castle's value was clear in 2007 when it was put up for sale at the astonishing price of three and a half million pounds, at a time when very few Scottish properties fetched over one million pounds.

In 1981, Stewart Cruden forecast that MacGibbon and Ross's 'classification and chronology of Scottish castellated and domestic architecture . . . by and large will never be upset'.[23] But of course eventually it was challenged, as established theories always are – although not until a century after its first publication, when Charles McKean wrote *The Scottish Chateau*:

Many of the chateaux that so delighted eighteenth century naturalist and topographical author Thomas Pennant's eye were greatly altered, reduced to ruins, or vanished within a century of his visit. The rain that washed away their mortar washed away their domesticity, leaving ruins with overemphatic battlements, gunloops and turrets. They were now confirmed as 'castles' and it was as such that architects David MacGibbon and Thomas Ross categorized them.[24]

But MacGibbon and Ross describe the castles of Doune, Tantallon and Dirleton – all massive grey ruins with a fortress-like appearance – as 'palaces and mansions of great extent and magnificence' (1: 418), and talking of their third period (1400–1542), say: 'The later castles of this epoch . . . not only contain the numerous halls and suites of apartments common at the time in French and English mansions, but they are also built and decorated in a style almost as ornate and sumptuous as their foreign prototypes' (1: 418).

As David Walker points out, 'there always has been a school of thought which valued the tower house as a powerful symbol of ancient lineage'.[25] This school of thought has been thoroughly explored by both Charles McKean in *The Scottish Chateau* and Charles Wemyss in *The Noble Houses of Scotland*.[26] Wemyss proposes that the ancient Scottish nobility, like the French *noblesse d'épée*, retained the old styles of building as symbolic of their lineage, while – in France at least – the newly wealthy and ennobled (the *noblesse de robes* in France) were open to more modern fashions in architecture.

The other main thrust of criticism was aimed at MacGibbon and Ross's theory of chronology. Castellologist Joachim Zeune argues against an exclusively typological-chronological approach: 'The individuality of a specific object, though, is almost bound to lose itself in the wealth of structural detail: concept and plan of the building often fit in so beautifully with typological-chronological classifications that one tends to overlook or disregard architectural details pointing to a far more complex chronology of building.'[27] He goes on: 'The discovery that an object might have been erected in several distinct phases is another potential victim of an exclusively typological approach. What one notices is often only the final shape, the

castle as it presents itself today; and this may be supported by carved dates referring, in fact, to a phase of alteration or extension. An older nucleus may thus escape attention.' Here again, though, MacGibbon and Ross are mostly not guilty. Again and again, they point out the different phases of building in the castles they survey, sometimes admitting defeat at the complexity of a building that contains layer upon layer of accrued work over centuries, such as Aboyne.

Richard Oram has charted the development of castle studies through the twentieth century, where a longstanding emphasis on chronology and form, which led to a one-dimensional view of castles and 'an obsession with dating', was gradually being replaced by a broader perspective: 'In this evolving methodology, the emphasis is moving away from chronological typology towards consideration of broader social, cultural, economic and political contexts alongside the structural analysis and an examination of the other physical manifestations of lordship in the surrounding landscape.'[28] MacGibbon and Ross may have been anxious to provide dates for their individual buildings and a theory of dating for Scotland's castellated architecture as a whole, but their scope is considerably wider and more nuanced than a simple chronology and they do take care to provide context. They stressed the domestic nature of Scotland's grander buildings at a time long before revisionist theories of castles were put forward by the historians of the late twentieth century. In many of the entries for the buildings that were still occupied, they give details of the owners and inhabitants and of changes that had taken place over the centuries, so that one gets a real sense of the intimate domestic scale and function of the buildings they describe, in a way that previous and subsequent castellologists rarely provide. For example, in their entry on Traquair House: 'Lady Louisa Stuart, the late liferentrix of Traquair, kept up the customs of a bygone age down till her decease in December 1875, within four months of her attaining her hundredth year, and her old spinnets, spinning wheels and distaffs, which she used to the last, ignoring most of the modern ways, still remain in the house' (2: 440).

McKean claims that 'Until very recently, the case for Renaissance architecture in Scotland was simply put – there was almost none'.[29] But MacGibbon and Ross repeatedly refer to the Renaissance style of architecture in their 'fourth period'. The general index shows numerous entries under 'Renaissance style'. Early twentieth-century castellologists may have been informed by a Victorian imperialistic world view that characterised fifteenth- and sixteenth-century Scots as essentially warlike and their buildings as reflections of this, but the text of MacGibbon and Ross is much more measured and restrained in the expression of this world view than many of those who were later inspired by them. For the next hundred years or so, the scholarly literature on castles focused almost exclusively on the structure of the buildings. Both form and function were important, but only as long as the latter was military or defensive. Geoffrey Stell developed this point:

Castle studies were long dominated by issues of design typology and military capability, while military strategy was likewise seen as the key to determining and understanding a castle's location. For more than a century from the middle decades of the nineteenth century these views prevailed among successive generations of castle scholars . . . the military standpoint reached its peak in the person of Dr William Douglas Simpson (1896–1968), who stands out as an uncompromising protagonist of such views.[30]

Stell goes on to link Simpson's views with his German mother and his links with East Prussia, 'from where in the 1930s he and his generation were confronted with the contemporary reality of mobile, ruthlessly efficient professional armies'.[31] The contemporary conditions within which historians operate necessarily frame their outlook, but some are more trammelled than others.

The castles literature, both academic and popular, generally stops dead at a point, usually several hundred years ago, when individual castles were either first built or finally abandoned or burnt out. The histories are stuck in the distant past and have become as fossilised as the buildings they describe. Yet most of Scotland's castles have changed quite radically during the past century. Some have decayed or disappeared altogether, while others have changed form, function and/or owners. Buildings are as dynamic as those who inhabit them; they do not stand still, but build up a semiotic biography of change. MacGibbon and Ross understood this in a way that most castellologists in the next century were unable or willing to; they acknowledged the dynamic nature of the buildings that they surveyed, at the same time as trying to assign them to historical periods and they spoke of current and past owners, sometimes with affectionate or admiring anecdotes.

At the end of Volume 2, MacGibbon and Ross make an effort to understand the course of domestic life in the castles they describe. Referring to their second period, they muse, 'How they managed to live, with their families, retainers, domestics and cattle, in these small fortresses, most of which contained practically only three apartments, it is difficult to imagine' (2: 571). They spend four pages recreating in some detail the scenes of life within small and large castles and keeps, quoting extensively from the historian John Hill Burton's *The Life of Simon, Lord Lovat and Duncan*

Forbes, of Culloden (1847) and from J.H. Parker's *Some Account of Domestic Architecture in England from Edward I to Richard II* (1853).

Later Castle Surveys –
after MacGibbon and Ross

Despite the criticisms described above, almost every scholarly work of the twentieth century and beyond on the subject of Scottish castles acknowledges the debt owed to the prodigious work of MacGibbon and Ross, mostly in glowing terms. Sir John Stirling Maxwell, politician, philanthropist and founder member of the National Trust for Scotland, was a great admirer of MacGibbon and Ross's volumes: 'it is not too much to say that these authors found chaos and left order. The present writer is just old enough to remember the delight with which their first two volumes were hailed.' He wrote *Shrines and Homes of Scotland* explicitly in 'an attempt to convey their message to a wider circle'.[32]

In the 1960s Nigel Tranter also wrote and illustrated five volumes on Scottish domestic castellated architecture, although these are much shorter and simpler than MacGibbon and Ross's and lack plans. His work *The Fortified House in Scotland* covers 663 buildings, which he defines as the 'fortalices, lesser castles, peel towers, keeps and defensible lairds' houses'.[33] 'And inevitably, tribute falls once again to be paid to the stalwart writers of MacGibbon and Ross's *The Castellated and Domestic Architecture of Scotland*, whose magnificent work and untiring energy, in those days before motor transport, are a continual source of wonder and admiration.'[34] Tranter did, however, sketch and describe a number of buildings that MacGibbon and Ross missed – e.g. Strathendry Castle in Fife, Lennox Plunton Castle in Kirkcudbrightshire and Little (Old) Sauchie Castle near Stirling, the last restored from a ruin in 2001.

Echoing MacGibbon and Ross, Tranter railed against the neglect and wilful destruction of Scottish castles in the introductions to his five volumes:

Although there were, and are, so many of these buildings, the wastage in them today is grievous and deplorable, indeed disgraceful. They are very much a wasting, though irreplaceable, asset. Although we are the envy of so many from lands less favoured in this respect, all too few of our own people either know, appreciate or care for them. Especially, unhappily, local authorities, into whose hands many of them fall.[35]

Mike Salter has also produced a series of five volumes on the castles of Scotland.[36] He lists and describes in some detail 1541 castles altogether, twice as many as MacGibbon and Ross, with plans, sketches and photographs. Since 2008, the RCAHMS/HES Canmore website has produced easily searchable information and pictures on most of the castles of Scotland, including a bibliography for each, making information much more accessible for castle researchers.

Scottish castles are a popular subject for coffee-table books and there are many general books on the market, some with only a superficial commentary on each building. The best are well-researched and scholarly accounts containing carefully detailed and lengthy descriptions and analyses of specific areas, for example Alastair Maxwell-Irving's exhaustive volumes *The Border Towers of Scotland: The West March*[37] and *The Border Towers of Scotland 2: Their Evolution and Architecture*. In 1953 and 1954 Country Life Books published two significant books: *Scottish Castles of the Sixteenth and Seventeenth Centuries* by Oliver Hill – a lavishly illustrated work – and John Fleming's *Scottish Country Houses and Gardens Open to the Public*. Important works on Scottish castles by Robert

Clow, Stewart Cruden, Michael C. Davis, Richard Fawcett, Maurice Lindsay, W. Mackay Mackenzie, Richard Oram, W. Douglas Simpson, Peter Yeoman, David Walker, Joachim Zeune and numerous others have been published since the 1960s. The most recent is Martin Coventry's *The Castles of Scotland: A Comprehensive Guide to More Than 4,100 Castles, Towers, Historic Houses, Stately Homes and Family Lands*. This is an alphabetical gazetteer or encyclopedia of Scottish castles and other historic buildings, many of which no longer exist. It is a *catalogue raisonné*, as MacGibbon and Ross wished for, but without the detailed text, plans and sketches that they pioneered, and without any filter for buildings that have gone. They did consider 'that some account of those castles, or other allied structures in the country, which have now almost, and in many cases entirely, disappeared, would be desirable; but although such information would be extremely interesting, it has been thought that the subject falls more particularly within the province of the archaeologist' (4: vi). They did, however, provide details of a several lost castles – see Chapter 6.

The subsequent large-scale surveys of Scottish architectural history have all involved multiple authors and many years of incremental publishing. The *Inventories of the Ancient and Historic Monuments* published by RCAHMS (1909–92), which covered only about half of Scotland, were finally abandoned in 1992, *The Buildings of Scotland* series (the 'Scottish Pevsner') took 27 years to complete and the RIAS series of illustrated architectural guides of Scotland, started in 1986, is still incomplete. In response to a suggestion from the scholar and architectural historian Andor Gomme in 1959 that a *Buildings of Scotland* series should be produced, Nikolaus Pevsner, author of the *Buildings of England*, wrote:

If you are going to do this really, you will have for the rest of your life a ball and chain round your leg. You will be alternately depressed and elated and you will of course not find a publisher to pay for it. My organisation is that I have two full-time assistants who work for a year each in libraries extracting all that can be extracted. I then take over from them and do the travelling and the writing . . . Scotland has 33 counties, and although there may not be much in them I feel that, if you do it single-handed, you will need 33 years.[38]

In this letter, with his gloomy predictions, Pevsner nicely sets the context for the astonishing scale of the achievement of MacGibbon and Ross in completing their survey of *The Castellated and Domestic Architecture of Scotland* in only five years, while working full-time, without paid help and volunteer help for only some of their entries. They suggest in Volume 2, when floating the idea of a *catalogue raisonné*, that 'It would be to us a labour of love to engage in such a work.' A labour of love is surely what their work became. They were hampered by a metaphorical ball and chain perhaps, and had many challenges to overcome, but it is comforting to think that they must have experienced at least some elation and enjoyment on their castle surveying jaunts.

Some pressing questions that arise from an overview of the work of MacGibbon and Ross are these: What has happened to all the castles that MacGibbon and Ross surveyed? Were their prophecies of doom prescient? Did the twentieth century treat Scotland's built heritage better than the nineteenth century? And what will the future in the twenty-first century bring? Part 3 will address these questions.

PART 3

The Castles,
Then and Now

Introduction

They reveal to us the social relations of the people of Scotland, both in peace and war, during all the periods of our national life. They exhibit the state of comparative prosperity and adversity, of rudeness and refinement, of jealousy and suspicion, or of neighbourly confidence and friendship, in which our forefathers dwelt during all the vicissitudes and trials of the various epochs of Scottish history. (3: 2)

Castles were so much more than architecturally interesting buildings to MacGibbon and Ross. In the surveys they were social historians and architectural historians in equal measure. Their excitement about the social aspects of the castles is evident. In their entry on Fairlie Castle they point out that 'Confined and narrow as the accommodation of such a tower may seem at the present time, it is evident that a considerable amount of domestic comfort was undoubtedly experienced within its walls' (3: 181). They go on to describe the Testament of Katherine Crauford, Lady Fairnelie, which details her napery, wearing apparel, cooking utensils, barrelled meat and wine and many other items in 1601. In their entry on St Andrews Castle, they devote three and a half pages to a lively historical account of the goings on at the castle from 1200 to 1612 – using many more paragraphs about the social history of the people involved than about the building survey.

Given how alive they were to changes, would MacGibbon and Ross be astonished to see how many of the castles they surveyed have altered dramatically? Would they be surprised, or pleased, or sad at what has happened to Castle X in the intervening 140 years? They have given us very clear indications of their views on conservation and it seems perfectly plausible to imagine that they would be pleased, for example, about MacLellan's Castle in Kirkcudbright becoming a well-preserved museum in state care, or dismayed about the demolition of Elphinstone Castle. They would certainly be surprised at the wholesale removal of Castle Doon to a higher location to save it from

OPPOSITE LEFT. Kelburn Castle, Ayrshire, decorated with graffiti.

OPPOSITE RIGHT. Kelburn Castle, by Billings.

flooding when a new reservoir was created, or the opening of the ancient, remote and formerly ruinous Mingarry Castle as a luxury hotel. They might be pleased that Traquair House has still scarcely changed at all. 'Since the end of the seventeenth century, when the last additions were made, almost nothing seems to have been done to the building beyond the necessary repairs to keep it wind and water tight . . . The present proprietor, the Honourable H.C. Maxwell Stuart, has preserved the venerable aspect of the place as far as compatible with the comforts of a modern gentleman's residence' (2: 440). Traquair is still lived in by a member of the Maxwell Stuart family and although it has been adapted for modern living and visiting tourists, the current owner, Catherine Maxwell-Stewart, reported that her grandmother had lived alone at Traquair throughout the Second World War with no electricity and very limited heating.[1]

They would certainly be astonished at the transformation of the exterior of Kelburn Castle. The graffiti was installed in 2007, when the Earl of Glasgow invited four Brazilian artists to paint a temporary design on the walls before the concrete render was removed and the building re-harled. However, in 2021 the graffiti and the harling are both still there and the building has become a tourist attraction largely because of the exterior paintwork.

MacGibbon and Ross catalogued and commented on many changes in their surveys and understood that fashion and finance often dictate usage. The pace of change accelerated in the twentieth century, however. Haggs Castle underwent six transformational changes over the course of a century, for example. Castles changed hands regularly but not frequently in the nineteenth century, but in the twentieth century a brisk trade developed and some castles that have been restored

from ruins have been placed on the high-end housing market multiple times, such as Castle Grant.

The Churches

In addition to the three volumes MacGibbon and Ross produced on the ecclesiastical architecture of Scotland, Volumes 3 and 5 of *The Castellated and Domestic Architecture of Scotland* have short sections on churches. In Volume 3 they disclaim any attempt to give a general account of ecclesiastical architecture, but they make the case for the churches, from the fifteenth century onwards, incorporating the 'Scottish style' of architecture of houses and castles into their design: 'nearly every church of the fifteenth and sixteenth centuries being distinguished by its crow-stepped gables and corbelled and embattled parapets, precisely in the style of the castles and mansions' (3: 37). In illustration, they provide a sketch of Linlithgow Church (St Michael's Parish Church). As examples, they mention Greyfriars Church in Stirling and church towers in Pittenweem, Anstruther and Fenwick. Dysart Church, they say, 'has the complete appearance of a fortified keep' (3: 39), and they compare the corbelling of Dairsie Church to that of Crathes and Craigievar.

In Volume 5 the authors describe 25 church buildings, with sketches, 'for the purpose of showing the influence of the Domesticated and Castellated styles upon them' (5: 130). MacGibbon and Ross were explicitly in favour of the quaint and picturesque in church architecture and were not admirers of the plain Presbyterian style: 'The Puritan sentiment which prevailed during the latter portion of the seventeenth century being entirely destitute of interest in architecture or decoration of any kind, many of the above structures [churches] suffered during that sterile period' (5: 131).

5

Castles Across
the Country –
an Overview

———

The castle has always been a formidable image, a powerful intimidating fantasy of the human imagination. The fortress, the citadel, the craggy tower dominating the landscape: it is older than history, as natural to man as the eagle to the eyrie.

Rose Macaulay (1953) *Pleasure of Ruins,* Walker and Co., New York, p. 441

Of the castles described by MacGibbon and Ross about two-thirds were uninhabited and mostly in ruins. Those ranged from fragmentary ruins (e.g. Duchal Castle in Renfrewshire, still a fragmentary ruin), to well-consolidated buildings at minimal risk of deterioration. A few, such as Amisfield, Repentance and Stobhall, were empty but in good repair, being roofed and consolidated. Of the rest, the majority were inhabited by families, some only on a part-time basis, as shooting lodges or summer residences, e.g. Cawdor Castle and Brodick Castle. In some ways, castles were simpler buildings in the late nineteenth century. Apart from the great military fortresses, they were generally either ruinous or inhabited by wealthy families. Most were privately owned. Some buildings were more ruinous than others and some more fully inhabited than others, but the dichotomy was almost absolute. A few exceptions were Dundas Castle, which housed a distillery; Stranraer Castle, then still in use occasionally as a municipal prison; Kinnaird Tower, open as a

museum; Kinnaird Head, a lighthouse; and Merchiston Castle, in use as a boarding school. The great fortresses of Edinburgh, Stirling and Blackness were still used by the military. Forty of the castles that MacGibbon and Ross surveyed have since disappeared, mainly through demolition. Fifty of the ruined and uninhabited castles have been restored and are now mostly in use as family homes or holiday accommodation.

This overview, like MacGibbon and Ross's survey, is merely a snapshot in time. Castles described as inhabited, or in use as hotels, or unroofed ruins at risk of collapse, may change status dramatically over short periods of time. Even during the few years when MacGibbon and Ross were carrying out their survey, changes took place, mostly for the worse. In his history of Balbithan House, Gordon Slade concluded 'By 1841 Benjamin Gordon and his two sisters were living at Balbithan, and the history of building and alterations came to an end.'[1] But, of course, this was not the end of the alterations made to Balbithan, which resumed in the 1960s and may well continue again in the future. History never stands still, even in Scotland's castles.

The Geography of MacGibbon and Ross

The scope of the surveys carried out by MacGibbon and Ross encompasses the whole of Scotland, from Muness Castle in the Shetland Island of Unst ('the most northern specimen') to Dunskey Castle in the Mull of Galloway and Queen Mary's House in Jedburgh in the Borders. They visited remote and inaccessible castles all over the country, when they could have comfortably covered a large number of representative buildings within easy travelling distance of Edinburgh and still have produced a major body of work on Scottish castles.

The physical geography of Scotland can be challenging. At Ailsa Craig in Ayrshire the logistics and sheer effort of getting there would have defeated a less determined pair. MacGibbon and Ross provide two plans, a sketch and a detailed description of the small tower situated on a rocky shoulder on the side of an extremely steep volcanic island in the Firth of Clyde. Because of the barren nature of the island, they decided 'it must have been the fortress of a pirate chief, who issued from it to plunder the surrounding seas and coasts, for the island itself would never yield the sustenance necessary for the captain and his crew' (3: 207). In order to get there, they would have had to make their way by train to Girvan and charter a local fishing boat, then scramble up a precipitous and narrow rocky path before getting on with their sketching and measuring. The journey back down the path is even more difficult than the ascent.

Getting to Muness Castle on the island of Unst from Edinburgh would probably have meant a train to Aberdeen followed by a ferry journey of at least 12 hours to Lerwick, then a further two onward ferry journeys from Lerwick, making a weekend trip either impossible or utterly exhausting. Other island castles visited include Kismul, Castle Tioram, Brodick, Threave and Dunvegan.

Scotland has had several reorganisations of its counties and regions in the last 120 years. The first took place in 1890, just as MacGibbon and Ross were starting to publish their research, and is incorporated into their topographical index in Volume 5.[2] In the discussion in this part of the book I have chosen to use the 1890 county names (see Plate 5), rather than the current council areas, for ease of reference to the original volumes, and have used MacGibbon and Ross's spellings (e.g. Dumbartonshire instead of Dunbartonshire). MacGibbon and Ross's 33 counties are easy to locate; despite counties such as Forfarshire,[3] Linlithgowshire and Haddingtonshire having disappeared from current maps, their county towns give the clue to their location.

The graph on page 78 shows the distribution of MacGibbon and Ross's castles across Scotland.[4] As can be seen, the counties with the most castles are Aberdeenshire, Ayrshire, Fifeshire, Midlothian and Perthshire, all with more than 50. The complete list of castle entries, at the back of Volume 5, is organised by county. A further ten had gone before MacGibbon and Ross's time, but they chose to write an entry describing the former building, often lamenting its disappearance. Not all of the castles listed in the back of Volume 5 were actually surveyed – e.g. Bocharm Castle in Banffshire is one of a list reported as having been mentioned by Professor Cosmo Innes in *Scotland in the Middle Ages* (1: 63), but is not given a separate entry. MacGibbon and Ross may have used a professional indexer, who would have noted names from the text, but not necessarily have understood their degree of significance.

Location is often the most salient feature of buildings: the first question we ask about Castle X is 'Where is it?' Grouping castles together

Ailsa Craig Castle, Ayrshire, by MacGibbon and Ross. Note the steepness of the slope, although perhaps MacGibbon and Ross exaggerated the degree of it slightly.

Ailsa Craig Castle today, little changed since MacGibbon and Ross visited.

geographically has the additional advantage of providing insights into local building styles – the great Bel Family castles of Aberdeenshire being perhaps the best-known example – and location-specific building types, such as the mediaeval western seaboard fortresses or the small towers of the Borders. MacGibbon and Ross grouped together the entries on Fairlie, Law, Skelmorlie and Little Cumbrae castles and also Bonshaw, Robgill and Wardhouse towers, because of their location and similarities. They initially organised their surveys by historical period. However, within the historical sections they used a geographical approach. In Volume 3 they note in the section on the fourth period, 'Each series of buildings is taken topographically, in the same order as formerly – i.e. beginning in the west, we move by the south west along the south of Scotland, then take the central districts, and finally those further north' (3: 372). If they had conceived their great project as a kind of encyclopedia, or *catalogue raisonné*, as they later proposed, they could have used an alphabetical and/or a geographic approach – and alphabetical is the approach they took, for pragmatic reasons, in the Supplement in Volume 5. But a series of entries unrelated by any category other

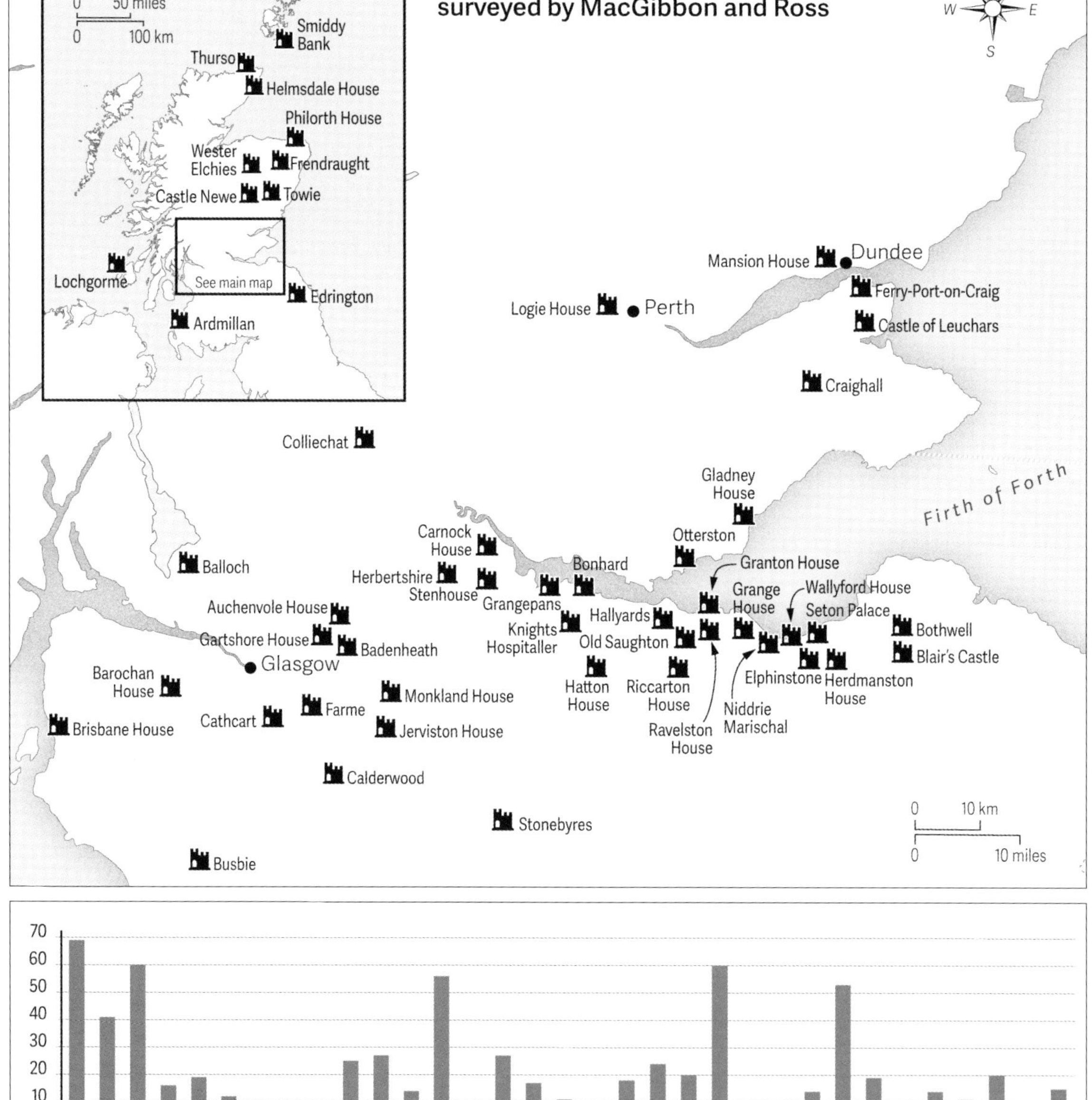

(*Top*) Castles surveyed by MacGibbon and Ross that were already no longer standing when surveyed, or have since been demolished. (*Foot*) Distribution of MacGibbon and Ross castles across Scotland.

than initial letter can be a barrier to creative historical analysis, their great strength.

The broad-brush statistics in this chapter demonstrate how much and how frequently the form and function of castles have changed by highlighting condition and usage, but they present a crude picture only. It is challenging to give definitive numbers for categories of castles, as their status is sometimes uncertain – it is not always clear from the descriptions or sketches whether or not buildings were inhabited when MacGibbon and Ross visited; their sketches often show them as spruce and clean, when in fact they were covered in vegetation and almost derelict – e.g. MacLellan's in Kirkcudbright (2: 149) and Queen Mary's House in Jedburgh (4: 112). Some castles, then as now, were occupied only as holiday homes or shooting lodges and were empty for much of the year. The category of 'ruinous' is a broad one, scoping everything from rickles o' stanes to recently abandoned buildings with intact roofs.

Different counties present widely differing statistics. In Argyllshire, for example, 75% of the MacGibbon and Ross castles are ruinous, whereas in Midlothianshire, the area around Edinburgh, the majority are inhabited, or in use as offices or hotels. The map opposite shows all the lost castles at and since the time of MacGibbon and Ross's survey. Unfortunately seven (12%) of MacGibbon and Ross's Midlothianshire buildings were demolished in the twentieth century. In Orkney and Shetland five out of the eight buildings are in the care of Historic Environment Scotland, whereas in almost equally remote Wigtownshire, none is. In Peeblesshire the majority of castles surveyed comprise small ruinous towers in remote fields. Aberdeenshire and Fifeshire each have nine castles that are open to the public, whereas Perthshire and Midlothianshire, also with large numbers of castles within their county boundaries, only have five each, and Ayrshire has only three out of 60,

none of which is in the care of HES. In both Buteshire and Caithness-shire only one castle in each (Ackergill and Dunbeath, respectively) is inhabited; the rest are ruins.

In this chapter Scotland has been divided into six geographical areas for ease of analysis: South Scotland; Western Central Scotland; Eastern Central Scotland; North Central Scotland; Northeast Scotland; North-west Scotland. Figures for the condition (ruinous or inhabited) of the MacGibbon and Ross castles, their usage and public accessibility are given for each historical county, producing a picture of the changes, for better or worse, over the past 130 years.

SOUTH SCOTLAND

The modern council areas of the Scottish Borders (historical counties Berwickshire, Selkirkshire and Roxburghshire) and Dumfries and Galloway (historical counties Dumfriesshire, Kirkcudbrightshire and Wigtownshire) make up this area. Across this region, MacGibbon and Ross surveyed 102 castles, the majority of which are small and ruinous. Referring to the period known as the 'Rough Wooing'[5] in the mid sixteenth century, they said

> Henry VIII . . . sent an army into Scotland, and devastated the southern counties in a fiercer and more unsparing manner than any of his predecessors. All the towers, castles and houses of every kind, and even the churches and monasteries, of the southeast of Scotland, were destroyed by the relentless hands of Surrey and Somerset. It is therefore not surprising to find almost no examples of domestic architecture in this region save desolated ruins. Those structures which are observable in a comparatively entire condition are either of later

date than the middle of the sixteenth century, or are restorations of ancient structures. (3: 364)

Berwickshire, Roxburghshire and Dumfriesshire border England and together with Selkirkshire and Kirkcudbrightshire these counties comprise the East, Middle and West Marches of Scotland. Within them lie the Border Towers, fortified strongholds representing scenes of reiving and bloody feuds. MacGibbon and Ross surveyed 44 castles in the Border Marches, many of them desolate ruins in the landscape. Kirkcudbrightshire and Wigtownshire together make up Galloway: beautiful, remote and sparsely populated, but with 58 castles surveyed by MacGibbon and Ross (and at least as many again that they did not get to), among which are five in the care of HES. A troubling statistic is that there are six Dumfries and Galloway castles on the Buildings at Risk Register.

Berwickshire

MacGibbon and Ross surveyed 19 castles in Berwickshire, of which nine were ruinous and one, Wedderlie House, partly ruinous and partly inhabited. It was restored in the 1940s and the 1960s and is now rented out as a weddings and events venue. Edrington Castle disappeared shortly after MacGibbon and Ross wrote that it was 'a mere fragment of an ancient castle' (4: 391). According to Sir Hebert Maxwell, 'Edrington Castle . . . once a place of great strength and importance, has been quarried away to near ground level'.[6] The ruined castles they surveyed are Billie Castle, Blanerne Castle, Cockburnspath Tower, Corsbie Castle, Evelaw Tower, Fast Castle, Greenknowe Castle, Home Castle and Whitslade. All remain ruinous today, with Billie Castle, now as then, only recognisable by a few grass mounds. MacGibbon and Ross describe Fast Castle as 'The crumbling ruins of a

great keep' (3: 222); unfortunately, it has crumbled further in recent years. Seven castles were inhabited: Bassendean House, Bemersyde Castle, Cowdenknowes Castle, Duns Castle, Hatton Hall, Nesbit Castle and Thirlestane Castle (Lauder). Nesbit Castle became unoccupied during the mid twentieth century but has recently been restored as a private residence; all the others have been continuously occupied. Cranshaws Castle appears to have been empty but in good condition when MacGibbon and Ross visited. It was restored shortly afterwards, in 1896, by Andrew Smith, an Edinburgh brewer. In 1978 it was refurbished by Robert Hurd and Partners and was upgraded again in the twenty-first century. It is now rented out for self-catering holiday accommodation.

Selkirkshire

MacGibbon and Ross surveyed 12 castles in Selkirkshire. Only one, Buckholm Tower, was inhabited when they wrote about it,[7] but now there are two, restored to domestic residences in the twentieth century: Kirkhope Tower and Oakwood Tower (re-named Aikwood by Lord and Lady Steel, who carried out the restoration in 1988–92). Whytbank Tower was recently restored but remains empty and well maintained. Buckholm Tower, meanwhile, now stands in ruins high on an exposed fellside above the valley of the Gala Water. Its condition deteriorates further every year. Fernielee (now Old Fairnilee) House, which was a roofless ruin when MacGibbon and Ross visited, was partially restored in 1904 and mostly demolished. It now stands as a consolidated ruin in the garden of Fairnilee House, an Arts and Crafts masterpiece built in 1904 by John J. Burnet. The remainder of Selkirkshire's castles were ruinous then and still

OPPOSITE. Cranshaws Castle in Berwickshire.

Newark Castle in Selkirkshire (Scottish Borders).

are: Blackhouse, Dryhope, Elibank, Gamelscleuch, Newark, Thirlstane (Ettrick) and Torwoodlee, which has been stabilised recently. MacGibbon and Ross report that 'The ruins of the old tower of the Scotts of Thirlstane stand behind the modern mansion of Lord Napier and Ettrick' (3: 402), i.e. Thirlestane House, which dated from 1812–13 and was demolished in 1965.

Roxburghshire

Only two Roxburghshire castles have been continuously inhabited since MacGibbon and Ross:

Branxholm and Darnick. Three are open to the public: Hermitage Castle and Smailholm Tower are in the care of HES and Queen Mary's House in Jedburgh has been a local council museum since 1930. It stands in a public garden. When MacGibbon and Ross visited they noted 'at present it is so overgrown with ivy, and so hemmed in with bushes and apple trees, that one can hardly see it' (4: 114). Their sketch, however, shows the building entire, with no vegetation to be seen.

Eight Roxburghshire castles were ruinous or consolidated then and still are: Cessford, Colmslie, Corbett, Goldielands, Langshaw, Littledean, Minto

RIGHT. MacGibbon and Ross's tidied-up sketch of Queen Mary's House in Jedburgh.

BELOW. Queen Mary's House, Jedburgh (2020), situated within a small public garden that still has apple trees.

and Timpendean. Fernieherst (now Ferniehirst) and Hillslap have undergone significant changes: Hillslap was restored from a ruin in the 1970s and Ferniehirst had changes of fortune before its restoration by Simpson and Brown in 1987–90. Ferniehirst opens regularly for public visits.

Dumfriesshire

MacGibbon and Ross surveyed 25 castles in Dumfriesshire, of which 8 were inhabited, 15 were roofless ruins and 2 were roofed but uninhabited. Four are now open to the public: Caerlaverock, Lochmaben and Morton are in the care of HES and Drumlanrig Castle is owned by the Duke of Buccleuch. Three have been restored from a ruinous state – Lochhouse Tower, Spedlins Tower and Comlongan Castle – and one, Hoddam (now Hoddom), has gone from being inhabited to a state of dereliction, in the middle of a caravan park. Fourmerkland was inhabited but was abandoned as a residence in 1896[8] and has been empty but consolidated and well maintained since then. Repentance Tower has also been consolidated and well cared for, as has Amisfield Tower. Achincass or Auchen Castle and Bankend or Isle Tower (5: 232) were both greatly ruined when MacGibbon and Ross visited, and remain so. Frenchland Tower, Lag Tower, Lochwood Tower, Sanquhar Castle, Torthorwald Castle and Wardhouse Tower have all been ruinous throughout. Hollows Tower, also known as Gilknockie Tower, was a roofless ruin, but was restored in 1979–80. It is now a visitor centre and houses the Clan Armstrong museum, with a section devoted to Neil Armstrong, the first man on the moon. Robgill, Closeburn, Isle Tower (3: 393), Bonshaw and Elshieshields have been continuously inhabited.

OPPOSITE. Spedlins Tower in Dumfriesshire.

Kirkcudbrightshire

The picture in this county is complex; there has been much change. When MacGibbon and Ross carried out their survey, 12 castles were ruinous. Of those, five are now in the care of HES: Cardoness, Carsluith, MacLellan's, Threave and Drumcoltern (Drumcoltran) Castle. The last, which was partly inhabited when MacGibbon and Ross visited, is now roofed and consolidated and part of a farmyard. It is a plain tower with a stern text inscribed in Latin above the door: 'Keep hidden what is secret; speak little; be truthful; avoid wine; remember death; be pitiful.' Two of the ruinous buildings were restored for occupation in the twentieth century – Abbot's Tower and Barholm Castle – and five are still ruinous, in varying states of disrepair. These are Old Buittle Castle, a fragment; Campston Castle (Cumston), Edingham Castle, standing in isolation in a field; the fragmentary remains of Garlies Castle, 'which has been a structure of considerable size and various ages' (5: 279), and Auchenskeoch Castle, a sad fragment in a farmyard. Earlston (now Earl-stoun) Castle was consolidated in the 1990s and had almost been restored by the Vivat Trust as a holiday home when the Trust went into admin-istration. Kirkconnell Tower is let as holiday accommodation. Barscobe House, Buittle Castle, Hills Castle and Rusco Castle were inhabited by farm labourers in the nineteenth century and fell into disrepair and abandonment during the twen-tieth century, when they were later restored for modern habitation by new owners. One castle, Kenmure, has suffered what is probably an irre-versible decline and has gone from a fine inhabited house to a deteriorating roofless ruin. It is such a large and complex building that the resources needed to save it are unlikely to be available, espe-cially given its remote location. It was a hotel in the mid twentieth century.

Stranraer Castle, now known as
the Castle of St John and used as
a museum.

Wigtownshire

The castles which were inhabited then and are still inhabited are: Isle of Whithorn Castle, Lochnaw and the Old Place of Mochrum, which is used for shooting parties and is rented out as a wedding venue. There were eight ruinous castles when MacGibbon and Ross visited and all are still ruinous, although plans have been made for the restoration of Myrton Castle and Dunskey Castle. The ruinous castles are Carscreugh, Castle Kennedy, Castle Stewart, Dunskey, Galdenoch, Killasser, Myrton and Sorbie. The Chief of the

Clan Hannay, which owns Sorbie Tower, would like to restore the tower and use it for events and accommodation. Castle of Park, which was tenanted by workmen, was taken into care by the Ministry of Works in 1951 and leased to the Landmark Trust in 1992. It is now rented out for holiday accommodation. Stranraer Castle, also known as the Castle of St John, was a prison and became a museum in the 1980s. MacGibbon and Ross noted that the surrounding houses 'hem it in closely on all sides, so much that the building is somewhat difficult to get at, and can only be seen from the back gardens of the adjoining houses' (3: 512).

These buildings have since been demolished and the tower now stands proud in the town centre. Castle Wigg was originally a sixteenth-century tower house, later encased in an eighteenth-century mansion. 'The older portion forms but a small part of the building as it now exists, extensive additions having been made at the close of last century' (5: 248). After a fire in 1933 it became derelict.

WESTERN CENTRAL SCOTLAND

This area stretches from the south of Ayrshire to the north of Dumbartonshire, plus Bute and Stirlingshire, with a mix of rural areas and densely populated towns, including Glasgow and Stirling. Ayrshire, although not a large county geographically, is very rich in castles. Of the 144 castles surveyed by MacGibbon and Ross in this region (60 in Ayrshire, 9 in Dumbartonshire, 19 in Renfrewshire, 20 in Stirlingshire, 24 in Lanarkshire and 12 in Buteshire), 15 have since been demolished or deteriorated badly, only 4 have been restored from ruin and 10 are now open to the public.

Ayrshire

MacGibbon and Ross surveyed 60 castles in Ayrshire. Three have since been demolished: Ardmillan Castle, Brisbane House and Busbie Castle. There are several buildings whose history is not well reflected by bald statistics. Rowallan Castle, for example, was partly ruinous and partly inhabited, or at least in good condition internally, when MacGibbon and Ross visited. It has a complex history and MacGibbon and Ross devote 14 pages to it, with 10 sketches and 2 plans. 'It is to be hoped that every means will be taken to preserve such an interesting house, containing as it does, within its walls, the memorials of so many periods and events connected with our national

history' (2: 389). Rowallan spent some time in the guardianship of Historic Scotland but was released from state care in 2015 after a legal battle by the owner, who has since restored it for use as luxury holiday accommodation. Aiket was restored in the 1970s, and Newmilns was restored in the 1990s. Portencross was bought by a local community group. Unroofed since 1739, it was described by MacGibbon and Ross as 'a fine example of an early Scottish stronghold, and, although entirely neglected, is in a fair state of preservation' (3: 153). The Friends of Portencross carried out extensive repairs. It is now a roofed museum. Barr Castle and Dean Castle also house museums. Brounstoun Castle is ruinous now and was ruinous when MacGibbon and Ross visited, but its condition has deteriorated badly since then, as has that of Auchans. Giffen and Hessilhead have all but disappeared. Other castles that were ruinous when MacGibbon and Ross visited, and remain ruinous, are Ailsa Craig, Ardrossan, Ardstinchar, Auchenharvie, Auchinleck, Baltersan, Carleton, Clonbeith, Corsehill, Craigie, Craigneil, Dalquharran, Dundonald, Dunure, Glengarnock, Greenan, Kilkerran, Kirkhill, Knockdolian, Loch Doon, Mauchline, Monk, Pinwherry, Stane, Terringzean, Thomaston and Turnberry.

MacGibbon and Ross dealt with Law, Fairlie and Skelmorlie castles together in one entry, along with Little Cumbrae Castle in Buteshire: 'These simple towers are all situated in the same locality, round the entrance to the Frith [sic] of Clyde, and have such a striking resemblance to each other, both in their internal arrangements and external aspect, that they will be best described together' (3: 173). Skelmorlie, however, was already 'restored and incorporated with a large mansion' in 1852 (3: 183), and Law Castle was uninhabited when surveyed by MacGibbon and Ross, but was restored between 1989 and 2005. Fairlie's owner has plans for restoration, and Skelmorlie has recently been

Crosbie Castle, Ayrshire: derelict and deteriorating.

renovated. Bargany House, Blair, Caprington, Cessnock, Cassillis, Crawfurdland, Hunterston, Kelburne, Kilhenzie, Killochan, Maybole, Newark, Penkill, Sorn and Stair have all remained occupied. Crosbie Castle was used as a youth hostel, but a fire in 2004 led to considerable damage and it is now on the Buildings at Risk Register.[9]

Dumbartonshire

MacGibbon and Ross surveyed nine castles, of which five were already ruinous and four were inhabited. All of the latter have since been demolished: Auchenvole House, Badenheath Castle, Cardarroch and Gartshore House. Darleith Castle has become partly ruinous. Two of the castles surveyed – Darleith and Dunglass – are on the Buildings at Risk Register. Inch Galbraith, Kilmahew and Rossdhu remain ruinous. Strangely, although Dumbarton Castle is an extremely significant stronghold with a stirring military history and a complex series of buildings dating from the seventeenth century (and easy access at that time by a pier from the town, built for Queen Victoria's visit in 1847), MacGibbon and Ross did not survey it. They do mention Dumbarton Castle in their section on masons and architects, but only in passing, whereas all other significant royal and military buildings, such as Stirling and Linlithgow, have full entries.

Renfrewshire

MacGibbon and Ross surveyed 18 castles in Renfrewshire. Only two were inhabited then: Haggs and Houston. Haggs has a history of multiple uses and Houston House was divided into six grand apartments in the 1990s. Five castles were ruinous then and still are: Barr, Duchal, Inverkip, Palnoon and Ranforlie. Barochan and Cathcart castles were demolished in the twentieth century. Three buildings have uncertain futures. Mearns Tower, owned by the Church of Scotland, is on the Buildings at Risk Register. Dargavel House is on a former military site and its interior is in a poor state. Stanely Castle is now in the middle of a reservoir, partially submerged, whereas when MacGibbon and Ross visited it stood on a promontory and was accessible to visit.

Blackhall and Leven castles were both restored from ruins for habitation in the late twentieth century. Crookston Castle, a ruin in the city of Glasgow, is now in the care of HES, as is Newark Castle in Port Glasgow. Newark was partly inhabited in the nineteenth century and is now a consolidated ruin surrounded by shipbuilding yards. Two buildings have changed function: Old Bishopton Castle was inhabited as a private house in the nineteenth century, but is now in use as a facility for vulnerable young people. Pollok Castle was also a private house, 'restored recently' when MacGibbon and Ross visited, but now in the care of NTS.

Stirlingshire

Three castles have disappeared since MacGibbon and Ross's survey: Carnock House was demolished in the 1940s, Herbertshire Castle in the 1950s and Stenhouse Castle in the 1960s. All three had been inhabited when MacGibbon and Ross visited. Those inhabited then and today are: Auchenbowie, Bardowie, Castle Cary, Duntreath, Touch and Old Leckie (which went through a period of being empty). Bruce's Castle, Mains, also known as Kilmaronock, and Torwoodhead were ruinous then and still are. Restoration plans were made in the mid twentieth century for Torwoodhead but it is now on the Buildings at Risk Register. The remaining tower of Mugdock Castle was restored by East Dunbartonshire Council in 2005. Stirling Castle and Argyll's Lodging are in the care of HES and Cowane's Hospital, used as a guild hall in the late nineteenth century, is run by a trust which has restored the historic fabric of the building and hires it out as an events venue. Airth Tower, also known as Dunmore Tower or Elphinstone Tower, has become increasingly ruinous since MacGibbon and Ross visited. Culcreuch became a hotel in 1984 and Duchray and Gargunnock have changed from private homes to holiday accommodation.

Lanarkshire

Nine Lanarkshire castles were ruinous when surveyed by MacGibbon and Ross and have remained ruinous and in much the same condition: Avondale, Boghall, Bothwell, Corehouse, Covington, Crawford, Douglas (tower only), Edmonston and Lamington. Four were inhabited then and are still inhabited: Bedlay, Calderwood, Dalzell (now in eighteen apartments) and Waygateshaw. However, more than half of the castles have undergone some kind of change. Garrion Tower was inhabited but has been sold several times in recent years to potential developers and it is now on the Buildings at Risk Register in a dilapidated state. Four castles have been demolished: Farme Castle, Jerviston House, Monkland House and Stonebyres Castle. MacGibbon and Ross said of Craignethan Castle, 'the whole of the castle will soon become a shapeless ruin' (1: 255), even though part of it was still inhabited. It was taken into state care in 1949 and is now run by HES. Gilbertfield Castle was inhabited but has become ruinous and has been the focus of community alarm at vandalism and proposals for nearby building development. Mains Castle was uninhabited but 'practically entire', and has since been restored as a private residence. Jerviswood was also rescued from near dereliction in the 1980s. Hallbar Tower was 'well preserved' but uninhabited and was restored by the Vivat Trust as holiday accommodation in 1998. Crossbasket Castle was inhabited and in the 1980s became the headquarters of an American religious organisation. It has recently been extensively and expensively refurbished as a luxury hotel and weddings venue. Bedlay Castle was inhabited but became increasingly dilapidated and was put up for sale as a 'restoration opportunity' in 2014.

Buteshire

Three Buteshire castles surveyed by MacGibbon and Ross are on the island of Bute and three are on the neighbouring Island of Arran. Kames Castle on Bute (not to be confused with Wester Kames) was inhabited, and still is, and Little Cumbrae on Bute was in good condition but uninhabited, and remains so. Rothesay Castle is now in the care of HES and open to the public. Loch Ranza Castle on Arran is also in the care of HES and Brodick Castle on Arran is in the care of the NTS.

EASTERN CENTRAL SCOTLAND

This would be the most convenient area for MacGibbon and Ross to survey, as most of the castles are within a few miles of Edinburgh. Northfield House is described as 'situated within a few minutes' walk of Prestonpans railway station' (2: 183), which meant that Preston Tower, across the road, was also very conveniently reached. This area comprises the modern council areas of East Lothian, West Lothian, Midlothian and City of Edinburgh (historical counties Haddingtonshire, with 27 castles; Linlithgowshire with 20 castles; Midlothianshire, including Edinburgh, a small but densely packed county with 60 castles; and Peeblesshire with 14 castles).

Haddingtonshire

There have been relatively few changes to the castles in this area since MacGibbon and Ross surveyed them – the majority have either stayed inhabited or stayed ruinous. The 11 ruins are Auldhame, Barnes, Gammelshiel, Garmylton (also known as Garleton), Hailes, Innerwick Castle Tower, Penshiel, Preston Tower, Redhouse, Saltcoats and Yester. Of these, Barnes, Gammelshiel, Garmylton, Innerwick Castle Tower and Penshiel are all fragmentary ruins. Two castles in this county have been demolished: Hermanston Castle and Elphinstone Castle, which is described in the text as being in Midlothian. The five castles restored were Ballencrieff, Falside, Fenton Tower, Stoneypath and Whittinghame Tower, all of which are inhabited as private residences, apart from Fenton, which offers holiday accommodation. Wintoun House has become an events venue. Dirleton Castle and Tantallon Castle, both large and significant mediaeval fortresses, were taken into state care in 1924 and are managed by HES and open to the public. Lethington, Luffness, Nunraw and Northfield House have all been inhabited throughout. MacGibbon and Ross noted that 'Northfield is still inhabited and is well maintained, and John Marjoriebanks' house is in this respect quite a contrast to that of his brother-in-law, Sir John Hamilton, . . . on the other side of the road' (2: 185). The property they are referring to, then owned by Sir John Hamilton, is probably Preston Tower,[10] still ruinous but in good condition and in the guardianship of East Lothian Council.

Elphinstone Tower, Haddingtonshire (East Lothian), by MacGibbon and Ross. It was demolished in 1955.

Linlithgowshire

Three buildings were demolished after MacGibbon and Ross surveyed them. The demolition of the House of the Knights Hospitaller in Linlithgow in 1885 was of particular concern to them and they campaigned vigorously, but unsuccessfully, to save the building. Grangepans House was demolished in 1906, and clearly very dilapidated by 1885, although MacGibbon and Ross sketched and described it as though it were in good condition: 'We are indebted for some of the following notes to Mr Hyslop, Castlepark, Prestonpans' (4: 81). Hippolyte Blanc, a good friend of Ross, had prepared a design for the restoration of Grangepans House for the owner, Mr Cadell, but it was never followed through because of mining subsidence.

Bonhard, which was 'used by families of farm labourers' and partly closed off, was burned out in 1959 and blown up in 1962. Kirkhill House,

OPPOSITE. Grangepans House, Bo'ness, Linlithgowshire (West Lothian) in 1885. It has since been demolished.

ABOVE. Grangepans House, by MacGibbon and Ross. Note the colliery buildings in the background.

which was a farmhouse when MacGibbon and Ross described it, was abandoned in about 1970 and subject to vandalism, but by 1976 it had been restored and turned into two apartments. Kipps House was not so fortunate. MacGibbon and Ross reported that 'A few years ago, when we first saw the house, it was occupied by farm labourers, but it is now tenantless and fast hastening to ruin' (4: 15). It is now a sad and diminishing ruin in a farmyard. Three buildings are now in the care of HES: Blackness, Kinneil Castle and Linlithgow Palace. Kinneil Castle was saved from demolition by the local council in 1936 when sixteenth-century mural paintings were discovered and taken into care by

the Ministry of Works. Binns Castle (House of the Binns) was donated to the National Trust for Scotland in 1944 and is open to the public. Dundas Castle was, unusually, a whisky distillery in the nineteenth century. It is now an events venue with luxury accommodation. MacGibbon and Ross noted that Barnbougle Castle had been 'reconstructed some 10 or 15 years ago . . . previous to that time it was in a state of ruin' (4: 379). It was used as a library for the collection of the 5th Earl of Rosebery and has recently been extensively restored again and is used to host events. Ironically, the owners were told by the Fire Service during the restoration that the books in the library were

Barnbougle Castle, Dalmeny Estate, South Queensferry.

a fire hazard and should be removed. Niddrie Castle, a very large early L-plan tower, has been partially restored from a ruinous condition to a family home, but work is ongoing. Duntarvie House, which was 'fast falling into decay', is now also being restored, albeit very slowly. Only two castles were ruinous when MacGibbon and Ross visited and still are: Haining Castle, also known as Almond Castle, and Hopetoun Tower, also known as Staneyhill Tower. Both towers are in reasonably good condition, the latter the remaining relic of a much larger mansion. Bridge Castle, 'converted recently from a roofless ruin', is now in four apartments. Houstoun House became a hotel in 1970. Elliston House, also known as Illiston House, has been inhabited throughout, but has been considerably upgraded for modern living in recent years, as has Ochiltree Castle, which was formerly a dilapidated farm residence.

Midlothianshire

This county includes Edinburgh city. A large percentage of the buildings have remained in much the same condition since MacGibbon and Ross surveyed them, although ten buildings which were private homes when they visited have changed their function. Baberton House and Dalkeith Palace are now used as offices, Dalhousie Castle and Carberry Tower have become hotels,

Hawthornden Castle has become a writers' retreat, Pinkie House is now a school, Newbattle Abbey is a college, Lauriston Castle is a museum and Inch House and the Dower House in Corstorphine are both community heritage centres.

Seven of Midlothian's castellated buildings were demolished in the twentieth century: Grange House in 1936; Granton House in the 1920s; Hallyards Castle in 1929; Hatton House in 1955; Niddrie Marischal House in the 1960s; Old Saughton House in 1920; and Riccarton House in 1956. Of these, five had been inhabited when MacGibbon and Ross surveyed them.

Three Midlothian castles are in the care of HES: Craigmillar Castle, Crichton Castle and Edinburgh Castle. Magdalen's House is in the care of NTS. The Palace of Holyroodhouse remains a royal residence and is open to the public when not in use by the royal family. Lauriston Castle is open to the public and Inch House is a community centre. Merchiston Castle and Moray House were both schools in the late nineteenth century and are now used as education offices. Pinkie House is part of Loretto School. A few castles have had rollercoaster fortunes: Ford House, inhabited and in good condition when MacGibbon and Ross visited, became neglected in the twentieth century and was restored in 1960. Caroline Park also fell into dereliction and was restored in the 1980s. Borthwick Castle was rented on an improving lease by the architect Peter Daniel in the 1960s, then restored from semi-dereliction and opened as a hotel in the 1970s by Helen Bailey; it has been further refurbished recently. Dalhousie Castle and Carberry Tower have also become hotels. Those restored from ruins are Cramond Tower and Liberton Tower, the latter used as holiday accommodation.

Those that were inhabited when MacGibbon and Ross visited and have remained so are: Bavelaw Castle, Brunstane House, Cakemuir Castle, Calder House, Cockburn House – then the property of George Watson's Hospital and now encroached upon by farm buildings, but recently renovated – Craigcrook Castle, Drum House, East Coates House, Gogar House, Halkerston Lodge, Inveresk Lodge, Keith House, Liberton House, Linnhouse, Lochend House, Monkton House, Peffermill House, Pilrig House and Southsyde Castle, where MacGibbon and Ross lamented the recent alterations: 'It is now reduced very much to the level of a modern villa' (5: 348). Several of these have undergone extensive renovations in recent years.

Eleven castles were ruinous when MacGibbon and Ross visited and have remained ruinous: Brunstane Castle, Colinton Castle, 'so closely environed with trees as to be hardly visible till the spectator stands beside it' (3: 541), Craiglockhart Castle, East Cairns Castle, fragmentary Ewes Castle, Falla Luggie Castle, Hirendean Castle, Lennox Castle, Newbyres Tower, Uttershill Castle and Woodhouselee.

Peeblesshire

Ten of the 14 castles that McGibbon and Ross described were ruinous when they visited and all are still ruinous now. They quote from Chambers's *A History of Peeblesshire* in their entries on Cardrona, Castlehill, Horsburgh Castle and Tinnies Castle. Drummelzier Castle was a standing ruin until 1972, when it was largely dismantled, for fear of collapse. Hutcheonfield, Posso and Wrae were fragmentary, and Drochil and Nether Horsburgh are still standing ruins. Barns Tower was uninhabited and was restored for holiday accommodation in 2001. Neidpath Castle, owned by the Wemyss family, is uninhabited but is let out for weddings and events. Haystoun House was used for farm buildings but is now inhabited, and Traquair House is the only building that was and still is inhabited; it is described as the oldest continuously inhabited house in Scotland.

RIGHT. Drummelzier Castle, Peeblesshire, by MacGibbon and Ross.

BELOW. Drummelzier Castle today, in a farmyard, largely demolished.

NORTH CENTRAL SCOTLAND

This area comprises the modern council areas of Perth and Kinross, Fife and Angus (historical counties Perthshire, with 50 castles; Fifeshire with 56 castles; Forfarshire with 37 castles, and the two small counties of Clackmannanshire and Kinross-shire, with 5 and 6 castles, respectively). This is the area that Thomas Ross would have known well from his childhood.

Perthshire

Perthshire is a county replete with castles. MacGibbon and Ross recorded 50 of them. Sixteen castles were inhabited then and still are: Aberuchill Castle, Ardblair, Ashintully, Balmanno, Blairlogie, Drummond, Edinample, Fowlis Easter, Garth, Grandtully, Lethendy, Meggernie, Methven, Murthly, Newton (Blairgowrie) and Williamstoun. Sixteen were ruinous then and still are: Balthayock, Bordie, Comrie, Drumlochie, Evelick, Finlarig, Gartartan, Glasclune, Innerpeffrey, Inverqueich, Kinclaven, Moncur, Moulin, Talla, Tullyallan and Whitefield. Five have been restored: Aldie, Kelty House, Menzies, Pitheavlis and Stobhall. Pitheavlis Castle, in Perth, has been turned from a poorly maintained farmhouse into apartments; the other three have become private homes. Glendevon, which was inhabited when MacGibbon and Ross visited, is now on the Buildings at Risk Register, having most recently been a restaurant with a 'Dungeon Bar', and with its demise became derelict. Colliechat Castle, which consisted mainly of a 30-foot tower adjoining a farmhouse when MacGibbon and Ross visited, had disappeared by 1968 when RCAHMS investigated. Logie House was demolished in the 1960s.

Three Perthshire castles are now in the care of HES: Doune, Elcho and Huntingtower. Culross Palace (Fife, but which MacGibbon and Ross placed in Perthshire) is looked after by the NTS, although the Abbey is in the care of HES. Huntly Castle has become a prison. Balhousie Castle, formerly a private home, is now a museum of the Black Watch regiment. MacGibbon and Ross provide a sketch of the house based upon a photograph of 1861, before the house was remodelled and baronialised in 1863. Kinnaird Tower, on the other hand, was a museum when MacGibbon and Ross visited, but is now a private home. Newton House (Doune) is let out for holiday accommodation.

Fifeshire

MacGibbon and Ross surveyed 56 castles in Fife. More than half, 31, were ruinous, some consisting of nothing but fragments. Ferry-Port-on-Craig Castle had already been demolished, in 1855, when MacGibbon and Ross wrote about it. Gladney House was demolished about 1930, Otterston Castle in 1946 and Craighall in 1957. Fife's castellated architecture includes several nationally significant buildings, seven of which have since been taken into the care of the state and are managed by HES: Aberdour, Balvaird, Dunfermline Palace, Inchcolm Abbey, Ravenscraig Castle, Scotstarvet Tower and St Andrews Castle. In addition, Kellie Castle and Falkland Palace are looked after by the NTS and Dunfermline's Abbot House is run by a Trust as a museum and heritage centre.

Balgonie, Dairsie, Fordel, Monimail, Pitcullo, Pitreavie and Rossend were restored from ruins or dereliction. Earlshall Castle was restored by Robert Lorimer in 1892, just after MacGibbon and Ross lamented the decaying state of the interior. Airdrie, Balcomie and Myres remain inhabited, Pitfirrane is a golf clubhouse, Preston Lodge is in apartments, Fernie has become a hotel, and Kilconquhar and Pitcairlie offer holiday accommodation. Aithernie, Ardross, Hallyards House and

Ballinbreich Castle, near Newburgh, Fife: already a ruin when MacGibbon and Ross visited.

Knockdavie Castle were fragmentary ruins when MacGibbon and Ross visited and are still visible. Collarnie is part of a farm steading. Standing ruins were Ballinbreich, Bandon Tower, Carden Tower, Corston Tower, Creich Castle, Denmilne Castle, Kirkton Castle, Largo Tower (consolidated), Lochore Castle, Lordscairnie Castle, Macduff's Castle, Mountquhanie Castle, Newark Castle, Pitairthie Castle, Pitcruivie Castle, Pitteadie Castle, Rosyth Castle, Seafield Tower and Struthers Castle. These are all still ruinous.

Forfarshire

Twelve of the castles surveyed in Forfarshire (Angus) were inhabited then and still are: Auchterhouse, Bannatyne, Careston, Colliston, Ethie, Gagie, Gardyne, Glamis, Guthrie, Kellie, Murroes and Pitkerro. Broughty Castle is a museum in the care of the local council, Edzell is in the care of HES, and Claypotts, which is also in the care of HES, can be visited on request. Glamis Castle, ancestral seat of the earls of Strathmore and Kinghorne, is open to the public. Eleven of the castles that MacGibbon and Ross visited have been restored from ruins or dereliction: Airlie, Cortachie (in part, after a devastating fire), Craig, Dudhope, Farnell, Forter, Hatton, Inverquharity, Mains, Melgund and Powrie. Airlie Castle and Craig Castle were part ruinous and partly inhabited in the late nineteenth century; in the twenty-first century both are luxury wedding venues. Forfarshire included the city of Dundee. Dudhope Castle in Dundee was a dilapidated military barracks in 1890. It has since been used for several institutional purposes and is now used as offices. Nine castles were ruinous or uninhabited then and still are: Affleck, Balfour (tower only), Ballinshoe,

Flemington House, Forfarshire (Angus), in 1959.

Ballumbie, Brackie, Finhaven, Invermark, Redcastle and Vayne. None of Forfarshire's castles has been demolished, but Brackie Castle has become roofless, previously consolidated, and Flemington House, 'a well-preserved mansion of the 17th century (which was occupied until recently)' (3: 592) has become derelict and is encroached upon by farm buildings.

Clackmannanshire

MacGibbon and Ross surveyed only five castles in this tiny county, of which two, Clackmannan and Castle Campbell, are in the care of HES. Alloa Tower is in the care of the NTS. Old Sauchie Tower is now restored and inhabited. Menstrie Castle was restored in the twentieth century, won a Civic Trust award, and now incorporates holiday accommodation, private flats, and a museum and café run by the National Trust for Scotland. MacGibbon and Ross had noted that 'Little is now left of this once very interesting building, and what little remains is turned to ignoble uses' (2: 409). These 'ignoble uses' are not specified. It had been abandoned about 1740.

Kinross-shire

The condition of Kinross-shire castles has not changed much over the years, but Burleigh and Lochleven castles are now in the care of HES. Two of the six castles remain ruinous: Arnot Tower, which stands in the grounds of New Arnot Tower, built in 1878, and Dowhill Castle: 'The present appearance of the castle is not at all picturesque, as it is reduced to the level of the first floor all round and is thus not unlike a large packing-box' (4: 41). Cleish Castle and Tullibole Castle were inhabited when MacGibbon and Ross visited, and still are, but had both been restored earlier in the nineteenth century. Cleish had been restored before MacGibbon and Ross visited: 'The building was allowed to fall into a state of complete ruin, and a pencil sketch . . . shows the castle as entirely roofless, all the windows empty, with the tops of the walls and chimneys ragged and broken. But about forty-five years ago Mr. Young had it renovated and converted into his mansion-house under the direction of the late Mr. John Lessels, architect' (3: 569).[11] In the 1970s Cleish was 'de-Georgianised' when the

owner, architect Michael Spens, commissioned the sculptor and artist Eduardo Paolozzi to devise wall hangings and a suspended ceiling to decorate the Great Hall. The next owners re-installed the Georgian architecture, and Paolozzi's ceiling can now be seen in the Dean Gallery in Edinburgh, part of the National Gallery of Modern Art.

NORTH-EAST SCOTLAND

'The north-east is like a country in itself: it is quite distinct from other parts of Scotland.'[12] Aberdeenshire advertises itself via Visit Scotland as having more castles per acre than anywhere else in the UK, with 263 castles across the county, although only 19 feature on its current itinerary for 'Scotland's castle trail'. MacGibbon and Ross surveyed 69 of these castles and 11 in Kincardineshire (now part of modern Aberdeenshire). They also surveyed 30 in Banffshire and Elginshire, and 5 in Nairnshire (modern council area of Moray). In an area of Scotland that is relatively remote and sparsely populated, the number of castles in the north-east of Scotland is astonishing, as is the diversity of building types.

Aberdeenshire

Eleven Aberdeenshire castles are now open to the public, the highest number of any county. Five of the most splendid castle mansions visited by MacGibbon and Ross are owned by the National Trust for Scotland: Castle Fraser, Craigievar, Drum, Fyvie and Leith Hall. All had been inhabited when they visited. Four Aberdeenshire castles are now in the care of HES – Corgarff, Huntly, Kinnaird Head and Tolquhon. Additionally, Mar (Braemar) Castle, owned by the chief of Clan Farquharson / Invercauld Estate and leased to

OPPOSITE. Hallforest Castle, Aberdeenshire.

Braemar Community Ltd, is open for tours. Four castles are no longer standing: Castle Newe, 'now almost entirely a modern mansion' (4: 388) was demolished in 1927; Philorth House, 'residence of Lord Saltoun', a mansion built in 1666, was burned down in 1915; the remaining fragments of Frendraught Castle were demolished in 1947; and Towie Castle (not to be confused with Towie Barclay), which was ruinous in the 1890s, was demolished in 1968. In addition to the four that have disappeared, the only building whose condition has significantly deteriorated since MacGibbon and Ross's time is Westhall Castle, which was inhabited in the 1890s, but is currently on the Buildings at Risk Register after attempts to sell it for development fell through, and it has become increasingly derelict.

After MacGibbon and Ross's survey, seven of Aberdeenshire's castles were restored from ruins. In 1896, Cairnbulg was restored. Birse Castle was described by MacGibbon and Ross as a 'fragmentary ruin' (2: 49), although their sketch shows a building in good condition to corbelling height. It was restored in 1906 and expanded in 1930. Towie Barclay, Harthill and Pitfichie were restored in the 1970s. The collapse of Pitfichie's east wall and south gable in 1936 made it a 'seemingly doomed ruin'.[13] However, it was rebuilt and restored in 1977. Tillycairn and tiny Terpersie were both restored in the 1980s. Meldrum House became a country house hotel in the 1950s and Craigston and Delgaty castles now offer self-catering holiday accommodation.

Of the castles described by MacGibbon and Ross 14 have been continuously inhabited: Abergeldie, Arnage, Balbythan, Barra, Corsindae, Craig, Craigston, Delgaty, Hallhead, Lickleyhead, Monymusk, Muchalls, Pitcaple and Shivas. Aboyne, Balfluig, Balnacraig, Druminnor, Keith Hall, Midmar and Udny were all inhabited when MacGibbon and Ross visited and are inhabited now, but all have suffered changes of fortune in the intervening years, and have been restored or renovated. The following Aberdeenshire castles have remained ruinous since MacGibbon and Ross surveyed them: Asloon, Balquhain, Boddam, Colquhonny, Corse, Dundargue, Dunnideer, Easter Clune, Ellon, Esslemont, Federate, Gight, Glenbucket, Hallforest, Inverallochy, Inverugie, Kildrummie, King Edward Castle, Knock, Knockhall, Pitsligo and Pittullie.

Kincardineshire

Most of the 11 castles surveyed in Kincardineshire have stayed much the same over the past 130 years. Fiddes Castle was 'fast falling into decay' when MacGibbon and Ross visited but is now in good order and inhabited. Crathes Castle was occupied by Sir Robert Burnett but is now owned by the National Trust for Scotland. Kincardineshire has two ruined castles. The spectacularly sited ruins of Dunnottar Castle have been open to visitors since the 1920s, when it was purchased in a rundown state by the Cowdray family and repaired to save it from complete ruination. MacGibbon and Ross reported that the ruins of Kincardine Castle 'still stand to a height of five or six feet above ground' (3: 111), but it is now no longer recognisable as a ruined castle, being so overgrown and fragmentary. Benholme Tower is a partially consolidated ruin attached to Benholme Castle, an eighteenth-century mansion which was restored from dereliction in the 1990s. The fifteenth-century tower suffered a collapse of the east wall, along with part of the north and south walls, in a storm in 1993. The castles inhabited when surveyed were Allardyce, Balbegno, Benholme, Hallgreen, Inglismaldie, Lauriston and Tilquhilly.

Banffshire

MacGibbon and Ross surveyed five Banffshire castles which were inhabited and 11 which were ruinous, although they probably did not visit Bocharm, which gets a bare mention (1: 63). Inchdrewer was ruinous when they visited and still is, but it has a relatively new owner who, like the last owner, has plans to restore the building. Cullen House, which MacGibbon and Ross describe as a 'great mansion', has been divided into apartments. Four of Banffshire's castles are open to the public: the ruins of Auchindoun and Balvenie are in the care of HES and Drumin Castle is owned by the Crown Estate. Ballindalloch Castle is privately owned and still inhabited by the MacPherson-Grant family, who open the castle and gardens to the public. Blairfindy, Boyne, Castle Oliphant, Eden, Findlater and Findochty remain ruinous. Fordyce Castle, Kilmaichlie House and Kininvie Castle remain inhabited.

Elginshire or Morayshire

The 14 castles surveyed in this county have not changed much, although there has been one loss. Wester Elchies Castle, which was inhabited when MacGibbon and Ross surveyed it, was demolished in the 1960s. Easter Elchies Castle remains inhabited, as do Castle Grant, Darnaway Castle and Innes House. Two buildings have opened for public access: Brodie Castle, which had been owned by the Brodies of Brodie for over 500 years, was donated to the NTS in 1978, and Spynie Palace, a magnificently preserved mediaeval bishop's residence, was taken into state care in 1973. The Bishop's House in Elgin, which stands opposite Elgin Cathedral, remains ruinous; a restoration scheme by Rowand Anderson in 1892 was never executed. Blervie, Burgie, Duffus and Lochindorb castles also remain ruinous. Aslisk Castle was 'a mere fragment' when MacGibbon and Ross visited, although they reproduce a 1799 sketch by J. Claude Nattes of 'an interesting and extensive pile' (3: 611). Part of the west gable remains.

Coxton Tower, 'one of the most remarkable buildings of its class in Scotland' (2: 23), was empty but in good condition when MacGibbon and Ross visited. They noted that it 'was occupied as a gardener's cottage till within recent years' (2: 26). It has been repaired and consolidated again recently and is still empty.

Nairnshire

MacGibbon and Ross reported on only five buildings in Nairnshire. Two were inhabited then and still are – Cawdor and Kilravock. Two were ruinous then and are still ruinous – Inchoch and Rait. Inchoch has deteriorated greatly since the visit of MacGibbon and Ross. Ardclach Tower, an extraordinary little bell tower, was consolidated in the nineteenth century and is now in the care of Historic Environment Scotland.

NORTH AND NORTH-WEST SCOTLAND

This region of Scotland (modern Highland region, Hebrides, Argyll, Orkney and Shetland) is sparsely populated, mostly remote and difficult to access. Nonetheless, MacGibbon and Ross used trains and ferries to survey 91 castles in the region: historical counties of Inverness-shire (17), Ross-shire (9), Sutherlandshire (8), Caithness-shire (8), Argyllshire (41) and Orkney and Shetland (8).

Inverness-shire

Out of 17 buildings surveyed by MacGibbon and Ross, three have been restored from ruins – Castle Stewart, Dalcross and Muckrach. All three now offer holiday accommodation. Three are now in the care of HES and open to the public: Kismul, Ruthven (aka Huntingtower) and Urquhart, the last a very popular tourist destination. Kismul was rebuilt in the twentieth century, albeit not to current conservation standards. It was leased to Historic Scotland in 2000. Although MacGibbon and Ross date it to the thirteenth century, recent analysis suggests a later date, probably fifteenth century. Nine Inverness-shire castles were, and still are ruinous: Borve, Castle Moy, Castle Roy, Duns-caich, Duntulm, Ellan-Tirrim (Tioram), Invergarry, Inverlochy and Loch-an-Eilan. Duntulm and Duns-caith castles are on the Island of Skye, as is Dunve-gan Castle. Dunvegan is open to the public for visits. Castle Stewart (Stuart) was restored in the late twentieth century and is now a hotel. Erchless Castle was continuously inhabited until recently, when it was refurbished for self-catering accom-modation.

Ross-shire

Castle Leod and Kinkell were inhabited when MacGibbon and Ross visited and both are still inhabited, although Kinkell later became derelict and was restored in the 1960s. Castle Craig and Dingwall were ruinous then and still are; Dingwall is fragmentary. Kilcoy was restored in 1890 and Ballone in the 1990s. Ellandonan (Eilean Donan) was restored in the early twentieth century and is now open to the public. Fairburn and Redcastle are both on the Buildings at Risk Register but Fair-burn is to be restored by the Landmark Trust. Fair-burn was ruinous when MacGibbon and Ross visited, but Redcastle, 'a modern mansion in which several portions of an older edifice have been incor-porated to good effect' (3: 623), was inhabited. It was abandoned after the Second World War.

Sutherlandshire

Only eight castles in Sutherlandshire were surveyed by MacGibbon and Ross. Two were inhabited then and still are: Dunrobin Castle, 'the palatial resi-dence of the Duke of Sutherland' (4: 300) and Tongue House, then the residence of his factor, until recently a residence of the the late Countess of Sutherland. Ardvreck, Edderchalder and Castle Varrich, 'a shattered tower of small size' (3: 253), were and still are ruinous, but Helmsdale House, which, when MacGibbon and Ross visited, was already 'so much damaged & demolished that little can be determined' (5: 294), was demolished in the 1970s to make way for the A9 road bridge. Balnakiel House has been restored: 'We here find the Scottish style of house lingering in this remote region till the middle of the eighteenth century' (4: 80–81). Dornoch Bishop's Palace, which was a private residence, has become a hotel.

Caithness-shire

This county stands at the north-eastern tip of Scot-land, remote and inaccessible. MacGibbon and Ross surveyed 14 castles there, of which one, Thurso Castle, had already been demolished in the 1870s. Three castles were occupied: Ackergill Tower, Brims Castle and Dunbeath Castle. Brims has since become derelict, although it was occupied until the 1970s.[14]

Ackergill was very little inhabited during the twentieth century and by 1986, when it was put up for sale by the Duff-Dunbar family, it had become almost derelict. It was upgraded for holiday accommodation by its new owners at the enormous cost of £800,000 in 1988, and functioned as a hotel for over 30 years. It has now returned to private ownership.

Dunbeath had been remodelled by John Bryce in 1881 and it was he who provided the plans for MacGibbon and Ross. Negotiations in the early 1990s to donate Dunbeath to the National Trust for Scotland fell through and its owner, the Amer-ican inventor and philanthropist Stanton Avery, sold it on to another private owner.

Muckrach Castle, near Grantown-on-Spey, Inverness-shire: restored from a ruin, it now offers holiday accommodation.

Downreay (Dounray) Castle had been inhabited until 1863, then allowed to fall into disrepair and ruin. MacGibbon and Ross noted that 'In every respect it seems to be almost precisely the same as the houses of similar capacity erected in the Lowlands about the same period' (3: 631). Berriedale, Braal, Bucholie, Dirlot, Forse, Girnigoe, Keiss and Old Man of Wick castles were all ruinous then and are still ruinous. Girnigoe (or Castle Sinclair Girnigoe, as it is now known) has had recent funding for its long-term conservation and access for visitors.

Argyllshire

This is a county of both ruins and restorations and illustrates well the dynamic nature of castles. Thirty-seven out of its 39 castles were ruinous when surveyed by MacGibbon and Ross and only two were inhabited: Craignish, 'part of a modern mansion' (3: 173), and Duntroon, 'much modernised' (3: 87). Argyll is a challenging county to travel across, but it was probably more accessible by public transport then than now. Even before the opening of the Callander and Oban railway in

1880, a network of steamship routes from the Clyde ports allowed access through Argyll waters. Eight castles have been restored from ruins to dwellings – Barcaldine, Breachacha, Dunderave, Kilmartin, Kinlochaline, Mingarry, Saddell and Stalker (Stalcaire). Carrick Castle is currently being restored. Saddell was 'well preserved, and cherished with pride by its owner, Colonel MacLeod' (3: 197), but many of the ruins surveyed were fragmentary, such as Fraoch Eilean Castle and Knockmaillie. Innellan Mansion has gone but the castles of Achallader, Achanduin, Ardchonnel, Ardtornish, Aros, Canna, Coeffin, Dog, Dunolly, Dunyveg, Fionchairn, Gylem, Killundine, Lachlan, Lochbuy, Mearnaig, Moy, Tarbert, Shuna, Swin (Sween) and Toward remain as ruins. Four castles are open to the public, all in the care of HES: Carnassery, Dunstaffnage, Kilchurn and Skipness.

Orkney and Shetland

MacGibbon and Ross describe nine buildings in Orkney and Shetland, although Smiddy Bank in Orkney had already disappeared when they visited. Of the other seven, six are ruinous, five of which are in the care of HES: Bishop's Palace Kirkwall, Earl Patrick's Palace Birsay, Muness Castle, Notland Castle and Scalloway Castle. The other ruin is Bishop's House, Breckness, which has modern farm buildings encroaching on its site. Only one building is inhabited, Carrick House, which MacGibbon and Ross 'sketched from a passing steam boat' (5: 97). It has been in the same family since 1854 and houses a small museum. Tankerness House has also become a museum.

Conclusion

This overview gives some idea of the dynamic nature of the changes that have taken place. Ruined towers have become domestic houses, then faced ruination again, castles have crumbled and been demolished, threatened buildings have been saved by being re-purposed as luxury hotels or museums, or have been consolidated as ruins by heritage organisations. Castles have changed hands in the property market at an astonishing rate. Since the advent of user-friendly accommodation websites, more and more owners are signing up for occasional bed and breakfast or short-term lettings of the whole property, dipping in and out of the tourist market as their finances ebb and flow. The picture across Scotland's counties is not at all homogeneous, with physical geography one of the many factors which impact upon the fortunes of heritage buildings. Some counties have cherished and protected their cultural capital better than others. Once a building is left empty and unheated, especially if the roof is removed, decay can be swift; although the majority of those buildings which were ruinous in 1890 look similarly ruinous today, there has inevitably been a degree of degradation through time and weathering, which will only continue without intervention.

The legacy of MacGibbon and Ross's scholarly survey has allowed a comparative analysis – a kind of health check – of the buildings they surveyed then and now; while the results paint a rather gloomy picture of 52 castles demolished and others still at risk of further deterioration, they do allow a degree of optimism for the future, when one considers the numbers which have already been consolidated or restored and those which are at risk but potentially still restorable, although at a considerable cost. The changes of form and function in the castellated buildings of Scotland since MacGibbon and Ross carried out their survey are part of an inevitable and ongoing process. The following chapters will explore some of the most interesting stories that reflect the changes in these castles, in terms of risk, transformations and accessibility.

Plate 1. Costumed figures from David MacGibbon's Grand Tour sketchbook, probably painted in the mid 1850s.

Plate 2. The Royal Review of the Scottish Volunteer regiments in Holyrood Park, Edinburgh, 1860, attended by both David MacGibbon and Thomas Ross. Painting by Samuel Bough.

Plate 3. A romantic vision of Tantallon Castle in North Berwick, by Alexander Nasmyth 1816.

Plate 4. Tantallon Castle, by David MacGibbon, probably about 1850.

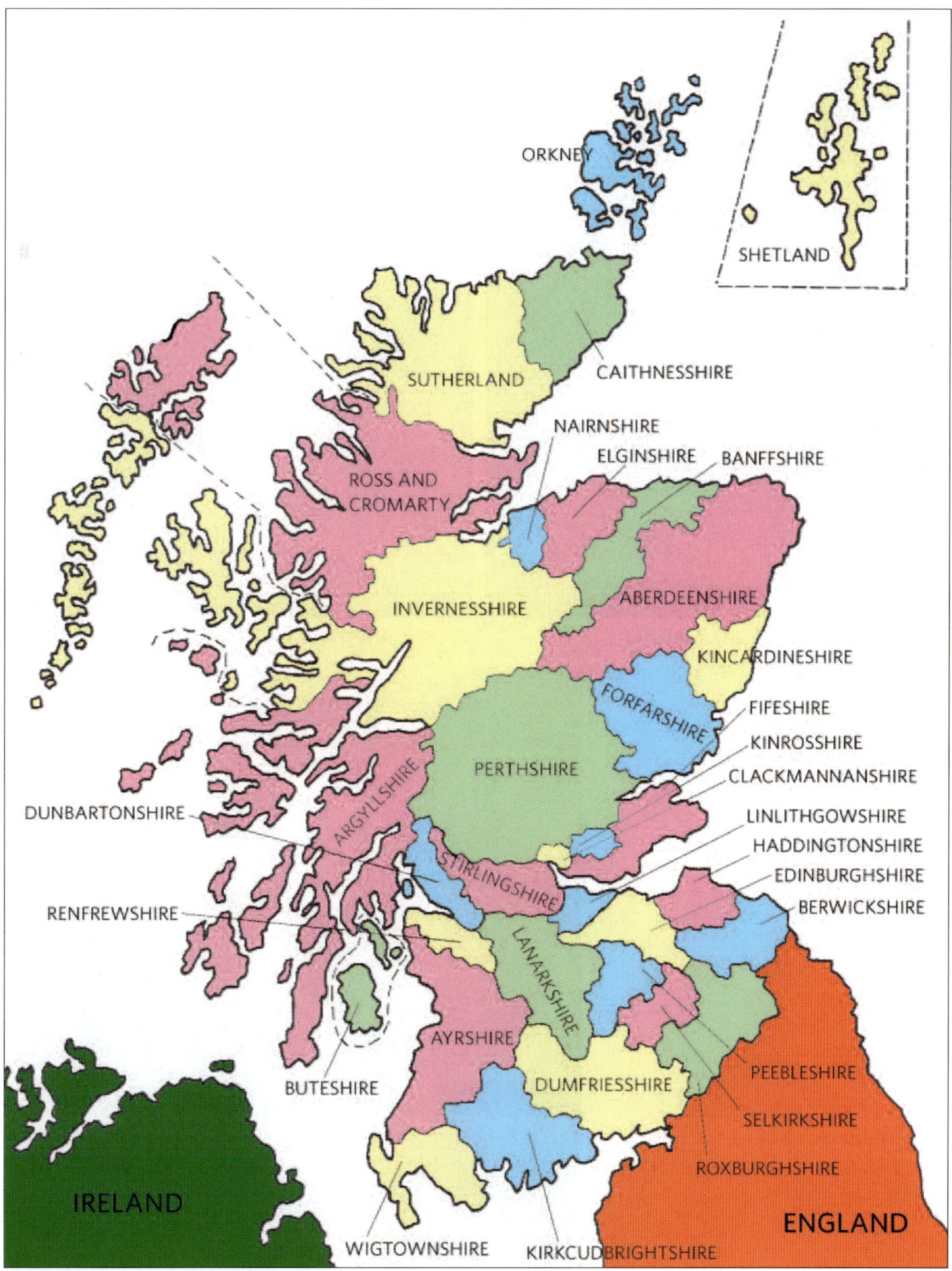

Plate 5. The counties of Scotland in 1890. (from *Family Tree Magazine*)

Plate 6. (Above left) Fernielee Castle, in the grounds of Fairnilee House.

Plate 7. (Above right) Sorbie Tower in Wigtownshire, decorated with knitted poppies to commemorate Remembrance Sunday.

Plate 8. (Right) Interior of Tower of Hallbar, Lanarkshire, restored by the Vivat Trust in 1998.

Plate 9. (Above) Colinton Castle, still 'closely environed with trees' in the grounds of Merchiston School, Edinburgh. It was partially demolished in 1800 to make a picturesque ruin on the advice of artist Alexander Nasmyth.

Plate 10. (Left) Blervie Castle, Moray, showing collapsed section.

Plate 11. Castle Wigg, Wigtownshire, around the beginning of the twentieth century.

Plate 12. Castle Wigg as a forlorn ruin. It has the remains of a sixteenth-century tower inside.

Plate 13. (Above) Inchcolm Abbey in the Firth of Forth, one of the many island sites visited by MacGibbon and Ross.

Plate 14. (Left) Elphinstone Hall in Aberdeen University, built in 1931 with stones re-purposed from Castle Newe, after its demolition in 1927.

Plate 15. (Above) Monymusk Castle in Aberdeenshire, which MacGibbon and Ross were not able to visit.

Plate 16. (Right) The 'Stirling Head' of Mary of Guise, a replica of one of the original ceiling decorations in the King's Inner Hall, now in place as part of the restoration of Stirling Castle.

Plate 17. Sanquhar Castle, Dumfriesshire, now a forlorn sight but once almost restored by the Marquess of Bute in the late nineteenth century.

Plate 18. Broughty Castle near Dundee, a former military fortress turned museum.

Plate 19. The restored library at Ferniehirst Castle, near Jedburgh. It had been in a 'deplorable state' when MacGibbon and Ross visited.

Plate 20. Cairnbulg Castle, Aberdeenshire, restored in 1896.

Plate 21. (Above) Cramond Tower near Edinburgh, restored in the 1970s. The east wing was added in 1992.

Plate 22. (Left) Merchiston Castle, part of Napier University in Edinburgh, hemmed in by modern buildings.

Plate 23. (Above) Lochnaw Castle, Wigtownshire, in 2015, much reduced from its Victorian vastness.

Plate 24. (Right) Liberton Tower, Edinburgh, restored in 1998 by the Castles of Scotland Preservation Trust.

Plate 25. Muckrach Castle, Moray, restored 1978–85.

Plate 26. Buittle Castle, Kirkcudbrightshire. The new sunken garden, created using only plants available in the fifteenth century, as listed in monastery garden invoices.

Plate 27. Interior of Tillycairn Castle, Aberdeenshire, restored 1980–84.

Plate 28. Drummond Castle gardens, Perthshire, much as they were when visited by Queen Victoria.

Plate 29. The skyline of Edinburgh Castle could have been very different had David Bryce's plans of 1861 been realised. Bryce's planned tower is in the centre of the picture.

Plate 30. Joseph Mallord William Turner, *Edinburgh Castle: March of the Highlanders*, c. 1834–35, illustration for Sir Walter Scott's *Waverley*.

Plate 31. (Right) Morton Castle, Dumfriesshire, used as a location in the film series *Outlander*.

Plate 32. (Below) Broughton Place in the Scottish Borders, a modern tower house designed by Basil Spence in the 1930s.

6

Castles Lost,
Castles at Risk and
Castles at War

———

It is a reverend thing, to see an ancient castle or building, not in decay.

Francis Bacon (1623) 'Of Nobility',
The Essays in Officina Ioannis Hauiland, London

The truth of this quotation can be witnessed in buildings such as Blervie Castle in Moray, which suffered a collapse of its west tower in 2006, and Innellan Mansion in Argyllshire. The roof and flooring of the latter had gone when MacGibbon and Ross visited, and by 1976, RCAHMS reported, 'All that now survives of Innellan House is an amorphous ivy-covered mound of stone rubble . . . No surveyable remains can be identified.' However, although one might imagine that most of MacGibbon and Ross's surveyed castles that are gone simply crumbled away, victims of neglect, attrition and the cumulative effects of weather, in fact most of the 52 lost castles were, like the mansion house in Green Market in Dundee and the Knights Hospitaller House in Linlithgow, actively demolished. They might have been saved had their owners put some resources into repairs, conservation or consolidation. One firm, Charles Brand of Dundee, demolished at least 56 country houses in Scotland between 1945 and 1965, as well as much of the 'built history' that still survived in Scotland in the 1950s and 1960s. Not just grand houses, but also factories, castles, railway stations, streets and municipal buildings. Charles Brand,[1] whose company began as a house clearance firm, ended up as a 'funeral director' of built heritage: 'The question must arise as to whether the Scots take a peculiar delight in blowing up buildings, in addition to simply demolishing them. Scottish sappers and lairds delighted in making a thunderous bang.'[2] Even in the case of Helmsdale Castle in Sutherland, which MacGibbon and Ross found 'so much damaged & demolished that little can be determined' (5: 294), the last remains of it were actively demolished in the 1970s to make way for a bridge over the A9 road.

McGibbon and Ross had suggested that the reason for the neglect of Scotland's castellated buildings 'probably arises, to some extent, from their bearing on the architectural and natural history of Scotland not being sufficiently understood and appreciated' (1: vii). In 1939 Scott-Moncrieff proposed a more robustly expressed explanation: 'all over the Lowlands the survivors of such houses [i.e. towers and mansions] are still left to fall into ruin: an awful reflection of our aesthetic sluggardliness'.[3] Lack of understanding and 'aesthetic sluggardliness' as explanations boil down to much the same thing: ignorance, which may be claimed as a justifiable excuse and also, perhaps, a cause for future optimism, if a heightened awareness of the value of heritage can prevail. In practice, the reasons given by owners for this destruction are to do with finance, convenience, safety (occasionally) or even ideology.

Castles Gone for Good

MacGibbon and Ross provide several sketches and surveys of castles that had already disappeared before publication of *The Castellated and Domestic Architecture of Scotland*. Lochgorme Castle was probably destroyed in 1615. Calderwood Castle in Lanarkshire fell in 1773. Thurso Castle was demolished in 1875 in order to build a new one; MacGibbon and Ross provide a sketch of the old one. The United States President Ulysses S. Grant visited the new Thurso Castle as part of his 1877 world tour, but it is now in ruins, having been partially demolished in 1952. Some of the walls of Balloch Castle, which disappeared about 1840, were incorporated into Taymouth Castle – MacGibbon and Ross provide a sketch of Balloch from 1780. Ferry-Port-on-Craig Castle (5: 271) was demolished in 1855. MacGibbon and Ross say of Lochgorme Castle that 'There seem now to be no traces of the fort(s) of Lochgorme' (5: 300), but they were relying on secondary sources for their information. The remains are now fragmentary and covered in vegetation, but are recorded as being extant by Geoffrey Stell in 1985 as part of an RCAHMS survey. Smiddy Bank in Orkney, described as 'an old dwelling-house' (4: 404), had already disappeared when they visited, but they provide an illustration, supplied by Mr Johnston, architect, of the ornate doorway. In the Earlshall entry they

mention the Castle of Leuchars, 'of which not one stone remains standing on another' (2: 289). Seton Palace was destroyed in 1789 to make way for Seton Castle, and Ravelston House was destroyed by fire in the early part of the nineteenth century. In their entry on Bothwell Castle, Haddington (demolished in 1966), MacGibbon and Ross also mention that 'There was another old house in Haddington – now unfortunately destroyed – called "Blair's Castle"' (5: 61).

The National Monuments Records of Scotland (NMRS), which was founded in 1941 to record Scotland's historic architecture in case of wartime destruction, records 280 houses of architectural significance that were demolished, blown up or burnt out, mainly in the 1950s and 1960s.[4] Of those surveyed by MacGibbon and Ross only a handful (Bonhard, Herbertshire, Herdmanston, Old Saughton and Stonebyres) are mentioned in the NMRS list, but the extent of the demolition of large country houses highlights the expendability with which they were viewed. One castle that had narrowly escaped demolition was Crookston Castle near Paisley, 'The upper part of the north-east tower is new, having been restored . . . by Sir J. Maxwell. A portion of this tower near the base is also new, having been cut out when it was at one time intended to blow up the tower!' (1: 538). In the orgy of destruction that took place in the 1950s and 1960s, some particularly poignant, even tragic, tales stand out.

Granton House was abandoned in the late eighteenth century and became a picturesque ruin in the nineteenth century. 'This house is a good example of the amount of fortification still considered necessary in the troubled times when it was built,[5] as well as of the improved domestic and residential accommodation which were being introduced in the early part of the seventeenth century' (2: 192). Despite being scheduled for listing by the Ancient Monuments Commission in 1915,

Granton House, Edinburgh, 1890.

due to a series of terrible blunders it was demolished in the 1920s. Firstly, the scheduling letter was delivered to the wrong address, a different Granton House, owned by the Gas Commissioners. No follow-up action was taken by the Office of Works and meantime the Duke of Buccleuch sold the property to a building firm which intended to quarry the rock below the foundations and then erect industrial buildings. Quarrying began in June 1921, and led to a public outcry. So, on 23 June, the Office of Works sent out another scheduling letter to the building firm, which replied:

> We are employing a large body of men for this work and we take it that your order means that operations will have to stop, and these men will have to be placed among the ranks of the unemployed. As tax payers, we cannot agree that it is necessary to preserve a mass of old stone work rather than provide a livelihood for the men who helped to carry the country through the last war. We therefore give you notice that we intend to demolish and remove the whole of Royston Castle [i.e. Granton House], and failing an answer from you within one month we will proceed to level it to the ground.[6]

Browbeaten, the Office of Works caved in to the builders and replied that they proposed to take no action to prevent demolition. Subsequent pressure

Craighall Castle, Fife, by MacGibbon and Ross. It was demolished in 1957.

on Edinburgh Town Council to purchase the castle failed and the Office of Works noted in 1927, 'No vestige of the Castle now remains. The site is now a disused quarry with a quarry hole filled with water.' Nevertheless the walled garden of the original house survived, albeit in a neglected and ruined state. A local group, the Friends of Granton Walled Garden, is currently aiming to have the castle's Renaissance garden restored as a community garden, with the aid of a team of volunteers.

MacGibbon and Ross were worried about Craighall Castle and rightly so: 'The ruinous condition of this castle exhibits a striking result of the destructive forces at work which are steadily bringing our castle and old houses to the ground. The

latest portion of the building is not yet two centuries old, and it now stands a naked, melancholy ruin, and has been so for many years' (2: 554). Craighall Castle was situated near Cupar in Fife. The early tower house, on the right of the picture, was built by Sir Thomas Hope in 1637. In 1697 it was converted into a country house with a theatrical Renaissance balustraded screen wall between the wings with three arches in each storey of the arcade. But by 1793 Craighall was recorded as being 'in ruin' and in 1956 it was noted 'the castle is likely to be demolished shortly owing to its dangerous condition'. In 1957, despite its Category B listing, it was indeed demolished, during a decade when too many castles, towers and great houses

Stonebyres Castle, Lanarkshire, demolished in 1939–40 to make way for a power station.

were lost. The stones were removed and nothing remains today.

Elphinstone Castle was described by MacGibbon and Ross as 'one of the most remarkable and best preserved of the Scottish keeps of the fifteenth century' (1: 233). Although it was a ruin, traces of paint could be seen throughout the great hall, they said. With a terrible lack of prescience, they added: 'It is a pleasure to add that the building is well cared for, and the roof, which is modern, is in good order, and is perfectly water-tight.' The tower was, however, dangerously undermined by the nearby Elphinstone Collieries in the twentieth century and was demolished in 1955. MacGibbon and Ross described Herdmanston Castle in Midlothian as 'A

modernised mansion which contains some of the walls of an older structure' (4: 393). It was used as a military billet during the Second World War, and was so extensively damaged by the 'Rude and Licentious Soldiery' – mostly Polish officers, who were billeted there – that it had to be demolished after the War by the Royal Artillery. An early seventeenth-century painted ceiling was discovered in the ruin and presented to the National Museum of Antiquities of Scotland by Lord Sinclair.

Stonebyres in Lanarkshire was demolished in 1939–40 and a power station built upon its site. MacGibbon and Ross's sketch is a reproduction of an old lithograph predating 1850, when, as they report, 'the present mansion encasing the old struc-

Bothwell Castle, Haddington, by MacGibbon and Ross. It was demolished in 1966.

ture was erected' (3: 438). As can be seen from the illustration on page 111, Stonebyres had been transformed from a fifteenth-century tower house into an enormous top-heavy Baronial mansion. 'The whole edifice . . . has been an imposing and characteristic example of a Scottish mansion of the Fourth Period' (3: 439).

MacGibbon and Ross devoted four pages to their survey of Bothwell Castle in Haddington and finished by saying, 'This is one of the best specimens of old Scottish domestic architecture left in the town, and it is to be hoped that it will not share the fate of most of the others. It would still make an interesting residence for anyone over whom historic associations had any sway and, if kept in proper order, would preserve a most picturesque feature to the town, and help to maintain its historic and interesting character' (5: 61). Their

hope was in vain. By 1913 it was in ruins and it was demolished in 1966. All that remains is a small park on the site.

Busbie Castle in Ayrshire, 'A shattered structure of the Fourth Period' (3: 372), had been a ruin since at least the 1770s and was demolished in the 1950s, as it had been unsafe for many years. Busbie House was erected as a replacement for the old castle in the early nineteenth century. MacGibbon and Ross described Gladney House in Fife as 'a fine specimen of the early Scottish Renaissance. The fortunes of the house have changed with the locality, and it is now used as a penny lodging house' (5: 286). It had indeed changed fortunes, as it had once been the residence of William Adam and it was the birthplace of his architect sons, Robert and James Adam. An extraordinary pencilled draft letter of reply from Thomas Ross to a letter (dated

Barochan Castle, Renfrewshire.

14 July 1927) from A.R. Powys, Secretary of the Society for the Protection of Ancient Buildings, states: 'today I paid a visit to Gladney House, Kirkcaldy [sic.]. It is in most dilapidated most abominable condition, there is nothing inside but dirt and squalor – a slum of the slums – the sooner it is wiped off the earth the better.'[7] Gladney House was demolished c. 1930.[8]

Farme Castle was located in Rutherglen. MacGibbon and Ross reported that 'It has the appearance of having been built in the fifteenth century, and is a good instance of the persistence of the simple keep style of building' (1: 131). The castle acted as one corner of a courtyard, formed by an extension in the form of a castellated mansion. High walls and subsidiary buildings completed the courtyard. There was an ornate arched gateway to the courtyard adjacent to the castle, which was

of three storeys and a garret, above a corbelled-out parapet with machicolations and water spouts. An old ceiling was removed in 1917 to reveal an ancient wooden ceiling, which carried writing alluding to the Stewarts, and the date was 1325. Farme Castle was demolished in the 1960s, by which time it was being used as a repository for redundant mining equipment.

Other castles demolished since MacGibbon and Ross's survey include Barochan Castle in Renfrewshire, 'a large modern mansion' (4: 380), demolished in 1947, and Gartshore House, demolished in 1955.

Castles Abandoned for Something Better

Although tower houses were often subsumed into the architecture of larger, grander, more fashion-

Ardstinchar Castle, Ayrshire, watercolour
by David MacGibbon.

development of stables, gardens, a gatehouse and a home farm. The Campbells of Barcaldine Castle abandoned it for Barcaldine House in 1709; David Scott, treasurer of the Bank of Scotland, built Benholm Castle to replace Benholme Tower in 1760; Blervie Castle was abandoned for Blervie Mains in 1776; Burgie Castle was abandoned for Burgie House in 1802; Busbie Castle for Busbie House in the early nineteenth century; Cathcart Castle was abandoned for Cathcart House in 1740; Colinton Castle for Colinton House in 1800, Campston (Cumstoun) Castle for Cumstoun House in 1802; and Preston Tower for Preston House in 1663. All of the original castles except Busbie and Cathcart survived. Barholm and Barcaldine were restored from their ruinous state, Barholm in 2005 and Barcaldine in 1897–1911. Fordell House, however, the Georgian mansion that was built to replace Fordel Castle, was lost (see page 66); the castle remains, inhabited as a fine house.

Castles Recycled

> From Lord Cockburn's *Circuit Journeys* we learn that the building [Tullibole Castle] stood unroofed for some time previous to 1801; the old roof, he adds, having been removed and placed on the castle of Glendevon. (4: 112)

The exploitation of fine dressed stone and other materials from buildings seen as having no further purpose has been happening for centuries. In the 1770s Ardstinchar Castle in Ayrshire was largely demolished and the stone was used to build a bridge over the River Stinchar. As a young man, David MacGibbon sketched it in watercolour, probably in 1849. Evidence of the robbed cornerstones can clearly be seen in the sketch. Edrington Castle disappeared shortly after MacGibbon and Ross wrote that it was 'a mere fragment of an ancient

able houses such as Drumlanrig, Castle Wigg and Lochnaw, some were simply abandoned and left to their fate when the owners built themselves a fine mansion nearby in the eighteenth and nineteenth centuries. In almost every case, the name 'castle' or 'tower' was replaced by 'house'. Barholm Castle was abandoned by the McCullochs in about 1750 for Barholm House, a mansion a few miles along the coast on a level site with space for the

Lochmaben Castle, Dumfriesshire, by MacGibbon and Ross.

castle' (4: 391). According to Sir Herbert Maxwell, 'Edrington Castle . . . once a place of great strength and importance, has been quarried away to near ground level'.[9] What little is left has been incorporated into the walls of farm buildings.

Castle Newe was a castellated mansion house in Aberdeenshire, built in 1831 by Archibald Simpson. It was based on an existing Z-plan castle from 1604, which had square towers. MacGibbon and Ross were quite dismissive in their short entry: '[Castle Newe] dates partly from 1604, but is now almost entirely a modern mansion' (4: 388). However, it took on a new life when it was sold to Charles Brand of Dundee for demolition. On 15 March 1927, the *Aberdeen Press and Journal* carried this notice of a roup:

Demolition of Castle Newe. For sale – 200 splendid doors of all sizes, 120 windows, wood and marble mantelpieces with grates; stained glass: panelled shutters and other wood fittings: baths: wash hand basins: w.c.sets: NP. Towel rails: radiators; fire hoses: heating and other pipes, boilers and sinks. Large quantity of woodwork of all classes: slates linings pavements: slabs and dressed stonework, sills, lintels, corners etc.

What had been a magnificent mansion 'lit by electric light' was reduced to a list of fittings in a catalogue. But the slabs and dressed stonework, of Kildrummy freestone, were bought by the University of Aberdeen and used to build Elphinstone Hall at King's College in Aberdeen (Plate 14). A century after Castle Newe had been built, the new creation was complete, in arcaded late Scots Gothic style, in time to celebrate the quincentenary of Bishop Elphinstone's birth in 1931.

Seton Castle, East Lothian, Robert Adam's final project in Scotland, was built in 1789 using the stone from Seton Palace: 'This once magnificent structure, which was regarded as by far the finest Scottish residence of the sixteenth and seventeenth centuries, has unfortunately entirely disappeared' (4: 187). It was at various times occupied by Queen Mary, James VI and Charles I.

The stones of Lochmaben Castle in Dumfriesshire were systematically robbed by locals for building material over the centuries. In 1788 Adam de Cardonnel wrote about Lochmaben Castle: 'What

ABOVE. Burgie Castle, near Forres, Morayshire, in 1799, by Jean Claude Nattes.

OPPOSITE. Burgie Castle in 2015.

walls remain are stript of the outside facing, so that a few years will reduce this fabric to a heap of rubbish. Great pieces of the wall are tumbling down daily.' By the time MacGibbon and Ross visited, the castle had been further reduced, although it was not then – and still is not, in the care of HES – 'a heap of rubbish'.

In their entry on Burgie Castle, MacGibbon and Ross reproduce a drawing by Jean Claude Nattes of 1799. A couple of years later, all but the north-west tower was demolished in order to use the stone to build nearby Burgie House: 'The angle turret shown in the sketch on the corner of the main block is of very unusual form, and must have been quite unique and remarkably picturesque. This makes it all the more a subject of regret that

the building should have been removed, in order, as we understand, that the materials might be used elsewhere' (2: 262). MacGibbon and Ross describe the remaining tower as 'well-preserved', but its condition has deteriorated and it is unstable. Burgie Castle was in imminent danger of collapse until recent stabilisation work. Major vertical cracks had appeared in the fabric, the roof was in very poor condition and mortar had failed in the walls at roof level. The owner would like to restore it, but the tower is suffering from significant structural movement, which is currently kept in check with scaffolding.

Blervie Castle, a very similar tower house not far from Burgie, suffered a major collapse of the west tower in 2006. It had also had a large amount

of its stone used for the construction of a new and grander house, Blervie Mains, in 1776.

In their entry on Dunglass Castle, MacGibbon and Ross note that 'The castle has suffered a great amount of demolition and spoliation, so that now only a very imperfect idea can be formed of what it was before 1735, when the Commissioners of Supply made an order for using it as a quarry for repairing the quay. This work of destruction was only stopped when the place was purchased by Mr Buchanan of Auchentorlie' (3: 306).

When MacGibbon and Ross visited Houston House near Paisley, only the east side of what had been a large quadrangular structure remained. 'The three other sides of the courtyard were taken down in 1780 by a Colonel Macrae, who had purchased the estate. The old village of Houston lay close to the palace, and he offered and gave the villagers the materials, on condition of their moving two or three hundred yards away' (4: 227). Thus a new village of 35 cottages was built as a planned community, along two main streets, from the stone of Houston House. The remains of Houston House were purchased by the tobacco lord Alexander Spiers of Elderslie and used as a shooting lodge until 1872, when Lady Anne Spiers built the present mansion, which incorporates the remaining part of the original castle in the West Wing. In 1994–97, the house was subdivided into six separate grand residences with co-ownership.

Following the death of Sir James Drummond, in the 1970s, Hawthornden Castle in Midlothian was left to the butler and in the 1980s acquired by an American philanthropist. Architects Simpson & Brown were commissioned to carry out restoration work, including repairs to the stonework, for which they used salvaged stone from the demolished Caledonian Station in Edinburgh.

The 1905 restoration of Dean Castle in Kilmarnock was carried out using material from Balcomie Castle, which is still in use, but considerably smaller than it once was, as a consequence. Abbot's Tower in Kirkcudbrightshire was restored in the 1990s, but the rebuilding was necessarily speculative:

The structure is in a state of ruin, and the ground floor, which has been vaulted, is choked full of débris. Almost all the moulded and wrought stones within easy reach . . . have been torn out and applied to the usual common purposes. The general walling of the tower is of the large unhewn granite boulders of the district, while the dressed work being of freestone the wonder is not that so much has been taken away, but rather that any is left. (5: 215)

Barscobe Castle in Kirkcudbrightshire, 'an interesting example of the kind of house which gradually evolved itself out of the old pele tower towards the end of the seventeenth century, and shows the extent of the accommodation which was then considered sufficient for a country laird' (3: 524), was built in the 1640s with stone from Threave Castle. Taymouth Castle, a neo-Gothic mansion of 1842, was built on the site of Balloch Castle and has some of its stone walls incorporated into the structure. At Flemington House in Forfarshire the stair jamb had to be taken down, as the weight of a farm cistern had cracked it. The treads of the stair were re-used in the restoration at Allardice Castle in the 1990s. Abbotsford, Sir Walter Scott's baronial mansion in the Borders, was constructed 'with sculptured stones from ruined castles and abbeys across Scotland built into its walls'.[10] Even St Andrews Castle was not immune from recycling. MacGibbon and Ross report that, after its importance began to wane at the start of the seventeenth century, 'the Town Council in 1654 ordered part of its venerable materials to be used in repairing the harbour walls' (3: 336).

Fire

> Fire continues to present a grievous threat to every country house; a moment's inattention and centuries of history can be wiped out in a flash.[11]

When candles, open hearths and oil lamps were in daily use and interiors clad with wood panelling or draped with tapestries, destructive house fires were common. The danger of catastrophic fires should have reduced enormously with electric lighting, central heating and the technology of modern fire alarms and suppression systems. However, modern buildings are not immune. The late twentieth and early twenty-first centuries witnessed several devastating fires in important historic buildings: Windsor Castle, Clandon Park House, Uppark House, Glasgow School of Art (twice) and Notre Dame Cathedral were all seriously damaged by fire. The outpouring of anguish after the last three fires was made the more public through social media, which spread the word – like wildfire, one might say. Centuries earlier, in 1672, a fire in Willem Blaeu's warehouse in Amsterdam destroyed a number of Timothy Pont's intricate manuscript maps, with their detailed pictures of Scottish castles. This was arguably an even greater loss than the loss of buildings, which can eventually be rebuilt – but only if the original plans and drawings survive.

Fires Reported by MacGibbon and Ross

The list of Scottish castles that have suffered fire damage is a long one. MacGibbon and Ross reported on several fires that had gutted buildings *before* their surveys. Alloa Tower burned in 1800; Druminnor in the 1750s and again in 1804; Knockhall was gutted by fire in 1734; Dean Castle in 1735; Castle Kennedy in 1715: 'The castle was their resi-

dence [the Earls of Stair] till 1715, when it was burnt by accident, since which time it has remained in a state of ruin' (4: 370). The Earl of Stair had returned from one of his visits to France unexpectedly, prompting a servant to attempt to dry out his bedding in front of an open fire. It caught light and the subsequent blaze gutted the castle, which was never restored. Ballencrieff was also set on fire by a careless servant:

> The old house at Ballencrieff, in which Johnson 'passed two nights and dined thrice,' as Boswell accurately records, is now a melancholy ruin. It was burnt down about twenty years ago. For many years previously, deserted by its owners, it had been left in the care of a woman who lived in an outbuilding, which in the old days had formed the kitchen. . . . Though the flames no longer roared up the chimney as they had done for many a long year, still a fire was kept up and soot accumulated. One day the old woman tried to get rid of it by setting it alight, a primitive mode of chimney-sweeping not uncommon in that part of the country. A spark, it is conjectured, was carried into the main building through a broken pane, and falling on some straw brought in by the birds who nested there, set an upper room on fire. The summer had been unusually dry. The flames spread rapidly from one end of the house to the other; so fierce was the blaze that a large beech-tree which stood at some little distance was burnt also.[12]

Ballencrieff lay in ruins until it was restored in the 1990s. MacGibbon and Ross provide an entry on Ravelston House, although it no longer existed: 'Of this edifice, which was destroyed by fire in the early part of this century, the only portion now

OPPOSITE. Cortachie Castle, Forfarshire (Angus), on fire in 1883. Picture from the *Illustrated London News*.

ABOVE. Wallyford House, Haddingtonshire (East Lothian), just before demolition.

remaining is a lofty narrow staircase tower, with crow-stepped gables' (4: 8). They provide five sketches of the garden ornamentation – including parts of the house preserved in the 'fine garden' of the 'modern house'. In 1916 Ross led a trip for the Old Edinburgh Club to the 'modern' house and gardens, where he doubtless pointed out the ingenious use of parts of the old house in the gardens: 'The fireplace of the old hall is built up as a summer house in the garden, with the tympanums of three of the dormer windows placed on top' (4: 9). In their entry on Brodie Castle they report: 'The house was burned by Lord Lewis Gordon in 1645, but some of the ancient parts have been preserved in the restoration which took place thereafter' (4: 64). Fast Castle in Berwickshire 'has the appearance of having been blown up, as a large mass of masonry, with eight corbels embedded in it, has been thrown to the ground and completely turned upside down; but we understand that this

was the result of thunderstorms in 1871, when the battlements were struck by lightning, and the whole of the upper part of the structure was ruined' (3: 223). MacGibbon and Ross report that Cortachie Castle 'was ruined by Argyll in 1641, and has since its subsequent restoration been again destroyed by fire' (4: 50).

Abandonment eventually followed by destruction overtook another Midlothian historic house, Wallyford House, 'a mansion about one and a half miles eastwards from Inveresk Railway Station' (4: 64), which MacGibbon and Ross had surveyed in some detail with a plan and a sketch of the fine Renaissance doorway dated 1672. They noted, 'It has unfortunately been almost completely destroyed by fire within the last year or two.' Wallyford House survived as a ruin until 1948, when the Ministry of Works gave permission for it to be demolished in order to build a housing estate on the site. Pollok Castle in Glasgow had also very

Niddrie Marischal House, Edinburgh, occupied until 1942 but now demolished.

recently been almost completely destroyed by fire, in 1882, 'and, after standing some years in ruins, has again been restored and extended by the present proprietrix, Mrs Fergusson Pollok of that Ilk, under the careful supervision of Mr Charles S.S. Johnston, architect' (4: 217).

Aberdour's staterooms in the south wing were gutted by a fire in 1710, but MacGibbon and Ross do not mention this, nor the fact that Barnbougle was used to store explosives, and was subsequently left as a ruin after being damaged in an accidental explosion. Preston Tower was burnt accidentally in 1663, and then abandoned.

Fatal Fires after MacGibbon and Ross

The fires that raged after MacGibbon and Ross's surveys were also numerous, seven of them result-ing in the complete loss of the building. Old Saughton House, which contained 'probably the best preserved of any painted stone ceiling in Scotland' (5: 337), was completely burned out in 1920 and demolished a few years later. Barochan was demolished in 1947 after a fire. Herbertshire was finally demolished in 1950 after fire in 1914. Bonhard was burned out in 1959 and blown up in 1962. MacGibbon and Ross devote four pages to their survey of Niddrie Marischal House in Midlothian (2: 62), mainly telling the story of the family from details found in a notebook in the house's charter chest. They also give uncharacteristically detailed descriptions of the interior: 'It is a fine staircase, with rounded pilasters at the end of the newel, somewhat like those of the latest staircase of Crichton Castle. The landing of the stair is very stately and massive, probably being one of the finest things

Hatton House, West Lothian, from John Slezer's *Theatrum Scotiae*.

of the kind that we have left us' (2: 64). They provide a sketch of it and also describe the ceiling and the walls of the dining room, with its portrait of 'the great hero', William Wallace. It was occupied until 1942, gutted by fire on Hogmanay 1959, and then completely demolished so that a housing estate could be built on the site.

In their description of Ardmillan Castle near Girvan, MacGibbon and Ross quote Abercrumie's *Historie of the Kennedyis*, written in the seventeenth century: 'the castle of Ardmillan, so much improven, of late, that it looks like a palace, built round, courtwayes; surrounded with a deep, broad ditch, and strengthened with a movable bridge at the entry; able to secure the owner from the suddain commotions and assaults of the wild people of this corner, which upon these occasions are set upon robbery and depredation . . .' (4: 253).

Ardmillan Castle caught fire in 1973 and was subsequently abandoned. Although the eighteenth-century mansion was largely destroyed, the sixteenth-century tower had stood up well to the fire and might have been saved. However, in 1977 the estate was purchased and the tower was not seen as having any value. Ardmillan Castle was finally demolished in 1990 and the grounds converted into a holiday and caravan park.

Hatton House in West Lothian (old Argyle House) was one of the great Renaissance houses of Scotland, expanded from an original tower and later Renaissance courtyard by Lord Charles Maitland in 1650. MacGibbon and Ross, unaware of its impending doom, give almost eight pages to its description. It burned down in 1952 and was demolished in 1955. All that remains are the ogee-roofed pavilions at each end of the terrace, which

Cassencarie Castle, Wigtownshire (Dumfries and Galloway).

are on the Buildings at Risk Register and classified as at high risk. In 2008 they were described as 'rapidly deteriorating, exposed to the elements and inhabited by pigeons'. More recent inspections have found further deterioration.

The Unfortunate Survivors

Some buildings survived their fires, but were mortally wounded by the damage and descended into dereliction and ruin. Crosbie Castle was badly damaged by fire in 2004, and was partially demolished in 2007. It is now on the Buildings at Risk Register. It seems likely that Cassencarie in Wigtownshire, also surrounded by a holiday and caravan park, may follow the same unfortunate path as Ardmillan. Cassencarie suffered a fire in the 1960s, but this was after its elegant interior had already been abandoned and used instead for storing hay. It is now derelict and unsafe and on the Buildings at Risk Register.

Castle Wigg was rendered derelict by a fire in 1933. It has the appearance of an eighteenth-century country house, but within the walls the remains of a sixteenth-century tower house can still clearly be seen. Loudoun Castle in Ayrshire was gutted by fire in 1941, days before it was due to be leased to the War Office as a military headquarters. Beyond repair, it has stood in ruins since then; it now sits in an abandoned theme park,

Cassencarie Castle interior, 1958.

surrounded by rusting rollercoasters and decaying rides. Philorth House was burned down in March 1915, 'a fine example of a simple but picturesque Scottish mansion of the 17th century' (2: 508). The earliest part was destroyed and the nineteenth-century part still stands as a burned out shell.

Crathes Castle suffered a serious fire in 1966, ironically only ten years after Sir James Burnett of Leys had donated the castle to the NTS in order to preserve it for future generations. The old tower survived, although the painted decoration was blistered and damaged by soot, but the Victorian and Queen Anne wings were gutted. The Trust faced a dilemma for the future: to rebuild them, tear them down, or tear them down and replace them with a modern structure? Schomberg Scott's solution of rebuilding the Queen Anne wing only, but to its original, lower proportions, was adopted. The Victorian wing was sacrificed, at a time when there was almost a moral imperative to rid the country of such architecture. It would doubtless be much admired now, had it survived.

The Lucky Survivors

Other buildings not only survived their fires, but were renewed, with the damage being repaired and the buildings rebuilt where necessary. Shivas (now known as House of Schivas) was burned out in 1900 and restored for Lord Aberdeen by Sydney

Mitchell. Monzie Castle was engulfed by fire in 1908 and only the outside walls remained. It was restored by Robert Lorimer using Edinburgh crafts-men. Robert Lorimer also restored Dunrobin Castle after a fire in 1915, when the building was being used as a wartime naval hospital. Ian Gow reports that 'Robert Lorimer was not shy of tele-graphing distressed owners in the aftermath of fires'.[13] Glamis Castle also suffered a fire during the First World War when troops were billeted there. In September 1916 two soldiers discovered a fire in a room under the castle roof. As they ran to raise the alarm, the first person they came across was Lady Elizabeth, later to become the Queen Mother, who telephoned both the local and Dundee fire brigades. She then organised a chain to convey buckets of water from the river and helped with the removal of the valuables out onto the lawn. Aiket Castle had two separate fires in one day in 1957; it was restored from dereliction in the 1970s. Pilrig House burned down in 1971 and was rebuilt in 1982; it is now in apartments. Cullen House was badly damaged by fire in 1987 and was restored by 1989; Liberton House in Edin-burgh was gutted by fire in 1991 and subsequently restored by Groves-Raines architects; Castle Grant had its south-west wing destroyed by fire in the mid twentieth century; it became derelict but has subsequently been restored. In 2009 Kelburn Castle had a fire which spread to the roof as a result of

an electrical fault. Twenty-five firefighters battled the blaze through the night before it was extinguished; only minor damage was sustained. Cramond Tower suffered a fire in the roof space in December 2011, causing damage to the roof. Pitcaple Castle in Aberdeenshire had a fire in the east wing in 2014; eight crews of firefighters managed to prevent it from spreading to the roof and the fifteenth-century tower house. It is a tribute to the Scottish fire services that in all of these fires no lives were lost, apart from a pet cat at Pitcaple.

War

Most of the castles surveyed by MacGibbon and Ross had been domestic residences throughout their history, although a few of the older fortresses had seen military action in previous centuries. The last battle fought on Scottish soil was Culloden in 1746 and the last castle besieged and damaged by enemy attack was Blair Castle, Perthshire, also in 1746, long before MacGibbon and Ross started their survey. Since then, castles had been generally peaceful places, apart from some continuing Border skirmishes, mainly to do with sheep. They reported of Corgarff Castle, in Aberdeenshire, 'Till 1831 the castle still contained a garrison of two officers and fifty men; but these were no longer required to put down rebellion; they were merely employed to support the civil authorities in the suppression of smuggling' (2: 68).

The larger fortresses, Edinburgh and Stirling castles, had always been used to house troops, but military activity had not been seen by most castles for several centuries. However, in the twentieth century, during the First World War, and more so during the Second World War, castles were pressed into service for a variety of military requirements, ranging from a rest centre for entertainers for the troops (Erchless Castle) to the headquarters for the liberation of Norway (Riccarton House). Those castles that had always been strategic military strongholds – Edinburgh, Stirling, Blackness, Broughty, Inchcolm – were pressed into service whenever national conflicts arose.

At Edinburgh Castle, for the first time since it started in 1861, the one o'clock gun stopped firing from the Castle esplanade during the First World War. This was in order to avoid distressing the Castle's hospital patients and, indeed, the residents of Edinburgh during a time of war. The Castle hospital had beds for 57 patients, along with secure rooms for 'prisoners and lunatics'. In August 1914 the first prisoners of war arrived; a German vessel was sunk off Germany's North Sea coast and 16 injured seamen were brought to the Castle. There were also civil internees – the Red Clydesider David Kirkwood, later Baron Kirkwood of Bearsden, was imprisoned in the dungeon in 1916, after being arrested in Glasgow for making speeches contravening the Defence of the Realm Act, fomenting a strike at Parkhead Forge. According to him, the German prisoners on the floor above him 'seemed to want for nothing'.[14] (The prison was closed in 1923 when the Castle ceased to hold a permanent garrison.) By August 1914, in addition to the garrison in place already, reservists were arriving to help the battalion get up to the strength of 1,000 men. Since the Castle officially had accommodation for only 750 men, it would have been under great pressure. It acted as a recruiting depot for new troops getting processed and undergoing basic training.

The first foreign troops to garrison at Edinburgh Castle arrived as a regiment from Newfoundland, Canada. Despite all the war-related activity, it is extraordinary that the Castle operated as a visitor attraction throughout the 1914–18 period, so that civilians were able to continue to look around the historic areas. The Scottish Regalia was only removed when the first Zeppelin raids started in 1916. In the Second World War Edinburgh Castle was again used as a military hospital and the Crown of Scotland was hidden in a mediaeval latrine closet in David's Tower. In 1939 Luftwaffe pilots shot down over the Firth of Forth were taken to the Castle and treated in the military hospital.

In 1881 Stirling Castle became the depot for the Argyll and Sutherland Highlanders. On 4 August 1914, the day Britain declared war on Germany, the Castle's annual garden party was held as usual – a last moment of normality before the horror that was to come. The order to mobilise the battalion of Argyll and Sutherland Highlanders came on the evening of the garden party, reportedly just as the last of the guests left. Within days the Castle, as the regimental depot, was crowded with reservists and new recruits. Thousands of young men from all over Scotland gathered at its gates to sign up to serve king and country. Recruits generally stayed there for a few days, were medically examined, issued with their equipment and then shipped off to more permanent bases or to the trenches. Stirling Castle fulfilled a similar role in the Second World War.

Blackness Castle, known as the 'ship that never sailed' because of its long, narrow shape and its position jutting out into the Forth, was also a military site, but by the mid 1800s, army use of the site had declined considerably. It was revived, however, when it became a key ammunition store in 1870, causing MacGibbon and Ross problems with their survey: 'In the seventeenth century the castle was made into a prison for distinguished Covenanters. It is now converted into an ammunition depot. For this purpose its structure has been changed, and, owing to the precaution now necessary for safety, it is with difficulty that its ancient portions can be examined and defined' (3: 225). They must have had considerable difficulty, because, given the significance of the site, this is an uncharacteristically short entry at under two pages. Blackness remained as an ammunition store throughout the First World War. It was finally

vacated by the War Office in 1919. During the 1920s the Office of Works carried out a major programme of repair and restoration to reverse most of the late nineteenth-century army interventions (e.g. by removing the courtyard roof and blocking up the east entrance), which had been put in place under the threat of invasion by Napoleon III of France. During the work, a gruesome discovery was made in the pit-prison in the 'stem' tower – an iron manacle clasped around the wrist-bones of a long-perished prisoner.[15]

Inchcolm Abbey, which is on an island in the Firth of Forth, had briefly seen military use during the Napoleonic conflict. Because of its strategic location in naval warfare, new structures were built for a wartime role in the First World War: concrete gun emplacements, observation and control posts, ammunition magazines, searchlight positions and accommodation huts. The men stationed on Inchcolm lived in a 180-bed hutted camp around the abbey with some of the abbey buildings used as mess facilities. Separate accommodation was provided for 20 naval personnel and officers. The Ministry of Works dismantled much of these after the war during the 1920s, but the outbreak of the Second World War saw a rebuilding of defences with very substantial encampments laid out around the abbey; most of these have been subsequently removed, though some of these structures can still be seen on the island by visitors to the abbey. The current visitor centre was built as the engine room in 1916, principally to power the carbon-arc electric searchlights for night-time vision. During the Second World War it was converted to a telephone exchange and acted as a hospital. The HES Statement of Significance for Inchcolm Abbey notes that: 'Together these remains are of great interest to military historians, and to a more general pubic interested in wartime history. Many of the structures are dramatically sited, their brutalist concrete and uncompromising lines softened by undergrowth. While not to everyone's taste they add an undoubted atmosphere and contribute to a memorable visit.'[16]

At the outset of the Second World War, a Luftwaffe raid took place on the strategic Forth Bridge. Although no damage was done, the Ministry of Defence decided henceforth to protect the bridge with balloons. The Balloon Barrage, as it was called, needed a headquarters nearby and the position of Dundas Castle with its views over the Forth Bridge and along the river itself made the castle a natural place for this purpose. Five years of military occupation did no good for the structure and condition of the buildings, however.

Military Housing of Troops

Between 1940 and 1945, there was a friendly 'Polish invasion' of the towns and villages of Scotland, with troops billeted across the country. Seven of MacGibbon and Ross's surveyed castles were used to house Polish troops at various times: Castle Menzies was a Polish Army medical supplies depot and Cortachie Castle a hospital for Polish troops. Polish troops of the 3rd Flanders Rifle Brigade, part of the 1st Polish Armoured Division, were quartered on the third floor of Dalkeith Palace from 1942 onwards. Herdmanston housed Polish officers, Glamis had two field artillery battalions, Myres Castle in Fife housed Polish troops, and Tulliallan became the Scottish headquarters of the Free Polish Army. As a lasting memorial, the Great Polish map of Scotland sits in the grounds of Barony Castle in the Borders.

Other nationalities of troops were housed elsewhere: Indian soldiers were billeted in Castle Grant during the Second World War, during which part of it was badly damaged by fire, and Canadian soldiers were stationed in Coxton Tower. Dargavel House, 'a mansion, partly old and partly modern' (4: 21), was situated on land that was part of a compulsory purchase order by the Ministry of Defence at the start of the Second World War, in order to set up the UK's largest explosives factory, which only ceased operations in 2008. The castle was used for meetings and training. The site around the castle is now being developed as a brownfield regeneration housing project. Dargavel has become rundown through its long-term institutional use and future plans for the castle are unclear.

Balhousie Castle in Perth, a convent before the Second World War, housed officers' quarters for the Auxiliary Training Service during the war. This was the start of a lengthy military involvement – after the war, it housed a detachment of the Royal Army Service Corps and the Headquarters, Highland District, Corps of Royal Engineers. In the early 1960s there was a major army re-organisation. The Black Watch Depot at the Queen's Barracks was closed, and Regimental Headquarters and the museum came to the castle, where they remain.

At Crookston Castle the north-east tower was used by the Home Guard as an aircraft observation post during the Clydeside Blitz. Concrete floors were inserted into the tower and an army camp was set up in the parkland around the castle. The grounds of Loudon Castle were used to house a small military camp for training SAS troops.

In the First World War, Blair Castle and Glamis Castle were both used as hospitals. In the Second World War, Borthwick Castle was used to store the Scottish Public Records; Drumlanrig was used to house the girls of St Denis School in Edinburgh; Ferniehirst had troops billeted; Haggs was requisitioned by the army; Merchiston was used by the National Fire Service; and Stranraer Castle was an Air Raid Precautions base. Hoddom Castle, Herdmanston House and Redcastle never recovered from being requisitioned; after the war Herdmanston was demolished and Hoddom and Redcastle were never again occupied and are both now on the Buildings at Risk Register.

The Second World War did a favour for Newark Castle in Renfrewshire, however. Described by MacGibbon and Ross as 'closely surrounded and hemmed in by shipbuilding yards' (2: 425), it was hidden from public view for nearly 100 years. When the shipbuilding industry collapsed after the war, the great sheds came down to reveal an almost perfectly preserved late sixteenth-century castle, which is now in the care of HES and open to the public.

Castles Compromised

From the depths of the Border valleys to the farthest-flung islands of the Hebrides a trail of beleaguered country houses can be traced through Scotland. They may not all be unloved and forgotten, but most have been neglected and abandoned to the mercy of the elements. Deserted and left to decay after wartime requisitioning; cast off as cold skeletons in the aftermath of savage fires; crudely adapted for agricultural storage, hundreds have also fallen prey to vandalism and systematic looting, and many have been written off as lost causes.[17]

A distrust of all old buildings was prevalent among certain local councils in the 1960s and early 1970s. MacGibbon and Ross describe Rossend Castle in Fife as having become a 'hospitable mansion' (3: 559), and mention that Queen Mary had stayed there in 1563. But in 1972 Burntisland's Council decided 'that its ancient castle should be destroyed as a symbol of former feudal oppression'.[18] The story of the fight by conservationists to save it[19] exemplifies the struggles which went on in many places to save condemned historic buildings, in much the same way that MacGibbon and Ross had campaigned to save the Knights Hospitaller building in Linlithgow. In the case of Rossend, however,

the building was saved from demolition at the eleventh hour and restored as architects' offices. It is now a private home.

Nigel Tranter campaigned in his books against the neglect of Scottish fortified houses in the 1960s and 1970s and was particularly alarmed by 'a craze for demolition among certain of our local government authorities, which seem to prefer anything modern, however unattractive and poorly built, to anything ancient'.[20] It is not fanciful to compare the deliberate destruction of architecturally significant buildings that symbolised unwanted ideologies to book burnings or statue smashing – an attempt, powered by rage, to expunge despised objects and thus purge what they stood for. Edinburgh Council was to be commended, however, for a valiant but ultimately misplaced attempt to save Cramond Tower. MacGibbon and Ross reported, 'It is in an unfortunate condition, being entirely crowned with ivy, which has got such a hold of it (the branches in some places going through the walls) as to greatly imperil its safety; while on the top, in consequence of the roots of saplings penetrating the walls and arch, the masonry is becoming dangerous. This is greatly to be regretted, as the structure is somewhat unique, and might easily be preserved from decay' (3: 432). In the 1960s Edinburgh Town Council removed most of the vegetation and crowned the barrel roof with a concrete cap. On discovering later that they did not in fact own the building, they abandoned further work and it was again left to the ravages of the weather and vandalism.[21] Cramond Tower was restored to become a private home in the 1970s.

Cassencarie and Hoddom castles both sit in the midst of caravan parks, increasingly derelict. The ruins of Loudon Castle in Ayrshire became surrounded by a holiday theme park in 1995, but it closed in 2010. The building is enormous and mostly consists of an early nineteenth-century

Cathcart Castle, Glasgow, by MacGibbon and Ross.

Gothic mansion. 'Within the modern structure are incorporated portions of two older castles, the first a keep of the fifteenth or sixteenth century … and the other is apparently of the seventeenth century' (5: 321). The years of neglect have not been kind to Loudoun Castle and it is in a poor condition in urgent need of conservation. There are currently plans to develop the site as a tourist and leisure destination, using the building of new homes as 'enabling' development to fund the stabilising of the castle. There have also been plans to restore Dunskey Castle, but its doorway is situated a few yards from a right of way to the local caravan park – any restoration would have to take this into account. Pitfirrane sits in the middle of a golf course and functions as its clubhouse. Burleigh Castle, which is a property in the care of HES, sits on the A911 road, opposite a development of new houses in an old steading.

Cathcart Castle was purchased by Glasgow City Council in 1927 and then incorporated into Linn Park. However, Glasgow City Council pronounced it unstable and dangerous and demolished it in 1980. The castle was occupied until 1740 but it was vacated that year as its owner moved into a new mansion, Cathcart House, nearby. The castle's lead roof was removed, the structure fell into disrepair and was left to drift into ruin. When MacGibbon and Ross visited, it was a substantial and solid ruin, still standing to five storeys. 'The view shows the condition of the building about a century ago, and it is not very different now' (3: 235). Only low foundations now survive. There is a story, probably apocryphal, that Mary, Queen of Scots stayed in Cathcart Castle the night before the Battle of Langside in 1568.

Institutions, Housing Estates and Farmyards

Binney and Watson-Smythe warned of the problems of turning historic buildings over to institutional use:

> Experience shows that most forms of institutional use follow a remarkably clear pattern. First, the institution needs more floor space and begins to build in the grounds. The earliest extensions or additions may be discreetly sited and carefully designed, but very quickly the hut syndrome is underway and the house is rapidly surrounded by one- or two-storey flat-roofed extensions of the very utilitarian kind mercilessly caricatured by Osbert Lancaster.[22]

Castles which have been turned into institutions and suffered for it include Westhall, Craigcrook Merchiston, Pitfirrane (see page 144) and Huntly (Perthshire).

If a castle was rurally situated, it generally sat surrounded by policies, parkland or extensive

The fictitious Crotchet Castle, surrounded by industrial works, as portrayed by the twentieth-century cartoonist Osbert Lancaster.

gardens. As the population has increased and towns and cities have expanded their boundaries, inevitably driving the value of land up, many castles have had the policies surrounding them sold off and are now hemmed in by modern buildings. In rural areas, the outbuildings and walled enclosures which once would have surrounded the castles and towers have nearly all disappeared and many ruinous towers are left to stand out obtrusively in solitary splendour in fields, quite unlike their original situation. Farm buildings have edged up close to Barholm Castle and Carsluith Castle in Kirkcudbrightshire, Abbot's Tower in Dumfriesshire, the Bishop's House, Breckness in Orkney, Flemington House in Forfarshire, Garmylton Castle in East Lothian, Cockburn House in Currie and Tillycairn in Aberdeenshire. Housing estates surround Castle Levan and Blackhall, and housing is encroaching on Claypotts and Burleigh. The buildings of Napier University have hemmed in Merchiston Castle (see Plate 22). Haining or Almond Castle stood 'in the middle of a cultivated field' (1: 413) when MacGibbon and Ross visited. It is now on the site of a former brickworks, in a heavily used part of an industrial estate. Dunglass Castle in Dumbartonshire, on the Buildings at Risk Register, is in the

Almond (or Haining) Castle, near Linlithgow in West Lothian, surrounded by industrial works.

middle of an operational fuel depot on the Clyde and is inaccessible.

Other castles, such as Baltersan and Niddrie, have been sold for restoration projects by landowners who included only a tiny footprint of land surrounding the building, leaving them exposed to future development and with potential access problems. Gogar House, 'a well-preserved mansion' (3: 525) which is situated between the City of Edinburgh and its airport, was lived in by Lady Steel-Maitland for over 50 years. When she died in her nineties in 2003, she left the 14-acre property to the schoolteacher tenant of a gatehouse cottage in the castle grounds. He sold the castle and grounds for more than £800,000 and the new owners applied for planning permission to renovate

the castle and convert a ruined stable block into two homes. An office block and five houses were also planned as part of the scheme, enabling development to fund the restoration of the castle. Although Gogar House still sits in 3.5 acres it is close to the modern new housing and has lost the benefit of its former policies. The castle was for sale in 2021 for £2.5 million, and the surrounding modern newbuild houses have a very high re-sale value, suggesting that a large profit was made on the development.

Cardarroch in Dumbartonshire was a charming small laird's house which MacGibbon and Ross found significant as 'a connecting link between the old Scottish style of house and the modern' (2: 511).

Cardarroch House, Glasgow, by William Simpson.

The artist William Simpson visited this house in 1853 with some friends, including the writer Hugh MacDonald. The latter wrote that

The house is a queer-looking old structure, with peaked gables, crow-steps, narrow windows, and a picturesque old doorway, over which is the date of 1625. It is now occupied by several families of weavers and labourers . . . At length we inquire the name of the ancient structure immediately before us. 'That's Cardarroch, an auld gentle house,' quoth our informant. 'And who lives there?' 'Oh, naebody,' he replies; and coolly adds, after a brief pause, 'just some workin' folk.' There is certainly a dash of worldly philosophy in the little rogue's reply. 'Workin' folk' and 'naebodies' are synonymous terms, we are afraid, in the vocabularies of older heads than his.[23]

It is not known when and how Cardarroch finally disappeared, but it was in ruins by 1901 and does not appear on later Ordnance Survey maps.

Like Cardarroch, many of the tower houses MacGibbon and Ross worried about were occupied by farm workers or labourers and became, effectively, rural slums. Ruins and semi-ruins on farms were convenient places to store agricultural goods and to house farm tenants or low-status workers. Bonhard, near Linlithgow, which was partly inhabited by farm labourers when

MacGibbon and Ross visited (the top floor and attic were closed off) did not survive a fire in 1959 and was blown up in 1962. Although it had been modernised and is described as a 'fourth rank chateau' in Canmore, MacGibbon and Ross describe a charming house containing 'three handsome rooms with finely panelled ceilings, each of a different design, and ornamental fireplaces with stone and wooden mouldings, and pilastered panel above the mantelpiece. These finishings, together with the wooden panelling of the walls, impart to the house an air of antique refinement, which is frequently wanting in the interior of many of our old mansions' (3: 534).

Auchans Castle in Ayrshire had been portrayed by Billings as a handsome mansion, but had already started its slide towards dereliction when MacGibbon and Ross visited. 'In consequence of the mansion having been in recent years divided up into workmen's houses, the original arrangements have been a good deal interfered with' (2: 174), they report, and go on to mention 'a fine marble fireplace, which is now removed'. Auchans is now seriously ruined.

Saughton Mills, also known as Stenhouse Mansion, had 'been at one time a pleasant residence on the bank of the Water of Leith . . . but it has now fallen on evil days and has been cut up into small houses for labourers. It is a building of considerable size for a small estate and was until lately of larger dimensions' (4: 97). For a time in the 1930s it had a greyhound racing track in the grounds and having become derelict it was donated to the NTS by the Greyhound Racing Trust in 1937. It was restored by Ian Lindsay in 1937–39 and is used by HES as a conservation centre.

Tilquhilly Castle in Kincardineshire was 'occupied as a farm residence' when MacGibbon and Ross visited. The building was abandoned in the 1940s, after having been used to raise turkeys, and deteriorated very badly. The owner who restored

the building in 1991 noted that MacGibbon and Ross had recorded that 'some fragments of good old wood-work lying in one of the upper rooms were well worthy of being preserved' (2: 293). 'Unfortunately, their advice was not heeded.'[24]

Tenanted properties were often quoted by MacGibbon and Ross as being in need of care and attention. Any tenant may have been better than none, however. In Thomas Ross's notes on Balvaird Castle of September 1878, he was concerned: 'The main portion of the Castle is in a good state of preservation, this is in great measure due to the fact of its having been inhabited by small Farmers up till a comparatively recent period, but now that it is tenantless and uncared for, its destruction will speedily come about.'[25] Fortunately for Balvaird it was taken into care and is now looked after by HES. Kipps House in Linlithgowshire was another such case: 'When we first saw the house it was occupied by farm labourers, but it is now tenantless, and fast hastening to ruin' (4: 15). It is now completely ruinous and encroached upon by modern farm buildings. Glendevon Castle 'has quite lately been put in good repair, but unfortunately, owing to the absence of the occupants, we had no opportunity of inspecting the interior except on the ground floor, which is all used as byres' (4: 41). It is now derelict.

Auchenskeoch in Kirkcudbrightshire is still a fragment 'incorporated with the walls of a farm steading' (4: 376), as it was when MacGibbon and Ross visited. Evelaw Tower in Berwickshire is surrounded by farm buildings and in a dilapidated state, whereas MacGibbon and Ross described it as 'tolerably well preserved' (3: 546). Collarnie Castle in Fife, with its painted heraldic ceilings, remains in agricultural use, with a steading attached. In 1887 MacGibbon and Ross reported that the painted ceilings were already in a very neglected state, and following its visit in 1925 the officers of RCAHMS recorded that it was in bad

Midhope Castle, near Edinburgh: interior. Undated, but probably 1960s. Midhope Castle is known to millions as 'Lallybroch Castle' in the film series *Outlander*.

repair. In 1931–32 and in 1985–86 works were carried out to make the tower wind- and water-tight. The chamber tower is covered by a modern roof, though the floors, together with the important heraldic ceilings beneath two of them, are in a poor condition.

Midhope Castle became derelict in the twentieth century, described by Canmore in 1962 as fast decaying, but MacGibbon and Ross had reported that 'Midhope is in good preservation, and still inhabited by pensioners of the Hopetoun family, whose palatial residence of Hopetoun House is in the immediate neighbourhood' (2: 506). The 1851 census had revealed that there were 53 people in 10 families living around Midhope – some, no doubt, in the castle itself and some in surrounding farm buildings – including four game keepers, four foresters, two labourers, a groom, a carter, a gardener, a joiner, and a number of paupers. Some of these would be the 'pensioners' to whom MacGibbon and Ross refer. In 1926 the castle was still occupied, sub-divided into dwellings for estate workers. However, RCAHMS recorded the castle as deteriorating, including a fine oak staircase with twisted balusters 'now sadly dilapidated' rising in the East Range from the first to fourth floors. Some restoration work began in 1988, including the replacement of the roof on the East Range and a new roof for the West Tower, as well as the insertion of new window frames into existing openings, but the building is still not habitable.

Corgarff Castle in Aberdeenshire, now in the care of HES, was 'cut up into small houses for agricultural labourers' (2: 67) after the army left the building in 1831. The last tenants were two sisters, the Misses Ross, who lived there at least until 1911. After the First World War it became derelict until it was taken into state care in 1961. Cassencarie and Craighall were both were used as farm stores but not habitations. Of Brunstane House in Midlothian MacGibbon and Ross reported that 'the edifice is now cut up and divided and is partly occupied as a farm steading' (4: 176). The large mansion is still divided into two houses and is in good repair. At Aberdour Castle, now in the care of HES, 'The greater portion of the buildings, including those erected by the great Regent [Morton], are used as cow-byres and piggeries' (2: 477).

Scotland is not alone in having dilapidated rural towers and castles. James Charles Roy, an American historian who restored Moyode Castle, a mediaeval tower in County Galway, has been outspoken about the neglect with which most of the many unoccupied Irish castles are treated, apart from those maintained in the care of the government: 'most others lie scattered to the winds in fields and woods, farms and villages – deserted, cracking, falling apart, home to cows, pigs, chickens, mice, bats, crows, pigeon coops, peat piles, rusted farm tools, straw, refuse and plastic feed bags. The smell of manure is their hallmark, the dank of slop and dripping ivy their atmosphere.'[26]

Buildings at Risk

The Register of Buildings at Risk was set up in Scotland in 1990 by Mary Miers, under the auspices of the Scottish Civic Trust. It was initially a printed pamphlet, started in response to a concern at the growing number of listed buildings that were vacant and had fallen into a state of disrepair. It is now an internet-based resource, maintained by HES, providing information, sometimes provided by concerned citizens, on properties throughout the country of architectural or historic merit that are considered to be at risk. This is essentially a signalling exercise to raise awareness and has in itself no legal powers to enforce upkeep or repairs; but it has alerted concerned individuals and community groups who have been moved to campaign and fundraise and sometimes to purchase and restore. The owners of the castles at risk are not necessarily wilful. Some are farmers who happen to have an inconvenient ruin on their land and no capital with which to consolidate or restore it, as with Castle Wigg.[27] Some are recent owners who bought a ruin with an intention to restore it, but subsequently found themselves unable to manage the considerable financial and logistical demands that ensue. A few are large landowners who do not wish to sell a picturesque ruin but, equally, do not wish to run the expense of consolidating or restoring it. Eighteen of the

Kenmure Castle in Kirkcudbrightshire, by MacGibbon and Ross.

castles that MacGibbon and Ross surveyed are currently on the Buildings at Risk Register. MacGibbon and Ross would certainly have approved of the public listing of castles at risk, with the implicit appeal to conserve and/or restore. Five of the castles at risk have changed significantly for the worse since MacGibbon and Ross's survey – i.e. Hoddom, Westhall, Kenmure, Crosbie and Garrion, all of which were occupied at the time. The first three of these are large, sprawling buildings with an architectural history of several accretions and a poor outlook for the future.

Kenmure Castle had been 'modernised' before the time of MacGibbon and Ross's publication and they did not approve: 'Great alterations have been made on the structure during this century, and the antique character of the building is considerably obliterated. It suffered especially from a very complete remodeling about ten years ago' (4: 256). It was partly ruinous a century earlier when Francie Grose visited, but in the 1950s Kenmure Castle was a hotel with beautiful gardens. However, it is ruinous and deteriorating again now in 2022. Like Aboyne, its architectural history is

Westhall House, Aberdeenshire.

almost unintelligible due to the amount of destruction and rebuilding and deterioration that has taken place. Torwoodhead Castle (now known as Torwood Castle) in Stirlingshire, which was ruinous when MacGibbon and Ross visited, has been undergoing 'restoration' since the mid 1950s, but it has deteriorated recently and is classified on the Buildings at Risk Register as being at 'moderate' risk. It has suffered from recent vandalism.

MacGibbon and Ross described Westhall Castle as 'a mansion, to which a large modern house has been added, situated about one mile north of Oyne Station. The old portion is a very picturesque specimen of the Aberdeenshire style of the Fourth Period, showing a copious application of the "label" corbelling so common in the north' (3: 601). Now it is categorised on the Buildings at Risk Register as being in very poor condition and at high risk. Westhall started life as a sixteenth-century L-plan house and was greatly extended in both the seventeenth and nineteenth centuries. The estate originally belonged to the Bishops of Aberdeen. It was the point where work began on the Great North of Scotland Railway in 1852, invested in by the owner, Sir James Elphinstone. By the middle of the twentieth century it had become used for institutional purposes, as an agricultural college. It then became a hotel, with plans to develop it into a golf complex in 1996. Since then it has become increasingly derelict. In 2012 a group of lads attracted by derelict properties reported on their visit to Westhall and posted a series of harrowing photographs on the internet showing the extent of the interior decay: 'Me and a group of friends went up to this place at night to find the infamous swimming pool, after climbin in a second storey window in the dark we were in the main building we wondered about with bike lights to ead the way but failed to find the pool so we just went home'[28] (spelling as in the original post). A few months later they reported on the same website that they 'caught pikeys stealing boilers and a big heap of lead from this place i reported them to the police the man was charged and now it whole site is pretty much locked down. im planning to back soon to see if theres away in and will report back if i find one.'

When MacGibbon and Ross visited Crosbie Castle, on the outskirts of West Kilbride, they remarked that 'The house contains a good deal of old oak carving' (4: 119). Crosbie became a youth hostel during the 1970s, but was abandoned after a fire in 2002. In 2007 it was semi-demolished after storm damage to the external walls of the castle. Its condition is currently described as poor and its level of risk as high. Garrion Tower, 'a genuine old Scotch house' (3: 477) had also, like Crosbie Castle, been ruinous and then modernised in the course of the nineteenth century. MacGibbon and Ross

reported this via James D. Robertson, who supplied the plans and information. Originally Garrion Tower was the pre-Reformation summer residence of the Bishops of Glasgow and Galloway. It was left empty some time before 2008, when it was put on the Buildings at Risk Register, and has deteriorated since then.

When MacGibbon and Ross visited Glendevon Castle it was inhabited, but is now on the Buildings at Risk Register. 'It has quite lately been put in good repair, and is inhabited, but unfortunately owing to the absence of the occupants, we had no opportunity of inspecting the interior, except on the ground floor, which is all used as byres' (4: 41). The Buildings at Risk entry for February 2014 reported: 'External inspection finds the building has been disused for some time. Some windows are broken, doors boarded up. There are some slipped slates evident, rainwater goods are missing in places and there is dampness to walls. A single storey building adjacent has a collapsing roof. The property is thought to have operated as The Dungeon Bar/ Restaurant latterly.' John Gifford described it as a 'mutilated tower house'[29] but it surely deserves a better fate than this.

Gilbertfield was intact when MacGibbon and Ross visited, although it is not clear whether it was inhabited. The far-right gable and angle turret (see page 142) collapsed in the 1950s and the other angle turret fell off in the 1960s or 1970s. It is currently at the centre of a controversial application for the building of 400 houses in land close by. In 1916, four men from the Cambuslang area were charged with having maliciously destroyed and pulled down its south bastion. In their defence the accused claimed to have spotted a stone sticking out from the building's turret, and said they thought it was a hazard – so removed the object with a rope, pulling down a mass of other material with it. The vandals were each fined £1, the equivalent of almost £100 today.

Gilbertfield Castle, Lanarkshire, by MacGibbon and Ross.

In addition to those on the Buildings at Risk Register, Brounstoun Castle and Loudoun Castle in Ayrshire, Cassencarie Castle in Wigtownshire and Inoch Castle in Nairnshire (2: 246) are all deteriorating. MacGibbon and Ross were concerned about Thomaston Castle in Ayrshire: 'It is unfortunate that such a good specimen of our domestic style of the sixteenth century should have been allowed to fall into the neglected and semi-ruinous state in which it now is' (3: 291). Thomaston is still neglected and semi-ruinous. They also pointed out that Downreay (Dounreay) Castle, the only castle in the north-west part of Caithness-shire, 'continued to be inhabited till 1863, but has since been allowed to fall into ruin' (3: 630). Since it is now situated on the site of a (former) nuclear power establishment, the archaeological monitoring carried out in 1997 had to be done without direct access to the site, using video footage of machine excavation of inspection pits and photographs taken by on-site staff. As for Arnot Tower in Perth and Kinross, they found that 'All the floors are gone, and the whole building much dilapidated – no doubt the work of violence' (3: 246). Yet it was, and is, in a rural setting, not near any large town, so opportunities for vandalism should be limited. Arnot Tower now stands in the grounds of Arnot House, built in 1878.

In the case of Crichton Castle, the complaint about vandalism came from elsewhere. Although MacGibbon and Ross were actively reporting on castles at risk in the late nineteenth century, they were not quite alone. John Dickson, author of *The Ruined Castles of Midlothian* (1894), wrote a heartfelt complaint about the state of Crichton Castle: 'Time, vandalism and neglect have literally choked it with debris . . . It would be well if the proprietor were induced to remedy still further the condition of things. A little was done upwards of twenty years ago, when here and there the crumbling walls were fortified by fresh masonry. But much more requires to be done. The courtyard stands sadly in need of being relieved of its mass of rubbish.'[30] However, a footnote states: 'This has now been done'. Perhaps the proprietor, Mr Callender, was shamed into action by the threat of publication. MacGibbon and Ross devote 11 pages to Crichton Castle, but make no mention of rubbish and the 'stinging nettles and branching elder bushes' that Dickson also complained of. Crichton Castle is now in the care of HES and is free from debris and overgrown vegetation.

Castles that were *Almost* Rescued

> Suppose one of you wants to build a tower. Will he not first sit down and estimate the cost to see if he has enough money to complete it? (Luke 14:27–29)

Many plans to restore ruined castles have been drawn up and acted upon, but some have never gone beyond the planning stage. MacGibbon and Ross report of Pitfirrane Castle in Fife that 'At one time it made a very narrow escape from destruction by alteration. Sir Arthur Halkett (the proprietor) has in his possession plans prepared by an architect about the end of last century, or beginning of this, which if carried into effect would have utterly ruined the old house. Another set of plans for additions to the mansion also exist, which were probably prepared in the seventeenth century, and are of considerable merit, but were never carried out' (3: 573–74). However, MacGibbon and Ross would doubtless be aghast at the twentieth-century flat-roofed extension built for the golf clubhouse that Pitfirrane became (page 144).

Plans for restoring Barholm Castle, drawn up by Ian Lindsay in 1953, were shelved by the owner as being too expensive to realise. Fifty years later a new set of plans – minus Lindsay's new large windows and the housekeeper's wing, which would not have received planning consent in 2001 – were drawn up and this time they *were* executed. In 1949 Ian Lindsay also drew up plans for Dundargue Castle in Aberdeenshire, with an extension, which were never brought to fruition. James Gillespie Graham prepared proposals for a new entrance hall at Methven Castle in the first half of the nineteenth century. 'Fortunately this romantic symmetrical Gothic building was not built since the plans show the earlier south-west tower rebuilt as a square tower and finished with Gothic crenellations.'[31] Methven Castle was restored by K.L.S. Murdoch in the 1980s.

In their entry on Baltersan, MacGibbon and Ross report: 'In the description of Carrick by Mr William Abercrummie, minister of Maybole, written towards the close of the seventeenth century, Baltersan is described as "a stately fyne house, with gardens, orchards, parks, and woods

about it"; but these unfortunately are now all gone, and the castle stands deserted in the middle of a corn field' (3: 504). And so it still stands, ruinous and deserted. Its current owner has made strenuous efforts to see it restored, but without success. For 16 years he tried to raise the finance to restore it but finally gave up and put the castle on the market in 2008. 'I'm just an ordinary man from a working-class background,' he said, 'but I've been gazing balefully at castles since I was five years old. After discovering McGibbon & Ross's classic, five-volume work on Scottish castles, I began scouring Scotland for somewhere I might buy . . . Then, in the late 1980s, I found Baltersan. And it was then that I began to learn that a dream can become a heavy burden.'[32] Baltersan was still for sale in 2021. Its large size – and consequent high rebuilding costs – coupled with an unfortunate situation close to a busy road, with a tiny amount of ground and no access road, mean that it is particularly challenging to find a buyer with the appetite and finances to restore it. It is on the Buildings at Risk Register.

Other ruined castles that have had unrealised plans for restoration include Inchdrewer, which was partially restored in 1971. The project was abandoned before completion by owner Robin Ian Evelyn Milne Stuart le Prince de la Lanne-Mirrlees[33] and was subsequently placed on the Buildings at Risk Register. In February 2008 it was reported that external inspection found the castle showing signs of a lack of maintenance. All glazing was broken and the property unsecured. In October 2010 an external inspection found that the semi-restored building had deteriorated and was now on the cusp of ruination. The ruins were purchased in 2013 by a Russian woman, sight unseen. She was reported to have plans to restore the castle, but little progress had been made by

OPPOSITE. Pitfirrane Castle, Fife, with the modern addition of a golf clubhouse.

2022, despite the advice and support of the late Marc Ellington, who restored Towie Barclay Castle in the 1970s.

The owner of Fairlie Castle in Ayrshire bought it in 1999 from the Earl of Glasgow, with the intention of restoring it to a family home. Scheduled monument consent was finally granted for a revised set of restoration plans in 2019, minus the modern extension that had originally been hoped for. MacGibbon and Ross quote Pont, in *Cunningham Topographised*: '"Fairlie Castle is a stronge toure, werey ancient, beutified with orchards and gardins it belongs to Fairlie de eodem, chieffe of ther name." All traces of the orchards and gardens referred to by Pont have entirely disappeared, and the place has a neglected appearance by no means pleasing' (3: 179). They would find the state of Fairlie Castle still to be neglected, but it is possible that changes may come about.

MacGibbon and Ross were sanguine about the future prospects for Castle Tioram (or Ellan-Tirrim Castle as they call it): 'its old walls of the thirteenth century still remain almost intact, and as the structure is well taken care of, they may still survive for centuries to come' (3: 58). They were wrong about that, however, as emergency stabilisation works had to be carried out on a collapsed wall section of the north-west curtain wall in 2000. Castle Tioram became a very public focus for the arguments between pro and anti-restorers when a new owner applied to rebuild the castle to provide living accommodation in 1999. The clashes between Historic Scotland and the late Lex Brown on behalf of Castle Tioram divided communities between those who supported his plans and those who believed that the castle should be left as a consolidated ruin; the divisions crossed party political boundaries and aroused fury among Brown's many high-profile supporters, such as Ranald Macdonald, chief of Clanranald (of which Castle Tioram is the traditional seat). In an article in *The Scotsman* in 2004, entitled 'High time to demolish the ruin that is Historic Scotland', Gerald Warner poured vitriol on 'the Jobsworths and olde worlde Luddites whose pedantic tyranny has made Historic Scotland an object of loathing to everyone who has the conservation interests of our heritage at heart'. He went on to articulate an overtly anti-SPAB view of conservation: 'It is a doctrinaire view that the landscape should be ornamented with ivy-clad ruins, in the style of nineteenth-century illustrations of the Waverley novels, rather than with accurately restored heritage. It is the mentality of those who, two centuries ago, built follies on their estates and employed bogus hermits to inhabit them.'[34] The media was overwhelmingly supportive of Lex Brown; Warner's views were echoed in numerous newspaper articles, particularly in *The Scotsman*, with titles such as: 'Hysteric Scotland? Planning quango's competence is called into question' (*The Scotsman*, 20 December 2007). Finally, Historic Scotland decided, 'having considered this case, we do not believe that a scheme of adaptive re-use for residential accommodation can be found which is acceptable in terms of impact on the monument'.[35] Their decision was upheld by an independent reporter who recommended refusal, and Scottish Ministers took the decision to reject the application in 2002. However, the fallout of the row over Tioram probably paved the way for the restoration of Mingarry Castle, another ancient fortress of the western seaboard which would previously have been unlikely to receive permission for an alternative-use scheme from Historic Scotland, and also signalled a political change that finally, in 2015, led to the inauguration of Historic Environment Scotland as a new body.

Sanquhar Castle has also had a difficult history: 'Sir William Douglas, the first Duke of Queensberry, (1637–1695) who built Drumlanrig, stayed in Sanquhar Castle till his death, preferring it to the splendid structure he himself had reared, and within

which he is said to have slept only one night. On his death the second Duke abandoned Sanquhar, and it then fell a prey to the depredations of the burghers, from whose rapacity the few remaining ruins have been saved in comparatively recent times' (1: 417). Sadly, this is again the case in the twenty-first century, with vandalism posing a threat. When MacGibbon and Ross mention it being saved in comparatively recent times, they are probably alluding to what turned out to be an unlucky near-miss when Sanquhar was *almost* restored by John Crichton-Stuart, 3rd Marquess of Bute. He had successfully restored Cardiff Castle and Castell Coch in Wales and in 1895 he purchased Sanquhar Castle, started to plan and execute its restoration, and had almost finished the south-west tower. Unfortunately, the work was abandoned after his death in 1900 and its future is now again at risk.

When MacGibbon and Ross visited Earlstoun they noted, 'It is now in a sadly ruinous state' (3: 521). They were dismayed because 'people not yet old, who were born in the house, remember it in perfect preservation' (3: 522). In 2009 the Vivat Trust carried out emergency work to stabilise the exterior with a view to restoring the building for holiday accommodation. Unfortunately, the Trust went into liquidation in 2015 and the restoration of the interior was never started.

There have also been unrealised intentions in the twentieth and twenty-first centuries to restore Westhall in Aberdeenshire; Monk Castle in Ayrshire; Newark Castle, Pitteadie Castle, Kirkton Castle and Lordscairnie in Fife; Lennox Plunton in Kirkcudbrightshire; Uttershill near Penicuik; Torwood Castle in Stirlingshire; and Dunskey, Myrton and Castle Stewart in Wigtownshire. Dunskey and Torwood are on the Buildings at Risk Register. Some schemes came to nothing for want of finance, others due to a complex mix of problems involving logistics, time commitment and planning consent. Any or all of the castles in this section might be restored at some time in the future. Duntarvie near Linlithgow and Carrick Castle in Argyll are undergoing slow restorations which were started some years ago. Other possible restoration projects include Knock Castle and Knockhall Castle in Aberdeenshire and Gilbertfield in Lanarkshire. HES suggests that, in the case of Gilbertfield, 'Authentically based reconstruction of the missing elements as part of a scheme of adaptive re-use would be possible, as the house was recorded in a complete condition by MacGibbon and Ross in the 1890s. Later photographs also exist. It is considered that the planning of the castle would lend itself to modern requirements quite easily.'[36]

Conclusion

Was the pessimism of MacGibbon and Ross justified? When one reads the sorry tales of so many castles neglected, at risk, burned, blown up and demolished, it is difficult not to conclude that they were indeed right to worry about the future. They strove so hard to protect the buildings they saw as at risk and perhaps a few were saved because of their interventions. There was a flurry of castle restorations in the ten years after the publication of *The Castellated and Domestic Architecture of Scotland*, which can possibly be attributed to the interest that MacGibbon and Ross generated in castellated architecture. However, the sad fact is that 52 castles have completely disappeared since MacGibbon and Ross surveyed them and at least

as many again are currently at risk of vandalism and further deterioration from an already poor state. Built heritage will inevitably deteriorate unless actively managed and cared for. 'Neglected castles and towers never remain static; the elements are harsh and no respecters of time: if a ruin is left to its own devices, it will continue to decay and collapse until it ends up a heap of rubble.'[37]

But for each of these castles at risk that are still standing, there is at least the hope that the future will see an individual owner or group who will bring the building back from the brink of ruin and lavish sufficient resources to restore it to fulfil a useful purpose, or at least keep it well consolidated. The dark days of the post-war 1950s and 1960s, when buildings were demolished simply because they were deemed to be an unfashionable nuisance, are over, but architectural heritage is still under threat, from climate change, from economic forces, and from a continuing ideology which gives conservation an unyielding status above restoration and adaptive re-use. MacGibbon and Ross were pessimistic, but tempered this with a dash of optimism: 'We are not without hope that this work may serve to direct the attention of proprietors and others to the value of our ancient domestic remains, and may thus help to preserve some of them from the decay and demolition which at present threaten speedily to overtake the greater number' (1: vii).

The next chapter contains much more positive news about the fate of some of MacGibbon and Ross's castles.

A · NICE · WYF · AND
A · BACK · DOORE
OFT · MAKETH · A · RICH
MAN · POORE

7

Castles Transformed

———

Do not let us talk then of restoration. The thing is a Lie from beginning to end. You may make a model of a building as you may of a corpse, and your model may have the shell of the old walls within it as your cast might have the skeleton, with what advantage I neither see nor care: but the old building is destroyed, and that more totally and mercilessly than if it had sunk into a heap of dust, or melted into a mass of clay.[1]

John Ruskin, *The Seven Lamps of Architecture* (1889)

As has been seen in Chapter 6, MacGibbon and Ross's castles were not safe from careless owners, neglect, demolition, predatory property developers or the devastation of fire. Nor were they safe from restoration. Ruskin and Morris may have disapproved, but MacGibbon and Ross were largely in favour, even pointing out buildings that they thought ought to be rescued and restored. They were very concerned about Earlshall in Fife, a fine sixteenth-century tower house which was ruinous but untouched. MacGibbon and Ross were desperate for it to be saved:

It is most unfortunate that the beautiful ceiling of the gallery, containing as it does quite a treatise on Scottish Heraldry, and throwing, with its wise proverbs and quaint

conceits, many side-lights on Scottish character, should be allowed to fall piecemeal to utter ruin . . . The woodwork of the ceiling and roof is rotting from the effects of damp, while the whole has been most rudely patched up with wooden straps nailed across the ceiling in the most unsightly fashion. (2: 289)

Very soon after this was written, Earlshall was rescued by R.W.R. Mackenzie, who gave the young architect Robert Lorimer his first major commission, along with a generous budget, to restore the castle. Mackenzie was a wealthy bleach merchant from Perth and was a friend of the Lorimer family who lived at nearby Kellie Castle. Like Lorimer he had great sympathy with the Arts and Crafts move-

OPPOSITE. The ceiling of Earlshall Castle (Fife) – wise proverb or quaint conceit?

ment and commissioned him to not only restore the ruined tower house but also design the furniture. Lorimer also designed and planted the gardens with yew trees which now stand topiarised as an extraordinary legacy of his work.

Lorimer's restoration of Earlshall is very much of its time. He must have known that the exterior harling was original yet he removed it from Earlshall, so that the building looked more 'authentic' with its unadorned stone revealed.[2] Ranald MacInnes examined the meaning of rubble, or unadorned stone, in Scottish architecture in a paper entitled 'Rubblemania':

> Rubble has tended to signal 'historic' Scots culture in a way which, conscious of its 'Scottishness', asserts itself in a manner which emphasizes naïveté, homeliness or simplicity. This is a view of Scottish architecture constructed during the post-'North Britain' period when the country's rebellious past was at a safe distance. Rubble also has become a sign for 'heritage', an appropriate emblem for tourist-orientated buildings.[3]

After the re-harling of Law Castle in Ayrshire, when it was restored in the late twentieth century, local feeling was offended: 'A neighbour, who asked not to be named, said Mr. Phillips had wrought havoc. "He has absolutely ruined what was a lovely old stone castle. It was a work of art, with beautiful stonework that had been there for 500 years, then he came along and roughcast every inch of it."'[4] This anti-harling attitude is hardly surprising; knowledge about harling is privileged information, accessible only to those with an understanding of the historical antecedents. And even they do not always get it right. The Ministry of Works was culpable for advising the owners of Stobhall and Kisimul to use non-porous cement and reinforced concrete in their restorations in the 1950s, causing

serious problems with damp ingress in later years. The owner of Rusco Tower was not allowed by Historic Scotland to harl the building in the 1970s, because it would not be 'authentic', again leading to problems with damp. Most restorations put the stamp of the time upon the re-purposed building, both externally and internally.

Thomas Ross threw himself into the restoration debate with his customary passion and enthusiasm:

> Then, as individuals, there are two classes of men: the Restorers and the anti-Restorers. In the former class there are those who are strictly conservative who would alter nothing of the old work which is in a condition to endure, and others who will take any liberty to cut and carve as they choose. It will probably be admitted that this latter kind of restoration is not so frequent as it once was. The creed of the anti-Restorer is to leave things very much as they are, cement the tops of the walls, and with the same material fill up all cracks, rents and joints. Both classes have wrought much evil which it is difficult to apportion justly between them . . . Now the purpose of these two parties is so far the same – to transmit these matchless and unique buildings to posterity, and the question comes to be, how is this to be best done? To accomplish this end something must be done. To leave them alone is to ensure their fall, later or sooner.[5]

Around 50 of the castles which were ruined or derelict when MacGibbon and Ross surveyed them have not been left alone, but have been restored and turned into homes, hotels, offices and other purposeful buildings, many of them projects on a heroic scale. Quite a few more have been transformed from wretched dwellings giving the most basic shelter to farm labourers, to comfortable and elegant homes – e.g. Hills, Buittle, Rusco. Many others that were not surveyed in *The Castellated and Domestic Architecture of Scotland* have also been rescued. Some have been on a rollercoaster of fortune: they may have been in good condition and inhabited when MacGibbon and Ross surveyed them, but subsequently became derelict and then were later restored. For example, Aiket, 'whose old Scottish character has been very much destroyed by alterations which, we understand, were made on it upwards of a century ago' (4: 365), was inhabited in the late nineteenth century, but went through a series of disasters, including two fires, which led to its becoming ruinous in the 1950s (page 152). It was later rescued from its ruinous state in the 1970s and restored to its sixteenth-century character (pages 153 and 154–5). Recently it has had an enormous series of extensions added. Other castles were ruinous but were later transformed into habitable buildings and then were abandoned and descended into dereliction once again, e.g. Kenmure and Crosbie castles.

Restorations before MacGibbon and Ross

Before 1886 there was also a great deal of rebuilding work going on. MacGibbon and Ross catalogue several castles that had been remodelled or restored in the decades before their survey. In Volume 4, they have a section entitled 'Altered and Fragmentary Structures' comprising 55 entries, of which the majority are castles that had been greatly changed before they visited – e.g. Penkill in Ayrshire, Barnbougle Castle near Edinburgh, Kellie Castle in Forfarshire and Kinnaird Tower in Perthshire. Inglismaldie was recently 'restored and converted into a modern mansion' (5: 295) in 1882 by the Aberdeen-based architect James Matthews. Crosbie Castle had been recently repaired. Bridge

Castle had 'been converted from a roofless ruin into a comfortable mansion in the recollection of living persons' (3: 276). Balhousie was repaired and added to by the Earl of Kinnoull, but 'until 1863 it was dilapidated, and only the first floor tenanted' (3: 586). Cleish 'was allowed to fall into a state of complete ruin . . . But about forty-five years ago Mr Young had it renovated and converted into his mansion house under the direction of the late Mr John Lessels, architect' (3: 569).

This was followed by a few other antiquarian restorations such as Castle Stewart in 1869, Old Place of Mochrum in 1873 and Kilcoy Castle in 1890. Hallbar and Elliston House were other nineteenth-century restorations which MacGibbon and Ross described as 'recent', while Bavelaw was somewhat earlier: 'The farmer who lives in it states that it was in a state of ruin about the beginning of this century, when it was in a great measure rebuilt' (3: 531). Pitcaple Castle 'had fallen greatly into ruin when, about 1820, it was restored and enlarged from plans by the late William Burn, architect' (4: 60–61). Of Garrion Tower they report: 'The interior of the house has been entirely modernised about the beginning of this century, at which time it seems to have been in a state of ruin' (3: 478). They report on Wardhouse Tower: 'Some years ago the building fell, through neglect and decay, but was immediately re-erected as we see it now' (3: 402).

In their description of Liberton House, MacGibbon and Ross start by telling the common tale of 'modern' alterations that changed the historic character of a house: 'This interesting old mansion has suffered grievously from alterations at various dates, more especially about sixty years ago, when, in order to accommodate the fabric to the taste of the period, nearly all of its ancient features were obliterated or concealed' (5: 317). They then go on to unfold the story of something rather wonderful that happened:

Aiket Castle, Ayrshire, in 1974.

Aiket Castle in 2009.

Aiket Castle in 2019.

The dining-hall, or, as it is now, the drawing room, shared the fate of the rest of the house, and no one suspected that behind the modern lath and plaster there were hidden the characteristic features shown in Fig. 1428. About three years ago, the present tenant commenced investigation, with the result that one interesting example of construction after another came to light. The quaint stone fireplace, the small, high, and deeply recessed windows on each side, with the long sloping sills, stone soffits and seats, and the finely arched recess, are thus once more visible and complete.

In Lochhouse Tower, when ownership changed recently, the new owner decided to strip back the interior walls. One of the bedroom walls was covered with wallpaper and it was soon discovered that the paper had been stuck on to large sheets of Perspex, which were affixed to the stone. Behind the Perspex, the interior stone walls were not just damp but running with water. He also found a very unusual double garderobe toilet behind the twentieth-century plaster. Barcaldine Castle in Argyll was in ruins when MacGibbon and Ross visited. It was restored shortly afterwards in 1897–1911 by Leslie Grahame Thomson and is now a luxury hotel. It appears to have had the harling removed and the exterior stone exposed recently.

Castles as Commodities

The Scottish castle has been commodified in a way that could hardly be imagined in the nineteenth century. There is now never a month when the Scottish property market does not have at least a handful of castles for sale, with the main country house estate agents doing a brisk trade in castellated mansions and tower houses. The market in castles started to take off in the 1960s and escalated to the point where dozens of sales were taking place annually by the start of the twenty-first century. Castle Grant, for example, has been bought and sold ten times since 1983 and is currently for sale again. Castle Law and Fordel Castle have both changed hands five times since the middle of the twentieth century. In the nineteenth century castles did change hands through sales as well as inheritance, but usually within a small group of aristocratic or landed elite, with the occasional incursion by a member of the nouveaux riches, such as the bleach merchant R.W.R MacKenzie who commissioned Robert Lorimer to restore Earlshall in 1892. It has since been sold four times. Sir Jack Stewart-Clark, the owner of a textile company, bought Dundas Castle in 1899. Unusually, it has stayed in the family since then. However, because of the position of increasing numbers of Scottish castles as commodities in the high-end housing market, rather than as physical expressions of ancient lineage, more are likely to be exchanged between wealthy buyers rather than deteriorate via generations of old families with decreasing resources.

Jamie Macnab of Savills, which markets many of the castles for sale, reported: 'I sold one castle where the facilities were so primitive that every bedroom needed a potty, which, when they were full, were put in wardrobes to keep the moths away!'[6] Nevertheless, it did sell. Castles change hands regularly on the high-end housing market, especially if they are adapted for modern living. Of the castles restored from ruins since MacGibbon and Ross surveyed them, the following are known to have been sold on to new owners since the restoration: Abbot's Tower; Aiket; Ballencrieff; Castle Levan; Craig Caffie (twice); Duncraig; Edinample; Fawside; Fordel; Fordyce; Forter; Gilknockie; Hatton; House of Aldie; Law; Leslie; Liberton House; Mains (Lanarkshire); Midmar;

Newmilns; Niddrie; Ochiltree; Peffermill House; Pitcullo; Powrie; Spedlins; Tillycairn; Terpersie. Several have been sold twice or more. In addition, Aiket, Baltersan and Barholm were sold on by would-be restorers before work started.

A nineteenth-century attempt to sell Broughty Castle, a coastal fortress near Dundee, as a restoration project failed: 'By 1821 it was a roofless ruin and was offered for sale in the Dundee, Perth and Coupar Advertiser on 21 December as a potentially "delightful residence" capable of restoration at small expense, or "which would make an excellent situation for an inn". There were no takers.'[7] It was bought by the War Office in 1855, at a time of renewed threat from the French, and was surrounded with batteries of large naval guns, remaining in military use until 1949. In 1969 Broughty Castle opened as a museum operated by Dundee Council.[8] This is a nice illustration of changes in attitudes towards ruined castles. If Broughty Castle had been for sale at any time from the 1970s, a century and a half later, there would almost certainly have been intense interest and competition to buy and restore it, despite the fact that the 'restoration at small expense' claim was as untrue then as it would be now. There would have been offers from a variety of would-be castle restorers with no landowning connections; a local community group would probably also have been formed to try to save it, as was the case with Portencross Castle in Ayrshire, a somewhat similarly situated building, in 1998. The reasons why these changes in attitude and behaviour came about are a complex mix of economic circumstances, social class changes and media involvement, coupled with the personal interventions of individual campaigners and architects.

Change may be inevitable, but it need not be debasing; castles in danger of decay and destruction have changed in many positive ways. In the twenty-first century the number of types of usage

of MacGibbon and Ross's buildings reflects a much more complex world in which heritage buildings can have multiple different functions, owners and types of access. Castles are still used as private homes, but have been adapted for re-use also as museums, community centres, self-catering accommodation, hotels, offices, visitor attractions, clan or regimental centres, prisons or development opportunities. They can be owned by private individuals, clans, businesses, charities, building trusts, developers, local councils or the state. Ownership and usage change, often within short periods of time, as economic and social and cultural factors impact upon them. But the challenges they face are similar to those which MacGibbon and Ross witnessed – neglect, vandalism, lack of finance, weather and climate.

Castles in Continual Change

Fernieherst (Ferniehirst) in Roxburghshire was already dilapidated in 1767 and half inhabited, half derelict in MacGibbon and Ross's time. It was repaired and partly restored in the 1920s. From 1934 to 1984 it functioned as a youth hostel, apart from use as an army billet during the Second World War. It was then repurchased by Lord Lothian and restoration plans were drawn up by the architects' firm Simpson and Brown. In 1984–86 the main part of the castle was repaired and restored as a single house, originally for holiday letting and opening to the public, and the ruinous kitchen wing was substantially rebuilt and extended as a small house for Lord and Lady Lothian. The chapel, which had been used as a stable when MacGibbon and Ross visited, was repaired and converted to a simple visitor centre and an office for Lady Lothian at the same time. The library was repaired, which would have delighted MacGibbon and Ross, who said, 'On the first floor of the round tower . . . there is a small circular apartment called the library. In this room is the beautiful wooden ceiling which, we are sorry to say, is in a most deplorable state of ruin' (2: 157); it is now restored (see Plate 19).

When MacGibbon and Ross visited Kirkhill House in Linlithgowshire it was in use as a farmhouse. In 1976, however, it had lain empty for five years and had been subject to vandalism. In 1974 an inspector from RCAHMS reported that the fine armorial panel showing the Erskine coat of arms, sketched by MacGibbon and Ross and described as being built into a hen house (4: 395), could not be located. However, in the late 1970s the tower house was restored and converted into two apartments and it was reported on Canmore that 'Built into the steading is a beautiful scrolled dormer-windowhead, and a balustered armorial panel.'⁹ So all was well in the end.

Haggs Castle is Glasgow's oldest inhabited secular building. Built by Sir John Maxwell, 12th Baron of Pollok, in 1585, it became neglected and then ruinous after 1752, when Sir John Maxwell, 3rd Baronet, moved to his new residence, Pollok House. By 1840 the lower floor was occupied by a smithy associated with the local coal mine. 'Till a few years ago this building stood a roofless and deserted ruin, a mile or two south from Glasgow; and about the time the drawings were made, a door was knocked through the north wall, and the ground floor was used as a smithy in connection with coal pits in the vicinity. The castle has lately been converted into a habitable dwelling house, and has become absorbed in the ever-spreading suburbs of the city' (3: 478). Sir John Stirling-Maxwell was the restorer in 1860; he used the castle for Pollok Estate's factor, who lived there until his death in 1899. After the factor died, Maxwell expanded the building, adding a drawing room and billiard room and a circular staircase. In 1943 the government requisitioned it for military purposes. After the war it was divided into four

residential flats by the Maxwell Trustees. The castle was bought by Glasgow Corporation in 1972 and was used to house Glasgow's Museum of Childhood. Since 1998 it has been a 19-room private house. MacGibbon and Ross submitted plans for the restoration in 1899, with drawings by Fred MacGibbon. 'By the middle of the nineteenth century it was being described as a "picturesque ruin", but soon afterwards was somewhat fancifully restored by the civil engineer Alexander George Thomson. A scheme by McGibbon and Ross to restore it to a more correct state was unfortunately not executed.'¹⁰

MacGibbon and Ross's sketches of Haggs before its restoration (3: 482–83, figures 412 and 413) were made from photographs supplied to them by John Baird, a Glasgow architect. They refer to the illustration (by 'Miss Mildmay'; see page 161) of Haggs Castle after its restoration in Sir William Fraser's book *The Maxwells of Pollok* (vol. 1 p. 4), but say 'it must be received with caution as a representation of the ancient appearance of the castle' (3: 482).

Until 1800 the castle buildings of Druminnor Castle in Aberdeenshire formed a courtyard, dominated by a massive square tower called the Old Tower, the oldest and most important part of the mediaeval castle. The surviving building was added to the Old Tower around 1440 to provide a much larger hall and residential suite, and occupied one side of the courtyard. The other three sides and the Old Tower were demolished in 1800, and in 1841 the remaining building, i.e. the 1440 hall block with its stairtower, was doubled in size and transformed into a modern country house. In 1960, the 1841 additions were demolished and the 1440 hall block and stairtower were restored, forming the present house.

When MacGibbon and Ross visited Barnbougle Castle near Edinburgh they noted that 'It was reconstructed some 10 or 15 years ago by Lord

Fred MacGibbon's drawing of Haggs Castle in Glasgow.

Rosebery . . . previous to that time it was in a state of ruin' (4: 379). They did not explicitly say that Lord Rosebery's 'reconstruction' was not at all faithful to the original, although they did place it in the section of 'altered structures' in Volume 4.

On the east wall is a carved panel with a quotation from the Book of Proverbs 22:28: 'Remove not the landmark which thy fathers have set', presumably added at the time of the nineteenth-century reconstruction. Barnbougle Castle was restored again

Haggs Castle, 1855, photographed by Duncan Brown.

Haggs Castle after restoration, painted by Miss Mildmay, from *The Maxwells of Pollok* by Sir William Fraser, published in 1862.

OPPOSITE. Druminnor Castle, Aberdeenshire,
in 1961, derelict and partially demolished.

ABOVE. Castle of Park, Wigtownshire
(Dumfries and Galloway), in 1912.

by the Rosebery family in 2019, from a state of
dilapidation rather than ruin, for use as an events
venue.

MacGibbon and Ross reported on Cairnbulg
Castle, Aberdeenshire, that 'This noble keep is
unfortunately in a very rent and torn condition' (1:
311). It had then been uninhabited since the late
eighteenth century. But just a few years after Mac-
Gibbon and Ross's visit, in 1896, Sir John Duthie
restored the castle using granite, which was his
wife's dowry from her father who was a stone
merchant. Their initials and motto are over the
present front door. In 1934 the late Lord Saltoun
bought it back into the family and modernised it.
From 1966 to 1997 it belonged to Lady Saltoun,

who made further modernisations in 1966. In 1989–
90 extensive repairs were carried out and both
towers, the staircase tower, and the west face were
re-harled. Since 1997 it has belonged to the Hon.
Mrs Nicolson, Lady Saltoun's eldest daughter.

Castles Expanded and Contracted

Castles are rarely static. Even the most intact medi-
aeval-looking building is likely to have had alterations at some stage in its history. Castle of Park
in Wigtownshire came into state care in 1949 and
had its low eighteenth-century wings demolished
in 1951 by the Ministry of Works, for reasons
which do not appear to have been documented.

In 1992 it was leased to the Landmark Trust and is now managed as holiday accommodation.

Cramond Tower, on the other hand, had a wing added. The tower had been restored from a ruinous condition in the 1970s and in the 1980s permission was sought from Historic Scotland to add an east wing, where there was architectural evidence of a three-storey addition. HS initially wanted the extension to be built using modern materials to distinguish it from the tower; it was finally built with matching stone in 1992, but reduced in height so as not to obscure the evidence of the original building.

When MacGibbon and Ross surveyed Aboyne Castle they noted that it had been in the family of the Earls of Huntly since 1449, 'till recently acquired by Sir William Cunliffe Brooks, who is now engaged in making extensive alterations on the castle' (4: 374). The 12th Marquess of Huntly bought back the castle and a small part of the estate in the mid twentieth century, but by 1949 it was falling into ruin, and by 1972 it was derelict. In 1975 the 13th Marquess of Huntly, the present holder of the title, rebuilt the castle completely, stripping it back by demolishing a large part of the structure, and made a building which looks the part of a traditional tower house but is not architecturally coherent. Even the vaulted ceiling in the drawing room was constructed in the twentieth century using wood and plaster. In 2016 plans were submitted by Groves-Raines architects for an additional wing to provide accessible family accommodation, which were approved by Aberdeenshire Council, thus paving the way for further expansion after centuries of previous expansion and contraction.

Merchiston Castle in Edinburgh was 'in use as an "eminent boarding school"' (3: 263) when MacGibbon and Ross visited. 'The town during the present century has gradually encroached on the solitude of the old tower, till now it is surrounded with suburban residences, above which, however, its bulky form is still a conspicuous landmark in the district . . . The castle is still surrounded with gardens and pleasure-grounds, which, together with the quaint lion-guarded gateway, still convey a fair idea of a Scottish gentleman's residence in the sixteenth century' (3: 263). They gloss over the nineteenth-century additions which dramatically changed the sixteenth-century outline of Merchiston Castle. It continues to be used for educational purposes, nowadays as part of Napier University's campus (formerly Napier College). It is no longer surrounded by gardens and pleasure-grounds, but 'exhibited like a trophy in the middle of the college',[11] hemmed in by 1960s buildings (see Plate 22). MacGibbon and Ross made a meticulous and detailed survey of the decorative features of the inside of the tower; fortunately, they did not have to report that at the west end of the Great Hall ceiling 'four nightmarish "drollities" sport outsize penises'.[12] These appear on a sixteenth-century painted beamed ceiling from Prestongrange, which was installed in Merchiston Castle in 1964.

Rosslyn Castle, the great fifteenth-century stronghold of the Sinclair Earls of Orkney, is largely ruinous, but one large range has remained roofed and contains fine interior work of the seventeenth and eighteenth centuries. When the present Earl of Rosslyn succeeded in 1977, the ruins were in a dangerous state and the roofed range derelict. Between 1984 and 1988 the ruins were repaired and equipped for holiday letting by the Landmark Trust. The geography of Rosslyn is daunting, as it sits on a high rocky promontory above a wild gorge, with a high access bridge, outer walls and a courtyard, all on varying levels and with varying dates of construction. It must have been both a physical and intellectual challenge for MacGibbon and Ross to survey and to draw up the plans. They devote more than ten pages to it, with seven sketches and two detailed plans.

Rosslyn Castle, Midlothian, by MacGibbon and Ross.

Kinkell Castle near Inverness was restored from a ruin by the sculptor Gerald Laing in 1969–70. He described it as 'a long and disorganised barrack block'.[13] Laing decided that the effect of the eighteenth-century extension was to make the whole mass horizontal and throw it completely out of balance and that it must go. Despite horrified advice to the contrary from his architect, Laing personally dismantled the wing with his stonemasons over a period of three days, by levering the stones loose with crowbars and dropping them over the edge of the building. He had no regrets: 'For the first time in more than two hundred years, Kinkell was revealed in the form its master mason had intended for it.'[14] Oddly, MacGibbon and Ross did not seem greatly aware of or troubled by the

Lochnaw Castle, Wigtownshire, around the start of the twentieth century.

eighteenth-century extension: 'It remains little altered, and is a fair specimen of the manner in which the Scottish style adapts itself to the simplest sorts of edifices' (4: 130). Their sketch shows the building from the south-west, with the extension only just visible in the background. It was used as a farmhouse for tenant famers when they visited, but abandoned in 1930. The extension had been built in 1766 for Lady Mackenzie after the death of her husband, Sir Alexander Mackenzie. She had wanted to move in with her son in his new house; however, 'The new Sir Alexander resisted her attempts and the matter was finally settled by an independent arbiter who decided that Lady Mackenzie should remain at Kinkell but that it should be modernised at her son's expense. At a cost of £300 the castle was re-roofed, an addition

of three storeys was added to one side, the floors were replaced and all the rooms were plastered and papered.'[15]

Lochnaw Castle near Stranraer was an enormous mansion incorporating a sixteenth-century tower and seventeenth- and eighteenth-century ranges when MacGibbon and Ross visited. They disapproved of the more recent additions: 'The old keep is completely cast into the shade by a large modern house which has been erected beside it, the towers of which are seen in the view' (3: 210). This had been designed by Archibald Elliot in 1820. MacGibbon and Ross even 'greyed out' the new towers, which, in their view from the east, did not look too intrusive. However, as can be seen from the illustration here, the extent of the additions was vast. These were mostly demolished in the

166

Methven Castle, near Perth, by MacGibbon and Ross.

twentieth century and the most recent owners have incorporated some of the remains of the extension into a walled garden with windows and a viewing tower.

Methven Castle had also been extended: 'The building . . . has been much added to and altered; but the original entrance doorway was probably in the position and of the style shown in the sketch' (4: 278). In other words, MacGibbon and Ross's sketch is speculative; they miss out the east and west wings, which were added in 1803. The west wing was demolished in 1953 and in 1984 listed building consent was granted for the demolition of the east wing, as part of a restoration project. The building had been deteriorating since the 1950s and the interior was infested with dry rot. It was restored as a private home in the 1980s and now offers bed and breakfast.

MacGibbon and Ross disapproved of the changes that had been made to Calder House in Midlothian: 'This ancient house, famous for its association with John Knox, still retains some of its ancient walls . . . But all the characteristics of ancient Scottish architecture, which no doubt

The gatehouse of Dean Castle in Kilmarnock, built 1935–36.

belonged to the structure, have entirely disappeared' (4: 387). Their views were echoed in 2008 by Stuart Eydmann et al.: 'This was a demesne of grandeur: here John Knox may have celebrated his first Reformed Communion in Scotland in 1556; here Frédéric Chopin stayed. By stripping off its harl, flattening the roof and slicing off its dormer windows, history has conspired to diminish a great palace into a country mansion.'[16]

Dean Castle in Kilmarnock, a huge mediaeval keep with a separate fifteenth-century palace block and a late seventeenth-century house, was ruinous

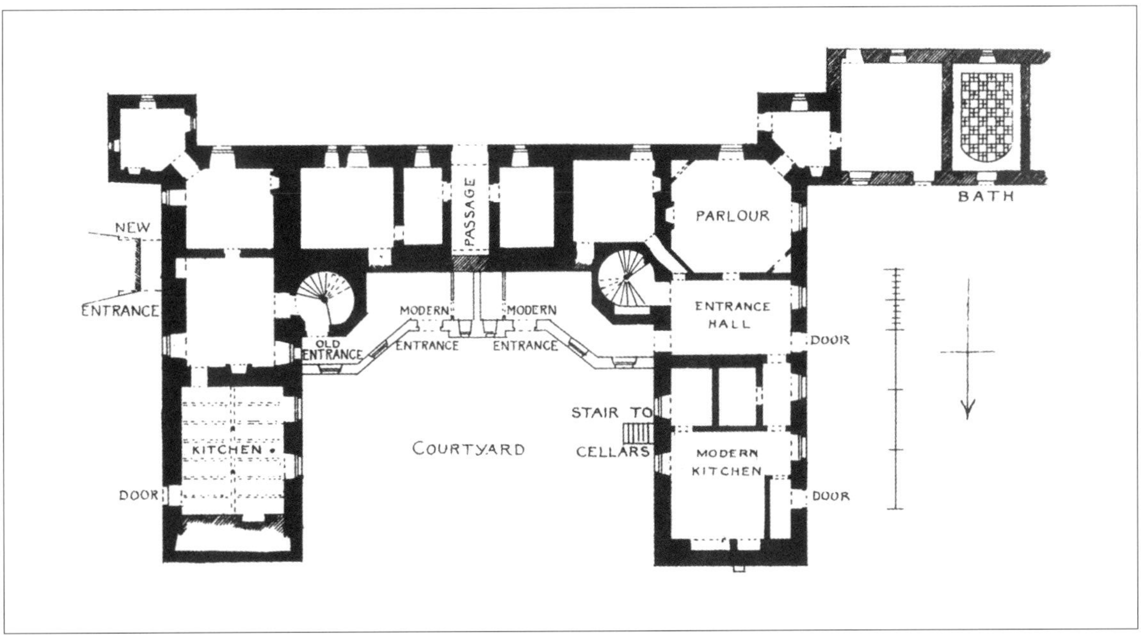

MacGibbon and Ross's plan of Brunstane House in Edinburgh.

when MacGibbon and Ross visited. The keep was restored by the 8th Lord Howard de Walden 1905–8 and the palace was completed by 1946. The gatehouse, which was no part of the original, was an addition built in 1935–36, copied from the gatehouse at Tolquhon Castle in Aberdeenshire. The entire building was donated by the 9th Lord Howard de Walden to the people of Kilmarnock in 1975. The castle now houses a museum of armour and weaponry and musical instruments.

Castles Divided Up

Some of the castles surveyed by MacGibbon and Ross were so large that they became inconvenient as family homes in the twentieth century. One solution that saved many buildings was to divide them up into apartments. Bridge Castle in Linlithgowshire is now in eight apartments and called Bridge Castle House; Pilrig House in Edinburgh rents out self-catering apartments for holiday lets; Menstrie Castle in the town of Menstrie had become largely ruinous by the 1950s. The NTS, in co-operation with Clackmannanshire County Council, played a large part in saving the building from demolition and in 1963 it was restored and divided into four apartments, with a further two rooms used as a small museum and café run by the NTS. Cullen House in Moray, 'a great mansion' (4: 294), had fallen into disrepair by 1972 and was bought in 1982 by Kit Martin and divided into 14 apartments. Keith Hall, 'a mansion, now much altered' (4: 61) in Aberdeenshire was also converted into 14 houses and apartments in 1984, also by Kit Martin as the developer. Pitheavlis Castle in Perth is now in four apartments. Kirkhill House in Linlithgowshire was divided into two apartments in 1976. Houston House in Renfrewshire, 'of considerable interest' (2: 512), was divided into six apartments in the 1990s. Brunstane House had already been divided in two when MacGibbon and Ross visited, as can be seen from the plan they drew, and it remains in two apartments.

Dalzell Castle in Motherwell became a boys' school – Gresham College – in 1952, until it was purchased by the local authority in 1967. It then lay empty until 1985, when it was converted into 18 private apartments. MacGibbon and Ross report that the large extensions to the house on the north side, 'were constructed by the late Mr R.W. Billings, architect, who stayed here for the greater part of three years superintending and working with his own hands at the carrying out of these and other extensive alterations then effected by Lord Hamilton' (3: 313–14). MacGibbon and Ross detail some of the difficulties that Billings encountered during his alterations, in particular the lack of secure foundations underpinning the castle. They disagree with him about the age of the south-west tower: 'This portion of the building was supposed by Mr Billings to date from the fourteenth century, and to be the oldest part of the castle; but there is nothing to indicate a period so remote. The walls are not of the massive kind found in structures of that date' (3: 318).

Powrie Castle, Dundee, was already in two distinct parts, dating to the sixteenth and seventeenth centuries, when MacGibbon and Ross visited. 'The old castle is a very massive building, but is in an unfortunately ruinous condition. The vaulted ground floor (now used as a piggery) is entire; so also is the first floor, with the exception of the south-west corner, which has entirely fallen' (4: 349). The newer building was, they noted, in fair order and inhabited by farm labourers. This was the north range, and it gradually became derelict. The story of its restoration is extraordinary. In 1977 the National Trust for Scotland launched a competition asking for suggestions as to how the building could be brought back to life. The winner was a journalist, Gillian Strickland,

who had recently married Peter Clarke, also a journalist, but who later became a Conservative MP. As winners, the Clarkes were given Powrie Castle for a nominal sum. They restored it as a private residence from 1978 to 1981, using plans by architect D.C. Leslie. The couple later restored Kirkhope Tower in the Borders from a ruinous state in 1996.

Castles for Holidays, Weddings and Events

In the 1960s, John Smith, a wealthy financier with a passion for historic buildings, was becoming somewhat frustrated by the limitations of the National Trust, whose General Purposes committee he chaired. He decided to set up his own conservation charity and in 1965 the Landmark Trust, of which King Charles is patron, was founded by John and Christian Smith. 'While the objects of the new Landmark Trust could have been realised in any number of ways, Smith had already formulated the very specific model that he had in mind: historic buildings would be acquired and repaired, and then let to the public for holidays. The intention from the first was that the preservation of the buildings and using them were to have parity of importance.'[17] The Landmark Trust was a trailblazer in the business of converting historic buildings into accessible holiday accommodation. Castles had been used as holiday homes and rented accommodation before this – for example, Kellie Castle in Fife: 'Previous to 1878 the house had been abandoned for many years, and had become an utter wreck, nearly floorless and roofless, and choked full of ruins and rubbish, the home of rooks and owls. It then fortunately passed under a long lease into the custody of James Lorimer, Esq., Professor of Public Law in the University of Edinburgh. By him it has been converted into a charming country residence' (2: 125). Kellie was finally bought by James Lorimer's grandson, the sculptor Hew Lorimer. It has been in the care of the National Trust for Scotland since 1970. However, the concept of actively marketing castles for short periods as holiday lets was new in the 1960s, as was the Landmark Trust idea of repairing and restoring historic buildings for this sole purpose.

Since the 1960s around 200 Scottish castles – not all surveyed by MacGibbon and Ross – have become holiday accommodation or events venues, generating income for the owners and providing a use for buildings that might otherwise have lain empty. Some have dipped in and out of the tourist accommodation market, as owners and their circumstances have changed. The castles that have become hotels are generally the larger ones which were once family homes but became too large to manage – e.g. Airth Castle, Dornoch Bishop's Palace, Dalhousie Castle and Carberry Tower. The Landmark Trust charity has restored five Scottish castles for self-catering holiday accommodation, four of which were surveyed by MacGibbon and Ross: Saddell Castle in Argyll, Park House (now known as Castle of Park) in Wigtownshire, Rosslyn Castle in Midlothian and Gargunnock House in Stirlingshire. Fairbairn Tower in Ross-shire is in the process of restoration.

The Vivat Trust was established in 1981 with objectives to 'secure for the benefit of the public at large, the preservation, restoration, improvement, enhancement and maintenance of buildings, sites, features and objects of historical, architectural and industrial interest'. Sadly, it went into liquidation in 2015, with the restoration of Earlstoun Castle as a holiday letting property only just begun. Castles make superb holiday letting properties for visitors to enter into a fantasy world as temporary lairds and chatelaines, linking into centuries of history without the heavy commitment and expense of maintenance and the long winter months spent in dark and often damp and cramped rooms. The thrill of sleeping in Mary Queen of

Scot's bedroom in Borthwick Castle hotel, say, is sufficient to persuade guests to pay premium rates.

Liberton Tower is only a few miles from Edinburgh city centre. MacGibbon and Ross mention its 'generally frail and dilapidated condition' (1: 226). It was constructed in the fifteenth century, but abandoned as a domestic habitation in the early 1600s and used as a farm store, byre and piggery until the 1990s. The Castles of Scotland Preservation Trust undertook its restoration in 1998 in order to let it out for holiday accommodation. Despite its imposing appearance, the tower can only accommodate four guests, because of the thickness of the walls and lack of interior space.

Mingarry Castle was a well-preserved ruin when MacGibbon and Ross visited: 'We have here undoubtedly one of the primitive castles of the Western Islands. The general plan of the enceinte – the small doorways – the narrow windows with their pointed arches . . . all indicate a date as old as the thirteenth century' (3: 46). It now bills itself as 'the most westerly hotel in the British mainland' after an astonishing transformation. It is also one of the most remote. In 2016 it was transformed from a ruin into a luxury hotel. The architect, Francis Shaw, had previously restored Hellifield Peel Castle in Yorkshire, a derelict manor dating to the twelfth century, in 2007–9.

Borthwick Castle, which was first restored as a hotel by Helen Bailey in 1972 and now operates as a luxury hotel, capitalises on its connection with Mary, Queen of Scots, marketing Mary's bedchamber enticingly as 'exquisitely decorated with golden opulence and a royal canopy hand carved oak bed modelled on Mary's bed displayed in Holyrood Palace'. Borthwick's walls are so thick and its window ingresses so deep that bathrooms have been created within them.

Lochhouse Tower near Moffat has been restored several times. When MacGibbon and Ross visited, it was unoccupied, but in 1879 it had been sold to William Younger of Auchen Castle. His son 'partially restored the roofless shell of Lochhouse Tower c. 1900 . . . The tower was eventually sold off as a separate house c. 1978. The new owner replaced the roof and carried out further restoration work, revealing a number of original features that had long been covered over.'[18] It was sold again in 1988 and in 2013, both times involving more restoration work. It is currently used as self-catering accommodation.

MacGibbon and Ross found Dundas Castle to be in a good state of preservation, but 'having been about the beginning of this century fitted up as a distillery, its interior arrangements are in various places concealed by the brick erections connected therewith' (1: 328). They make no mention of the 'new' castle, a Tudor Gothic mansion of 1818 designed by William Burn, but only survey what the current owners call the Auld Keep, and the fountain. In 1995 Sir Jack Stewart-Clark began restoration of both the Auld Keep and the castle. The Keep had not been inhabited for over 300 years. The parapet had to be taken down and restored and much stonework restoration took place. Electricity, banqueting and toilet facilities were installed. Dry rot had taken a serious grip in the main castle and many rooms had to be stripped to eliminate this. The castle is now a luxury events, 'exclusive use' and wedding venue.

A few other MacGibbon and Ross castles have also been restored explicitly to develop as holiday accommodation, mostly in the period since 1990: Barns Tower, Blair Castle, Castle Stewart, Comlongan, Cranshaws, Dalcross, Fenton, Forter, Leven Castle, Lochhouse Tower, Muckrach, Rowallan, Tower of Hallbar and Wedderlie. Muckrach was ruinous when MacGibbon and Ross visited; they said that 'This castle now belongs to J.Dick Peddie, Esq., R.S.A.' (2: 79), but the Dictionary of Scottish Architects states that Peddie rented the estate from the Countess of Seafield primarily for the fishing.

Whatever the case, the castle was not habitable at that time. It was restored in the 1980s.

So popular have castle holidays become that several websites specialise in offering accommodation in castles, which have become increasingly popular over the past 20 years, both as hotels and as self-catering properties. These websites also promote castles as wedding venues. A castle, ruined or otherwise, makes a romantic backdrop for wedding photographs. Around 100 Scottish castles – not all surveyed by MacGibbon and Ross – have become wedding venues including several HES and NTS properties. Comlongon Castle was restored in the 1980s and by 1994 it was hosting 200 weddings a year, although it has since been sold. The restoration probably saved the old tower, which had concerned MacGibbon and Ross: 'cracks and fissures are beginning to develop themselves in various parts of the building, which unarrested will soon bring about its ruin' (1: 239). Old Place of Mochrum, Balgonie Castle, Buittle Castle, Mingarry Castle and Wedderlie House all host weddings.

Castles Consolidated

Despite all of the transformations and losses that have taken place since *The Castellated and Domestic Architecture of Scotland* was published, the majority of castles would be instantly recognisable to MacGibbon and Ross. Ruinous castles such as Galdenoch in Wigtownshire have changed relatively little, having been kept in good order by their owners. Castle Stewart (aka Stuart) in Inverness-shire 'is one of the few ancient castles in Scotland which, although not occupied, are kept in good order and repair by the proprietors' (2: 481). It is now a hotel. Many of the inhabited castles have not changed greatly and would also be recognisable to MacGibbon and Ross, if a little smarter or somewhat more dilapidated – e.g. Wedderlie and Inch

Fatlips Castle in Roxburghshire (Scottish Borders), also known as Minto Tower.

House. Some castles are unoccupied but roofed and well cared for. These include Dryhope Tower in Selkirkshire, Fourmerkland, Repentance and Amisfield towers in Dumfriesshire, Castle Kennedy in Wigtownshire and Fernielee Castle in Selkirkshire. Torwoodlee Tower in Selkirkshire was stabilised and consolidated recently as a project spearheaded by the Pringle family, who have owned it since the fifteenth century. It remains ruinous. Whytbank Tower in Selkirkshire was restored and consolidated in 1987–92, but remains uninhabited. When MacGibbon and Ross visited they found that 'It is now reduced to one wall with a corbelled gablet, although as Mr Craig Brown

mentions, "so late as 1828 its walls stood unbroken, though roofless"' (4: 209). An archaeological survey in 1994 uncovered the courtyard and associated buildings, a terraced garden and several outlying structures, perhaps associated with the occupation of the tower during the eighteenth and nineteenth centuries.

At Fatlips Castle in Roxburghshire MacGibbon and Ross found that 'the upper part above the corbelling has recently been restored, but all beneath is old' (3: 420). The restoration to which they refer was carried out in 1857 by the Elliots of Minto. It was remodelled as a family museum and shooting lodge by Robert Lorimer in 1897. It fell

ABOVE. (New) Buittle Castle in Kirkcudbrightshire (Dumfries and Galloway), by Francis Grose, 1790.

OPPOSITE. Monimail Tower, Fife: the one remaining tower of a Renaissance palace has now been restored for community use.

into disrepair in the twentieth century and was in ruins by 1927.[19] Fatlips was restored again in 2013 and now lies empty but well maintained on a remote hilltop. It can be visited on request.

Castles Rescued from Farmyards

In a largely rural country, with a significant farming industry, it is not surprising that many of Scotland's ruined castles have been subsumed into farmyards, to be used as storage for silage or shelter for farm animals, or to house farm labourers. Agricultural workers were among the poorest paid members of society, with a lowly status, so it may seem strange that they should be housed in castles. In most cases these were semi-derelict tower houses within the farmyard, of little interest to the farmers, who had to employ large numbers of

labourers before the days of tractors, and, if in a remote area, find accommodation for them. Some farmyard castles, as has been seen in Chapter 6, did not come out of their agricultural situation well, or even survive at all, but a majority have been restored and continue to be inhabited. In 1881 the owners of (New) Buittle Castle decided to let the property, which had been restored earlier in the century, to a tenant farmer – but not before demolishing the angle turrets, seen in Grose's sketch above, as they considered these too grand for a farmhouse. The building became derelict some time in the twentieth century and was restored in the 1990s, then sold in 2018. The current owners are reconfiguring the property as an events venue and holiday accommodation.

At Monimail in Fife, only one tower remained

Fountainhall, Midlothian, by MacGibbon and Ross.

of what had been a much larger Renaissance palace, residence of the Archbishops of St Andrews. 'It is much to be regretted that . . . this tower has now been reduced to the unworthy position of a "bothy" occupied by gardeners of Melville Castle' (3: 449). Monimail's remaining tower was restored in the early 1990s for use by a community whose focus is on a sustainable way of life, growing fresh produce in the 16-acre plot and running courses on environmental issues.

Fountainhall (also known as Penkaet Castle) in Midlothian is now comfortably inhabited and well maintained. It was not so when MacGibbon and Ross visited: 'It will not surprise those who are conversant with the neglect which has fallen on too many of our old buildings, to know that this historic apartment [the ballroom, formerly a hall of justice] is now used as a hay-loft, and the rooms below as a stable' (2: 554).

Park House in Wigtownshire, which had been inhabited by workmen, and Liberton Tower in Edinburgh were both rescued from rural dereliction and are now rented out as holiday accommodation, the former by the Landmark Trust and the latter by the Castles of Scotland Preservation Trust. Barr Castle in Galston Ayrshire was a wool store, but is now a small museum and is in good condition (Barr Castle in Renfrewshire, which was not in a good state when MacGibbon and Ross visited, remains in ruins, but is designated as a scheduled monument and is now in reasonably good condition). Other castles formerly used for agricultural purposes which have been restored for private dwellings include Barholm Castle, Rusco Tower (which cows had been using as a 'house of ease'[20]) and Hills Tower in Kirkcudbrightshire, Aiket Castle and Newmilns Tower in Ayrshire, Haystoun House in Peeblesshire, Kinkell House in Ross and

Rural dereliction: Powrie Castle near Dundee in 1953.

Cromarty, Oakwood Tower (now named Aikwood) in Selkirkshire, Farnell Castle, Murroes House and Powrie Castle in Angus, Pitheavllis Castle in Perth, Craig Caffie Tower in Wigtownshire, Farnell Castle in Forfarshire and Kirkhill House and Ochiltree Castle in Linlithgowshire. Most of these towers have been bought by restoring owners who have been able to put resources into their buildings to make them fit for modern habitation and who are conscious of the need to preserve their heritage. However, Kipps House was not so fortunate: it was inhabited by labourers when MacGibbon and Ross first saw it but is now a ruin encroached upon by farm buildings. Balcomie in Fife is still in use as a farm building. Cockburn House in Midlothian is surrounded by farm buildings, but it has been renovated in recent years.

Former farmyard castles taken into care and now managed in a consolidated state by HES are Carsluith in Wigtownshire, Drumcoltran in Kirkcudbrightshire, Claypotts in Dundee and Balvaird in Perthshire. It is difficult to imagine Claypotts in its former rural situation, hemmed in as it now is by bungalows and a busy road skirting a commercial estate a few hundred yards away. Preston Tower, in the care of East Lothian Council, is similarly situated in a housing development.

Gardens Been and Gone

> Indications of the former beauty of the gardens and grounds are still observable in the snowdrops and other flowers which abound in the meadows, and the fine old trees which bordered the ancient avenues. (3: 546, entry on Greenknowe Castle in Berwickshire)

Gardens are ephemeral things, dependent largely on the energy, vision and resources of individuals and changing with fashion.[21] MacGibbon and Ross were interested primarily in the buildings they surveyed, but in a few entries they mention the gardens and policies surrounding the castles. In their entry on Fairlie Castle they say, for example, 'All traces of the orchards and gardens referred to by Pont have entirely disappeared, and the place has a neglected appearance by no means pleasing'

(3: 179). They report that Abercrumie admired the fine gardens and orchards which surrounded the mansion of Ardmillan and they noted with pleasure, 'These are still well maintained by the present proprietor' (4: 254). The gardens have now completely disappeared, along with the castle. At Balvaird Castle they noted that 'An enclosure to the south has evidently been a pleasure garden, and there is a large walled garden or orchard adjoining the castle on the east' (1: 342). Pitteadie Castle they described as a 'melancholy ruin'. 'It must have been a delightful residence, being surrounded by fine trees, and having an extensive garden sloping towards the sun' (3: 450). At Tolquhon Castle MacGibbon and Ross could still see traces of the pleasure gardens. 'In the southwest wall of the fore court, and on the side next the garden, there are recesses for flowers, somewhat similar to the well-known ones in the garden walls at Edzell Castle' (2: 301).

MacGibbon and Ross were impressed by Edzell Castle gardens, which are unique not only in Scotland but in Europe: 'To the south of the quadrangle is situated the pleasure garden. Such gardens were not unusual in connection with the Scottish castles of the time of Queen Mary and James VI, but there is no other so well preserved, or where the architecture has been so fine' (1: 363). This is the finest Renaissance garden to have survived in Scotland, although the planting dates to the 1930s. The garden was lucky to survive the Earl of Panmure's forfeiture of the estate, owing to his involvement in the Jacobite uprising of 1715. The final ruin came in 1764 after the company that had possessed it was declared bankrupt. The beech avenue, leading to the castle, was felled and the castle was gutted and sold on behalf of the creditors. When MacGibbon and Ross visited they noted that 'The castle now belongs to the Earl of Dalhousie and the ruins are well taken care of' (1: 366). In 1932 the garden was taken into state care

Entrance to the walled garden of Castle Kennedy, Wigtownshire.

first, due to its extraordinary significance, followed in 1935 by the rest of the castle. In 1936 the castle garden was laid out with the current planting scheme.

At Aberdour Castle, MacGibbon and Ross described 'the old-fashioned garden, surrounded with high walls, in which are several quaint doorways' (2: 474). The seventeenth century saw the ancestral building updated into a modern mansion with the showpiece additions of a long gallery and walled garden, one of the first walled gardens in Scotland. Castle Kennedy, which lies on an isthmus separating two lochs, had been ruined since a fire in 1715, and was an 'ivy-clad pile' when MacGibbon and Ross visited. They noted, however, that 'Everything that landscape art can do to beautify and adorn the surroundings of the castle has been done, and with no stinted hand' (4: 368). Castle Kennedy remains a ruin in an exceptionally beautiful landscape, although clad with more wisteria than ivy now. Field Marshall John Dalrymple laid out the formal gardens surrounding the castle after being impressed by the arrangements at the Palace of Versailles during his service as ambassador in France in the 1730s. The work was conducted by men of the Royal Scots Greys and the Inniskilling Fusiliers, who had been deployed to the area to suppress the Covenanters. It is possible that John Dalrymple himself had Covenanter sympathies and that his employment of his troops in the landscaping of his garden was a deliberate diversion of their focus away from the mission. After his death in 1747, both the ruined castle and the formal gardens were neglected. The gardens were restored, replanted and extended in the mid nineteenth century, initially by the 8th Earl when he stumbled upon a decaying copy of the original plan by William Adam in a gardener's cottage on the estate. They were further added to in 1840 by the 10th Earl, who also built Lochinch Castle and its gardens at the other end of the isthmus between the two lochs.

Queen Victoria visited Drummond Castle in 1842 and 'walked in the garden which is really very fine, with terraces, like an old French garden'. MacGibbon and Ross also mentioned the gardens: 'The beautiful terraced gardens on the south side of the castle are of world-wide fame' (1: 289). They are still very well maintained and open to the public (see Plate 28).

In 1960 Balbythan (Balbithan) House in Kintore was bought by the botanical artist Mary McMurtrie, who restored the house and transformed its gardens into a leading north-east nursery, specialising in rock plants, alpines and traditional garden flowers. She ran the nursery until she was in her 80s. It is now a private house with a private garden. At Cawdor Castle the walled garden was developed into one of the finest Victorian gardens of its kind, open to the public. But due to increasing number of visitors to the castle, and with many of them

reportedly helping themselves to the garden's treasures, it was eventually closed. Lying to the south of the castle is the Flower Garden, laid out c. 1710 by Sir Archibald Campbell, the Thane's brother. By 1725, Sir Archibald had completed his work including levelling a considerable piece of ground, in turn producing a beautiful garden where all sorts of fruit could grow. Hundreds of years later a few of the original fruit trees and the clipped yew hedges still survive. The Lady Cawdor of the day designed the oval lavender borders enclosing rose beds in 1850. Her plan shows long rows of gooseberries, which the family enjoyed regularly. To ensure colour and bloom remained in the garden, long herbaceous borders were developed, which are still in place.

HES oversees Scotland's *Inventory of Gardens and Designed Landscapes*, begun in 1987, a listing of 380 gardens of special significance and national importance. Seventy of the gardens and landscapes of MacGibbon and Ross's castles feature on the inventory. They have all been assessed against seven criteria, comprising artistic, historical, horticultural, architectural, archaeological, scenic and nature conservation interest. Only about a third of the 70 listed are grand gardens of the type that are open and attract visitors specially to see spectacular planting schemes. Those in the care of the NTS – Brodick, Castle Fraser, Craigievar, Crathes, Culross Palace, Drum Castle, Falkland Palace, House of the Binns and Kellie Castle – all have beautifully maintained gardens, as part of their package of attractions for visitors. The Arts and Crafts garden at Kellie Castle, now in the care of the NTS, was designed by Robert Lorimer in 1880, for his parents. He also planted the topiary yews at Earlshall.

Owners of restored castles tend to create gardens, to set off the newly inhabited building. The owners of Abbot's Tower, Aiket, Barholm, Blackhall, Buittle Castle, Craigcaffie (Craig Caffie),

Liberton House, Ochiltree, Spedlins and Towie Barclay have all have created domestic gardens where none had existed for centuries, although none is listed in the *Inventory of Gardens and Designed Landscapes*. Some owners try to recreate sixteenth-century gardens, restricting themselves to using only plants available to the early Scottish gardeners – a tough challenge, with the seductive lure of thousands of modern hybrids and New World plants perfectly suited to the Scottish climate and readily available. At Buittle Castle, the owners have successfully emulated the sixteenth-century approach in a new sunken garden, which has been developed behind the castle (see Plate 26).

The gardens charity Scotland's Gardens (the 'Yellow Book') started in 1931. King George V, who opened his garden at Balmoral Castle in the first year of the scheme, cried enthusiastically 'I hope you'll persuade everybody in Scotland to open their gardens!' In 2019, 11 of the castles surveyed by MacGibbon and Ross participated in the open gardens scheme, including Westhall, which is on the Buidings at Risk Register and too dilapidated to allow internal visits, but has maintained gardens. The other open gardens in the scheme are Megginch, Earlshall, Gardyne, Kilbryde, Duntreath, Castle Kennedy, Drummond, Kilcoy, Dunvegan and Barholm. Most open on one or two designated days every year for the charity.

Castles as New Homes from Ruins

Why do people purchase ruined towers with a view to restoring and living in them? In an extended essay that bridges literary theory, history and psychology, Theodore Ziolkowski described the towers owned by four great creative minds of the early twentieth century (Yeats, Jeffers, Jung and Rilke) and presented a seductive series of arguments portraying the significance of the tower as an anti-modernist symbol.[22] The poet W.B. Yeats purchased and restored an Irish sixteenth-century tower, Thoor Ballylee, in 1916–22, as a summer home.

When we consider the difficulties associated with the move into Thoor Ballylee – the expensive roof repairs, the need to have much of the furniture carpentered in situ because of the narrow stairway, the primitive sanitation, the constant flooding and dampness that finally drove the family out again – we are justified in assuming that it must have been a powerful compulsion that prompted Yeats to acquire the property. Indeed, the purchase was regarded as such a folly by his friends that Ezra Pound wickedly remarked that Yeats had undertaken his lecture tour to America in 1920 'to make enough to buy a few shingles for his phallic symbol on the Bogs. Ballyphallus or whatever he calls it with the river on the first floor.'[23]

A sixteenth-century tower house can be an uncomfortable place to live, even if efficient modern services have been installed. Owners must put up with steep and uneven stairs, almost inevitable damp, small windows with poor light and rooms that are often either too small or too large for convenience. Towers may look imposing, but the thickness of the walls means that the internal spaces are small, like a Tardis in reverse. The ground floor chamber in Barholm Castle, now a kitchen, is only one-third of the area of the footprint of the walls. Hardship during the restoration work is something of a badge of honour for those DIY restorers who camped out in miserable conditions, carrying out gargantuan projects. 'We moved in during the second coldest winter this century', recalls Stuart Morris of Balgonie Castle. 'We had a three-bar fire, but if we put the third bar on, it blew the circuit.

So the family was huddled round the two bars, and if you got cold, you grabbed a dog.'[24] Gerard Laing reported at Kinkell: 'Though there was little snow on the ground that year, it was bitterly cold. We made a brazier from an old oil drum and set it in the fireplace of the Great Hall . . . During our tea breaks we would huddle round it seated on blocks of wood or stone.'[25] Laing compared his problems favourably with those of Macneil of Barra, who was restoring Kisimul: 'A friend of mine visited Macneil and, as they were sitting around the fire talking, he noticed that, not only was the ceiling dripping with moisture, but small clouds were forming high up in the room.'[26]

In 1878 the Lorimer family took possession of Kellie Castle, rented on a 38-year restoring lease from the Earl of Mar, to use as their summer holiday home. 'All the windows were broken, the roof leaked like a sieve, and the fireplaces were stacked with fallen nests of decades of jackdaws and rooks . . . Living conditions were to be spartan and basic. An earth closet in the garden for the men, no baths with running water or electric light, just candles and paraffin lamps.'[27]

Can a tower house or castle make a comfortable modern home? MacGibbon and Ross pointed out that

in the larger mansions of the seventeenth century the amelioration of manners is very distinctly shown by the enlarged and improved nature of their accommodation. Besides the hall, drawing rooms, galleries, reception rooms, and private parlours, now became common. Bedrooms with dressing rooms and private suites of apartments were also not unusual. As the other public rooms increased in number, the size and importance of the hall gradually diminished, till at length it dwindled down to the dimensions of the modern dining room. (2: 574)

Those restorers who found a ruined tower with seventeenth- or eighteenth-century extensions, such as Ballencrieff, could make a commodious home. The original fifteenth- and sixteenth-century towers are much meaner in their accommodation – but the corresponding cost of building work and consequent upkeep is smaller.

Of the buildings that MacGibbon and Ross surveyed as ruins, 47 are now, in the twenty-first century, comfortable houses with modern services. After the reprinting of *The Castellated and Domestic Architecture of Scotland* by Mercat Press in 1977 the books were regularly used as a resource by would-be castle restorers looking for a suitable building to buy and rebuild. The list of those formerly ruinous towers bought, restored and adapted for modern living by individuals includes: Aiket, Aikwood, Balfluig, Ballencrieff, Ballone, Barholm, Barcaldine, Blackhall, Breachacha, Dairsie, Dunderave, Forter, Hills, Law Castle, Leslie Castle, Lochhouse Tower, Mains, Melgund, Methven, Newmilns, Spedlins, Powrie, Balgonie, Balmuto, Pitcullo, Pitreavie, Hatton, Inverquharity, Falside, Stoneypath, Terpersie, Kelty House, Rusco, Tillycairn and Tilquhilly. Others were restored by existing owners, e.g. Stobhall and Fenton, or by organisations such as the Landmark Trust.

Did MacGibbon and Ross romanticise castle living? To a degree, yes. But there is a surprisingly negative entry on Tillycairn Castle: 'from the disproportionate thickness of wall to a building of so small a size, the lowness of the vaults, and very sparing admission of light and air, it is but a dark, prison-like and uncomfortable mansion' (3: 602). However, the text was written for them by Mr Skane of Rubislaw and might not reflect their own views. Tillycairn was restored in 1980–84 and its interior is pleasantly bright, despite Mr Skane's foreboding (see Plate 27). Of Midmar, one of Aberdeenshire's grander castles, they said: 'Although quite antique in style and arrangements, it is now occupied as a comfortable mansion, and gives an excellent idea of what such houses were like in the days of James VI' (2: 375). Midmar is not a typical tower house at six storeys high, however, and they also admit that it 'has been a good deal added to'. Neither MacGibbon nor Ross appeared to have had any desire to live with their families in a castellated historic building, although the house that MacGibbon designed and built for his family home, Ashfield Grange (page 22), did have a whiff of Scots Baronial about it.

When MacGibbon and Ross surveyed Aldie, they found that 'The castle is practically entire and has evidently been inhabited up till a comparatively recent period' (2: 484–85). They refer to the additions made not long after the tower was erected, 'with the effect of increasing its accommodation threefold, and rendering it a house which would make a good residence even now' (2: 487). They even suggest extending it further to make a kind of conservatory: 'The very small open courtyard in the centre of the extended building is quite an unusual feature. If this were covered over with a glass roof, the plan of the building would present very much the character of many modern houses' (2: 488–89). In fact, Aldie remained empty for many more decades, becoming increasingly derelict, until it was bought in 1947 by Archibald Hope Dickson, when he returned to Scotland after working in the Far East. He employed the Edinburgh conservation architect Ian Lindsay to draw up plans for the restoration as a gentleman's residence and furnished the house with works of art. But he did not cover the roof of the courtyard with glass.

'Niddrie Castle is familiar to the thousands who travel by train between Edinburgh and Glasgow, from the glimpse obtained as the train emerges for a moment from the long rocky defile some three miles east of Linlithgow. The castle . . . is quite empty, ruinous and roofless' (1: 324). Niddrie Castle can still be glimpsed from the railway line,

no longer ruinous or roofless, but occupied by a family who have spent 20 years restoring the ruin into a family home as a massive DIY project. Niddrie has been a place of magnificence, seat of the princely Setons of East Lothian, where Mary Queen of Scots stayed after escaping from Loch Leven.

Authenticity?

Almost all castle restorers are preoccupied with a quest for authenticity, a return to an idealised original, a recapturing of what might have been. They furnish rooms with artefacts that 'fit' and often use reclaimed materials in the interior. It is impossible, of course, to pour the past back into a building or to recreate the precise interior of a sixteenth-century tower house, especially when modern services are involved. Those restorations that have taken a very light touch, such as Tilquhillie Castle and Hills Tower, are closest to looking as though a sixteenth-century intruder would not seem out of place.

However, not all castle owners were concerned with authenticity. Marigold MacRae, whose husband's grandfather restored Eilean Donan just after the First World War, told *The Scots Magazine*: 'Of course, there were one or two people, back in the 1920s, who grumbled to the newspapers complaining that the MacRaes were spoiling this picturesque old ruin with all their restoration. But all that's forgotten now and I think most people love what's been done.'[28] She is correct in a sense, in that the majority of visitors to Eilean Donan, the most popular iconic Scottish castle in terms of published imagery on biscuit tins, jigsaws, calendars, etc., are probably unconcerned about the rebuilding history and simply admire it uncritically. The restoration of Eilean Donan was very far from authentic, but it did require enormous logistical efforts, which might in themselves have been

authentic. Some of the largest stones for the rebuilding, weighing about 1.5 tons, were taken from the hills by Lochlongside; these were carried to the castle as they might have been 500 years ago. Horses dragged them to the shore, and when the tide was out they were secured by chains to the bottom of a boat. The incoming tide raised the boat, which was rowed over to the castle.

Unexpected Transformations

In the course of the twentieth century several castles took on unusual functions. Ferniehirst Castle became a youth hostel; Pitfirrane found use as a golf clubhouse; Dudhope became council offices; Hawthornden is now a writer's retreat; Castle Huntly is a prison; Dargavel House became a military training centre; and Old Bishopton Castle a secure unit for vulnerable young people. Buittle Castle has established an Orthodox shrine to Our Lady of Walsingham, as well as an events venue and bed and breakfast accommodation. Breachacha Castle on the Island of Coll became the centre for the Project Trust, a charity that provides young people with international volunteering experiences. Before going overseas, the volunteers stay on Coll for training, and in the early days of the project they stayed with Nicholas Maclean-Bristol and his wife Lavinia in Breachacha Castle, which the couple had restored from a ruin in the 1960s. Pitteadie Castle in Fife, which MacGibbon and Ross described as a 'melancholy ruin' (3: 450), was marketed for sale as a romantic ruin in the grounds of Pitteadie House; although it has certainly deteriorated since their visit, it is probably better cared

for these days, and may one day be restored.

Lochore Castle in Fife is one of the many castles whose state was lamented by MacGibbon and Ross. They describe it as a 'somewhat remarkable structure' and were particularly concerned about its recent deterioration: 'Complete ruin and desolation have overtaken Loch Ore Castle in the course of the nineteenth century. In the views by Cardonnel and Grose it is shown in much more perfect condition' (3: 243). They continue, 'The walls of enceinte are represented as entire [i.e. by Cardonnel and Grose] and they remained so within the memory of persons now living, till the removal of the earth outside brought the greater part of them down. The total ruin of the whole wall and keep itself seems imminent unless means are promptly taken to avert it' (3: 244).

Lochore is one of Scotland's oldest castles and of special interest historically. The twentieth century did the castle no favours – it was neglected and continued to deteriorate, just as MacGibbon and Ross feared. The Mary coal mine in Lochore Meadows was in action from 1904 to 1966 and its proximity must have detracted from the site. In 2014, however, the Heritage Lottery funded an archaeological and geophysical survey commissioned by the Living Lomonds Landscape partnership. As part of the project, digital artist Bob Marshall created a virtual 3D reconstruction of Lochore Castle, bringing vividly to life what it would have looked like in 1547 (page 186). MacGibbon and Ross would have appreciated that attention has finally been paid to what has become the fragile ruin of a once magnificent ancient fortress, and that resources have been found to investigate its history and stop further deterioration.

The wholesale removal of Loch Doon Castle to save it from flooding when a new reservoir was created was a tremendous feat of engineering. The castle originally stood on an island in Loch Doon. The entire castle was taken down, stone by stone,

OPPOSITE. Virtual cutaway model reconstruction of
Lochore Castle in Fife, by Bob Marshall.

ABOVE. Castle Huntly near Dundee,
by MacGibbon and Ross.

and re-erected on its present spot in 1935, in an
effort to save the castle's curtain wall as water levels
rose due to the local hydroelectric scheme.
However, the reconstruction does not include the
sixteenth-century keep, which had been added to
the inside of the west wall. It had consisted of a
simple wall of enceinte, of 11 unequal sides of
excellent coursed ashlar with the entrance in the
north, built in the thirteenth century. This had
been badly damaged and restored with inferior
rubble-work possibly in the first half of the
sixteenth century when the keep was added. The

Kinneil Castle near Bo'ness in 1936.

re-erected remains do not include this later work.

Castle Huntly has seen many changes through the centuries and it is clear from MacGibbon and Ross's account that they did not approve: 'In 1615 the estate was acquired by Patrick Lyon, first Earl of Kinghorn and in the latter half of the century the castle was much added to and "improved" by his grandson, the third Earl of Kinghorn and first Earl of Strathmore, who also "improved" the Castle of Glamis . . . In the end of last century the estate was sold to George Paterson, Esq., who added a modern mansion to the east side of the old keep, and renovated the exterior with the modern sham turrets and battlements which it now exhibits' (1: 322). Castle Huntly is now part of Her Majesty's Prison estate. It was refurbished

Kinneil Castle in the twenty-first century.

in 1947 as a borstal, or young offenders' institution, and is now the only open prison in Scotland and the only prison housed in a castle.

A Castle Saved by its Ceiling

MacGibbon and Ross reported of Kinneil Castle, 'It is said that the building was once richly deco-rated internally, but the upper floors of the keep seem never to have been finished – the standard partitions remaining unplastered till the present day' (3: 231). By 1936 the house had been abandoned and Bo'ness Town Council was in the process of demolishing it when Stanley Cursiter, director of the National Galleries of Scotland, heard that wall paintings had been discovered. The

Ministry of Works secured the wing with the paintings, and recovered the oak ribbed ceiling of the Parable Room. The paintings were restored, and the whole building has been consolidated and is now in the care of Historic Environment Scotland. It is open occasionally for visitors.

Conclusion

The transformational history of many of MacGibbon and Ross's castles might appear to be one of continuous, often intense drama: of walls going up and coming down, whole buildings being blown up, of owners selling up and new owners embarking on massive restoration projects, of rescue, repair and transformation coupled with opportunistic economic enterprises and creative ways to re-purpose awkward buildings. The recent history of many castles is as turbulent as the mediaeval period is often imagined to be. Many of the changes were made by individuals for personal benefit, although it could be argued that even the most private restoration project benefits us all simply by enabling a historic building to be better cared for. But in many cases the transformations that took place in Scotland's castles were about making them more accessible and involving communities. The next chapter looks at the democratic shift that has taken place in Scotland's castles over the past 50 years or so.

8

Castles for All

———

*Significant historic buildings not only should be saved, nor only saved
and used, but saved, used and made available to everyone and anyone.*
Founding principle of the Landmark Trust

When MacGibbon and Ross travelled across Scotland visiting castles for their great survey, they usually did so by invitation or at least with permission from the owners. The fact that they mention the owner's name in the majority of their entries suggests that, before setting out, they made contact whenever they could. How many letters must they have written, soliciting such invitations? And how tiresome were the logistics of arranging visits, especially to castles where the owners were in residence and a timed appointment would have to be made to tie in with railway timetables?

Seventy-six of the castles and mansions which MacGibbon and Ross surveyed were open to the public in 2020,[1] the majority in the care of either Historic Environment Scotland or the National Trust for Scotland. A few are cared for by charitable trusts or local authorities, or are in private ownership. Many of these were hopeless cases at the time of MacGibbon and Ross, like MacLellan's Castle in Kirkcudbright, a 'green haystack' smothered in ivy. Some were private residences or ruins on private

land, owned by aristocrats increasingly desperate about the upkeep of buildings no longer suitable for modern living. The Ancient Monuments Act of 1913 was a godsend to owners, as was the formation of the National Trust for Scotland in 1931, both offering opportunities to offload burdensome properties to the state or to a worthy charity. Indeed, between the wars both were at times in competition with each other to secure properties.

A few castles were already open to the public, including Edinburgh and Stirling. Before the twentieth century it was common for the grandest houses to offer guided tours by housekeepers or caretakers. The Victorians were keen tourists and took full advantage of opportunities to visit country houses and castles such as Cawdor, with its literary connection to Shakespeare's Macbeth. Other castles stood in fields, 'open' insofar as their owners did not fence them off. Many ruins are still in this position today. About half of HES castle properties are unstaffed and free to visit; examples include Orchardton Tower, Drumcoltran Tower and Carsluith Castle.

191

Between 1906 and 2000, 60 castles were taken into care, the majority in the 1930s and 1950s. By 1934, 33 were already in care, listed in a specially compiled article for the readers of the *SMT Magazine* ('A Monthly Magazine for All Who Travel by Road or Rail'). 'In presenting this volume to our readers we venture to express the hope that it will inspire in them a desire to visit and become intimate with the many ancient buildings in which Scotland is so rich.'[2] The democratising of access to Scottish castles was beginning, but initially access was to the ruinous properties only.

The History of the Acts

In 1873 Sir John Lubbock had started to try to introduce his national Monuments Preservation Bill in the House of Commons. He managed to get it to a second reading in 1875, but it was defeated by the arguments of those such as Lord Francis Hervey, who asked, 'Are the absurd relics of our barbarian predecessors, who found time hanging heavily on their hands, and set about piling up great barrows and rings of stones, to be preserved at the cost of infringement of property rights?'[3] The idea of putting public interest above private rights was seen as almost seditious. Finally, in 1882, Lubbock managed to push through the Ancient Monuments Protection Act – a relatively toothless piece of legislation, but nonetheless a signal that the national appetite for the conservation of historic buildings was growing in the UK. The 1882 Act focused on prehistoric and early historic monuments, protecting more than 20 monuments across Scotland in the 'schedule'. This Act created Commissioners of Works who had the power to acquire monuments either by gift, purchase or guardianship. It provided for the protection and preservation of monuments without disturbing land ownership rights. The Ancient Monuments Protection Act of 1900 formally extended the scope

of the legislation to include mediaeval monuments. This was followed in 1913 by a new Ancient Monuments Act, which extended and formalised many of the powers of the previous Acts. It had an ambitious overall aim, claiming 'the point to be kept constantly in view being that the evidence of the history of the country is the end to be secured'. To this end the acquisition of monuments was reinforced and a schedule of monuments of 'historic, architectural, traditional, artistic or archaeological importance' covered by protection orders was to be maintained and regularly reviewed, with direct power of intervention.

Public access was explicitly included in the 1913 Act for the first time so that the monuments could 'serve as object-lessons to the public'. This emphasis on the great mediaeval monuments saw a flurry of donations between 1910 and the outbreak of the First World War, of around 30 monuments including Jedburgh and Crossraguel abbeys, and the castles of Noltland, Threave and Urquhart. Although the First World War interrupted the momentum, it picked up quickly thereafter, as the cost of maintaining major masonry monuments fell on ever-stretched estates. The inter-war years saw 115 monuments – a third of the current estate – come into care. This period coincided with a period of intense interest and study of both architectural and archaeological monuments in Scotland and a further reinforcing Ancient Monuments Act in 1931. The serendipity of owners seeking to relieve themselves of the burden of repairs was complemented by Ancient Monuments staff who actively encouraged donation of monuments that they felt defined the character of built heritage in Scotland. This has, inevitably, led to an eclectic public collection, which displays both the bias of the time and the research interests of the individuals involved.

The Office of Works was first established in 1378. It evolved over the centuries into the Ministry of Works (1943–62), the Ministry of Public Building and Works (1962–70) and various other core government forms until Historic Scotland was established as an Agency in 1991, with a focus on conservation, regulation and designation, and developing the commercial potential of the estate. Most recently, Historic Environment Scotland was set up to become a new lead body for the historic environment. The responsibilities of HES were formerly split between Historic Scotland and the Royal Commission on the Ancient and Historical Monuments of Scotland (RCAHMS), which collected and managed records about Scotland's historic environment. Both were dissolved and their functions transferred to HES on 1 October 2015.

Historic Environment Scotland

The Historic Environment Scotland Act of 2014 delegated the function of managing the properties in care of Scottish Ministers to HES. The organisation was also tasked with a number of functions, including investigating, caring for and promoting the historic environment. The castle properties in the care of HES are mostly ruins, albeit carefully consolidated and made safe and accessible for visitors. Those buildings which were entrusted – or thrust – into the care of the state, mostly a century or so ago, have been carefully recorded, via their statements of significance,[4] and maintained and managed in a way that their owners might never have had the capacity to do. Tower houses and castles are disproportionately represented in the national collection, in comparison to, say, industrial buildings or churches or twentieth-century architecture. However, this is to the benefit of the castles surveyed by MacGibbon and Ross. Some buildings have undoubtedly been saved from dereliction and even demolition and most are open for public visits, with information and interpretation on site and on the HES websites. Thomas Ross, who was involved in the public recording of assets in the early twentieth century, would be delighted to see such extensive guardianship. Newark Castle in Renfrewshire is one building that would have cheered him.

> Newark is one of the finest specimens of the seventeenth-century architecture of Scotland, and being on the outskirts of a very considerable town it would surely be possible to find some use to which it could be applied other than an inconvenient residence for a few poor families on the one side, and a receptacle for dirt on the other. From its plan it is well adapted for many modern purposes required by such a community as Port Glasgow, and from its beauty it ought to be an object of just pride. (2: 431)

It is now in the care of HES and open to the public.

Thirty-eight of the castles that MacGibbon and Ross surveyed are now in the care of the state and looked after by HES. Claypotts and Kinneil are normally closed, but arrangements can be made to visit for researchers. Some of the buildings, such as St Andrews Castle and Urquhart Castle, would be entirely recognisable to MacGibbon and Ross, having changed very little over the past century. Those that have changed for the better include Aberdour, Blackness and Balvaird. Edinburgh Castle has undergone many changes, some for the better, others less positive. MacGibbon and Ross devote 19 pages to Edinburgh Castle, including 17 plans and sketches. In their introductory history of the castle MacGibbon and Ross reproduce copies of drawings by Sandby, Chambers, Wilson, Drury and Gordon to illustrate what it might have looked like before the nineteenth century. Chambers' 'restoration' drawing of the east part before the Lang Siege of 1573, including the towers, is 'to a large part imaginary, and it must not be supposed that they give a reliable representation of the demolished towers' (1: 449). The illustration of the Siege provided by MacGibbon and Ross, they report, was traced from a facsimile, published by the Bannatyne Club, of a plan of the siege of 1573, which accompanied a report prepared at the time by command of Sir William Drury. 'The ancient Castle was almost completely destroyed during this siege, and it is from the date of the rebuilding of the Castle by the Regent Morton after the siege that the existing modern Castle, whose appearance is so familiar, begins' (1: 451).

The modern castle is the jewel in the crown of the HES estate. It is part of the UNESCO World Heritage site of Edinburgh, 'dominated by a medieval fortress'. The first admission fee of a sixpence was introduced in 1915 during the First World War, but the Honours of Scotland had been on public display in the castle since 1818 when Walter Scott had rediscovered them in the Crown Room. MacGibbon and Ross were optimistic about the future for Edinburgh Castle, although damning about past actions:

> . . . the little Chapel of St Margaret has stood uninjured through all the various shocks and changes which have so altered all the other features of the Castle. But it has suffered severely at the hands of those in charge of the Castle, having been at one time divided into two stories, with a floor let into the masonry, so as to convert it into a powder-magazine. Some years ago, however, it was revealed by Professor Daniel Wilson, and was fortunately rescued by the efforts of the Antiquarian Society of Scotland from this unworthy use, and we understand that through the munificence of Mr. William Nelson [the publisher], a distin-

guished citizen of Edinburgh, it is about to be entirely restored to its original form, under the superintendence of Mr. Hippolyte J. Blanc, architect. (1: 461–62)

Blanc was a close personal friend of Thomas Ross. However, MacGibbon and Ross should have tempered their enthusiasm:

> St Margaret's Chapel was not the responsibility of the War Office but of the Office of Works. The approval of a committee was required, and the committee would approve only a much more limited scheme than Blanc had proposed. Work on the chapel had not begun at the time of Nelson's death in September 1887, but a codicil to his will bound his executors to complete the restoration already begun, and work on the Great Hall continued. It did not, however, bind them to pay for work which he had only intended to carry out, and since they 'looked with disapproval at his expenditure on a subject bringing in no return', the scheme for St Margaret's Chapel was dropped.[5]

MacGibbon and Ross were also hopeful about the future of the Great Hall (which they call the 'Parliament Hall'): 'there can be no doubt that when seen in its entirety this must have been a magnificent hall, of a similar type to those of the other Royal palaces at Linlithgow and Stirling; and it is satisfactory to know that the persevering endeavours of Major Gore Booth and others to have it so far as possible restored and fitted up as an armoury and military museum, are likely to be crowned with success' (1: 457). It was eventually restored

OPPOSITE. Chambers' sketch of the 'restoration' of Edinburgh Castle.

East Front of Castle, restored as before 1573
by R. Chambers.

IN · DE FENS
IACOBVS
REX · S

by Hippolyte Blanc, paid for by the publisher William Nelson's legacy – as the restoration had already begun, the executors had to allow the work to go ahead. But, from a twenty-first-century perspective, 'Although Blanc maintained his was an archaeologically-based restoration, what exists today is very much a late-Victorian masterpiece, and not in most respects James IV's Great Hall.'[6] The military museums in the castle did not start until after the First World War and after the erection of the Scottish National War Memorial in 1924–27, designed by Robert Lorimer. David Bryce's plans for a massive tower, dominating the castle, as a memorial to Prince Albert after his death in 1861 were never realised – a statue was erected in Charlotte Square instead (see Plate 29).

Stirling Castle has also seen enormous changes since MacGibbon and Ross visited. They recognised the significance of the great royal palaces of Scotland: 'We have in this Palace [Stirling Castle] (as in the other Royal palaces at Edinburgh, Linlithgow and Falkland) early examples of the taste for more extended and luxurious accommodation, which about this time began to be introduced, and of which we see so many specimens in the later mansions of the nobility' (1: 478). 'The fireplaces,' they wrote, 'are almost the only portions of the internal ornamentation remaining, and even these are much injured and defaced' (1: 474). They might have been surprised and pleased at how, not only have the fireplaces been repaired, but the luxury of the accommodation has been vividly brought to life by the Stirling Castle Palace Project, which has brought about the biggest change in any part of the national historic estate. Spanning the first decade of the twenty-first century, the project transformed the physical interiors and exteriors of the castle, using craftsmen and women to restore

OPPOSITE. Stirling Castle, restored fireplace in the King's Outer Hall.

the sixteenth-century interiors to their former opulence, at a cost of £12 million.

'The apartments of the Palace were all richly carved and decorated, the ceiling of the "presence chamber" being adorned with carved oak panels representing the heads of Wallace, Bruce and other Scottish kings and worthies. These were all removed in 1777, as some of them had fallen through decay, and unfortunately were much damaged and dispersed' (1: 473–74). The project to carve and paint 37 replica 'Stirling heads', now in place on the ceiling of the King's Inner Hall (see Plate 16), and to conserve and display the originals, was bold and successful. John Donaldson, master carver, spent five years creating the replicas, a measure of how costly the originals would have been for James V, who commissioned the ceiling.

Our knowledge of how the buildings were used and Stirling's place within Scottish and European culture was enhanced through several major historical peer-reviewed research programmes. In addition to the restoration of the buildings, a brilliantly executed new set of seven tapestries of the hunt of the unicorn for the Queen's Inner Hall was woven by an international team of weavers. The work took 13 years to complete and cost £2 million.

In the centre of the harbour town of Kirkcudbright, MacLellan's Castle was taken into care in 1912 and the Office of Works undertook major conservation works. Although it did not become the local museum that MacGibbon and Ross wished for (2: 149), it has been open to the public and remains a popular visitor attraction. Also in Kirkcudbrightshire, Threave Castle is one of south-west Scotland's most visited castles, a huge fortress tower situated on an island in the River Dee. The long walk across farmland followed nowadays by a short boat trip to the island 'help transport the visitor both physically and emotionally back in time to the later Middle Ages with all those images of war and blood-feud'.[7] But for MacGibbon and Ross there was no convenient boat trip, apparently, as they reported: 'The castle is reached by wading a ford on the eastern branch of the river about twenty yards wide' (1: 161). This could only have been done in a dry period, as the River Dee is fast-flowing, and must have been a difficult, even dangerous, crossing to make. Threave Castle was entrusted into state care in 1913 by Edward Gordon and the Ministry of Works immediately repaired the stone vault in the basement. MacGibbon and Ross had noted that 'unfortunately large portions of the vaulting have fallen and heaped the place with ruins' (1: 162), and their sketch of the interior basement floor shows the extent of the damage. In 1948 Major Alan Gordon, a cousin of Edward, offered the entire Threave Estate of 1,500 acres, including the island on which the castle stands and Threave House and garden, to the National Trust for Scotland. As part of the gift he helpfully offered to blow up Threave House, built by Peddie and Kinnear in 1871, and by then deeply unfashionable. Fortunately the NTS declined. Now, HES looks after the castle and the NTS the rest of the estate, including the house, and there are shared ticketing arrangements in place. The NTS has developed a local nature reserve around the island and Threave Castle has become a refuge for bats, ravens, ospreys, peregrine falcons and wintering geese.

In his notes, Thomas Ross expressed particular concern about Balvaird Castle:

> between measurements of the 1st floor this Autumn, great portions of the outbuildings have fallen and the whole of those buildings including the Staircase with its original roof may be said to be tottering to their fall. Also, one of the rybats of the Archway leading into the Court has been pulled out lately by a passing cart, which is a commencement of the destruction of this very quaint

and interesting portion of the structure. I was also sorry to observe that the Statue of Margaret Barclay, an ancestress of the noble Earl of Mansfield which was cut out of a single block of red sandstone, has been broken in two, this, I believe, must have happened very recently.[8]

In the text of *The Castellated and Domestic Architecture of Scotland* (1: 335) a somewhat different picture is painted, with no mention of these concerns. Did David MacGibbon make the changes? The section on the castle's sanitary arrangements is also quite different. In his notes, Thomas Ross writes 'But perhaps the most interesting features about the castle are those which throw some light on the sanitary arrangements of our Forefathers, and here they happen to be in exceptionally fine condition.' He goes on to explain in great detail and at length about the various closets, seats and pipes and the wide flue ('Of course a very disagreeable smell must have come up this flue') that terminated in a chamber below. This section has been considerably shortened, which is puzzling, as it is the kind of scatological detail that fascinates readers. The notes written by Thomas Ross are dated September 1878 and are written in elegant copperplate with flourishes, as if ready for publication (not all of his notes are written in this style; some look much more rushed and slightly scruffy). Perhaps there was simply not enough space to include everything, but the change of tone and emphasis between the note and the final publication does raise questions about whose was the final authorial voice.

Aberdour Castle was another building that had suffered neglect. MacGibbon and Ross were forthright about its risks:

> Aberdour is a charming specimen of an old Scottish residence, with quaint crow-

Balvaird Castle in Perthshire, by MacGibbon and Ross. Note the trees growing from the roof.

stepped gables, and corner sun-dial overlooking its fine terraced walks. Such a house, without sacrificing any of its characteristic features, might be inhabited to this day. But instead of being kept in the order which such a fine example deserves, the most complete and heartless neglect reigns over the whole place. The greater portion of the buildings, including those erected by the great Regent [Morton], are used as cow-byres and piggeries, while the church, one of the most complete Norman structures in Scotland, is in a similar state of heedless neglect. (2: 477)

In 1939 it was taken in state guardianship: 'The early castle structure is particularly important as the best preserved and most easily interpreted example of 12th century secular stone architecture in Scotland. Although much of the castle fell into ruin after 1700, this has had the benefit of preserving an unparalleled sequence of medieval and renaissance architecture.'[9] Now it is in the care of HES.

The National Trust for Scotland

In 1943, when Tam Dalyell of the House of the Binns was 11 years old, his parents asked to talk to him about something very serious. 'We are thinking of giving the house, which in the normal course of events when we die would belong to you, to an organisation called the National Trust for Scotland.'[10] This would be the first acquisition for the NTS's new Country House Scheme. The House of the Binns was transferred to the NTS by charter in 1944, with the proviso that Tam would be able to continue to reside there – which he did, until his death in 2017. In a solemn ceremony in 1946, watched by the young Tam, Mrs Eleanor Dalyell handed a clod of symbolic earth and stone to Lord Wemyss, acting Chairman of the Trust. MacGibbon and Ross were particularly interested in the splendid plasterwork ceilings and provide three sketches (4: 381–82).

The NTS was founded in 1931, much later than the National Trust in England, which had been set up in 1895. Sir John Stirling Maxwell said at the Trust's first annual general meeting in 1932: 'The National Trust for Scotland serves the nation as a cabinet into which it can put some of its valuable things, where they will be perfectly safe for all time, and where they are open to be seen and enjoyed by everyone.'[11] The first castle to be gifted to the NTS was Crookston Castle, donated by Maxwell himself. The NTS transferred Crookston into state care in 1963 and it is now cared for by HES. It is the only mediaeval castle to survive in the city of Glasgow. The local community now plays a major part in the management of the castle, under the auspices of the Crookston Castle Working Group. A storyteller-in-residence has been created, and a number of community events take place. Numerous local school groups are led on visits with a storytelling theme.

Of the buildings surveyed by MacGibbon and Ross, the NTS owns or manages Castle Fraser, Craigievar Castle, Drum, Fyvie, Leith Hall, Brodick Castle, the House of the Binns (Binns Castle), Alloa Tower, Falkland Palace, Kellie Castle, Crathes Castle, and Culross Palace. All of these, unlike the majority of the HES castellated buildings in care, are roofed and furnished.[12] Many of them house magnificent collections of artworks and furnishings, and are situated in beautiful gardens. These make up the kind of destination package which visitors find so enticing – in addition to a romantic and highly photogenic castle, there is a museum, well-maintained estate gardens, woodland walks, a tearoom, toilets, shop, ample car parking and regular events such as falconry displays, Christmas fairs and guided walks. Glossy illustrated guidebooks are complemented by volunteer guides, sometimes dressed in historical costume, audio tours and information panels. In 2017 Crathes Castle, which offers most of these attractions, received more than 120,000 visitors.

MacGibbon and Ross were particularly concerned about Culross Palace: 'This building has remained almost quite unaltered till the present day. It now stands untenanted, and is rapidly going to decay. The roofs are fast falling in, and the old painting will soon be a thing of the past. It is melancholy to see such an interesting structure thus left to its fate when a few pounds judiciously applied in time might save this valuable monument for many years' (2: 435). The restoration of Culross Abbey cost more than 'a few pounds judiciously applied', however. For a start, the NTS had to pay the Earl of Dundonald £700 for the palace in 1932. It was not a huge sum, even at today's value of about £50,000, but it was a significant expense for the Trust.

[It was] dependent on agreement with HM Office of Works that they should accept the guardianship of the property, relieving the

Trust of the expenses of repairing and maintaining the rich painted ceilings in the Palace. The purchase used up nearly half of the Trust's first legacy. This arrangement with the government body was the first of several subsequently entered into by the Trust. The advice and support of HM Office of Works was singled out for gratitude as an excellent example of cooperation without overlapping of interests.[13]

Culross was assessed as having the very highest rating of heritage significance in the NTS's 2012 Property Portfolio Review.

Not all attempts to acquire property for the Trust were successful. In 1994 negotiations were well advanced between the National Trust for Scotland and the owner of Dunbeath Castle, the Californian businessman Stanton Avery, who had bought the estate in 1977. The transfer of the 40,000 acres, including the clifftop Dunbeath Castle, was due to have been concluded by May 1994 but the offer was withdrawn by Avery. He claimed the sticking point was the failure of the National Trust to commit itself to underwriting the running costs. However, officials of the National Trust maintained that finance was not at issue, because £1.2 million of public funds was committed to the running of the estate if the transfer went ahead. Dunbeath Castle was put on the market and sold to a private owner in 1996. It remains in private hands, although its gardens are open to the public, by appointment.

The coronavirus pandemic in 2020 highlighted the fragility of the NTS funding model and caused it to take what many saw as drastic action: 'Until the unforeseen events took effect, the Trust was in a good position with reserves at an all-time high, growing membership and a programme of significant conservation works in the pipeline. The difficulties we are now in are wholly due to the loss of all our income streams at once and the imposed lockdown.'[14] It remains to be seen what the long-term fallout of the pandemic will be for the NTS and its properties.

Other Owners

Those castles open to the public which are not looked after by the NTS or HES are mostly either in the hands of trusts or local authorities. A few are still owned and occupied by longstanding owners. The glorious pink sandstone palace of Drumlanrig started as a sixteenth-century tower house. It was built between 1679 and 1691 by the 1st Duke of Queensberry and is owned by the Duke of Buccleuch, although he does not reside there. The Dowager Countess Cawdor lives in Cawdor Castle and opens it to the public. The MacPherson–Grant family owns Ballindalloch Castle and opens it to the public. Glamis Castle is the home of the Earl and Countess of Strathmore and Kinghorne. Glamis has the cachet of having been the childhood home of Queen Elizabeth the Queen Mother, which is its strapline on all advertising. The Queen Mother has been an attractive element of Glamis since she became Queen in 1936. MacGibbon and Ross mention an earlier draw: 'The castle of Glamis probably enjoys a wider fame than almost any other Scottish building, associated as it is all over the world with the tragedy of "Macbeth"' (2: 113). Their entry runs to 11 pages.

Two castles that open to the public are owned by recent owner restorers. One is Balgonie in Fife, purchased in 1984 by the late Raymond Morris, who engaged in a long-term restoration of the building with limited funds. MacGibbon and Ross carried out an extensive and detailed survey of the building, noting 'Balgonie has been a fine residence and has not long been abandoned. The keep in particular is one of the best in its class in Scotland. It may be regarded as quite entire in its masonry,

Glamis Castle, Angus, in a postcard marketing its connections with the Queen Mother.

only the wooden floors of the upper two stories being wanting' (1: 382). However, they also noted that the buildings along the north side and halfway along the east side were in ruins, while the remaining half of the east side was still inhabited as labourers' cottages. The buildings continued to decline and by the 1960s vandalism was a major problem. The current owner reported that when he bought the place 80 panes of glass had been shot out by air rifles. Castle Stalcaire (Stalker) was restored from 1965 to 1975 as a family project by the late Stewart Allward[15] and is open to visitors occasionally.

Community Castles

Two buildings surveyed by MacGibbon and Ross have become community centres in Edinburgh: Inch Castle, now a community centre and Corstorphine Dower House, which was taken over by the Corstorphine Trust in 1991 and is now a heritage centre and museum. Inch House has been a community centre since 1968; before that, from 1946–68, it was used as a primary school by the City of Edinburgh Council, to whom it had been sold in 1946 by Sir John Little Gilmour. Inch was restored and extended by MacGibbon and Ross. 'In 1891 (exhorted by the Society of Antiquaries of Scotland) they [the Gilmours] employed MacGibbon and Ross to restore the house and extend its character to the wing, which they did in no uncertain way . . . The room treatment is theirs too, but without consistency or outstanding quality.'[16] The interior is now depressingly neglected, and would need millions of pounds spending to bring it back to anything like its former state.

Mar Castle (Braemar) is leased by the Chief of Clan Farquharson to a local charitable foundation which opens it to the public. Barr Castle in Ayrshire, where John Knox preached in 1566, houses a small local museum and is occasionally open. It is also used as a Masonic Lodge. Dean Castle, also in Ayrshire, was ruinous when MacGibbon and Ross surveyed it, but now houses a local council museum and is open to the public. Balhousie Castle in Perth is also a museum, as is Broughty Castle near Dundee and Portencross in Ayrshire.

Inspirational Castles and Distinguished Visitors

MacGibbon and Ross usually mention the owners of the castles they surveyed, and occasionally the special visitors they attracted. Kinneil House, they said, 'is noteworthy in modern history as the place where Dugald Stewart [Enlightenment philosopher and founder of the Royal Society of Edinburgh] wrote many of his works, and where James Watt brought some of his improvements on the steam-engine to perfection' (3: 231). Merchiston Castle was 'widely known as the birthplace and residence of John Napier, the inventor of logarithms' (3: 263). Bannatyne House, 'A modernised and comfortable farm-house . . . owes its celebrity to its having been the residence, towards the end of the sixteenth century, of George Bannatyne, the author of the *Bannatyne Manuscript*, a collection of the writings of the older Scottish poets' (3: 592). In a postscript to their entry on Caprington Castle, MacGibbon and Ross mention that 'Between the castle and the village of Riccarton is the site of the "Bickering Bush", which was a thorn marking the spot where Wallace is said to have had a tangle with some English soldiers, who wanted to deprive him of the fish he had caught in the river' (5: 246). In their entry on Dalzell Castle, they report that 'William Cobbett, who visited Dalzell in 1832, in describing the castle and surroundings, says that it is the place at which, if he were compelled to reside in Scotland, he would choose to live' (3: 313).

Sir Walter Scott

The most distinguished connection to many castles, in the eyes of MacGibbon and Ross, would have been Sir Walter Scott, whom they mention several times: 'As is well known, Sir Walter passed the years of his childhood near Smailholm, at the farmhouse of Sandyknowe, and, in an introductory epistle to *Marmion*, he gives a graphic description of the tower and scenery around' (2: 38). It is now in the care of HES and houses a collection of charming costume figures and tapestries relating to Scott's *Minstrelsy of the Scottish Borders*. In the entry for Yester Castle MacGibbon and Ross say: 'The most remarkable building connected with the castle is a subterranean chamber . . . popularly known as "The Goblin Hall". This underground chamber is the hall referred to by Sir Walter Scott in the "Host's Tale" in *Marmion*' (1: 119). In their lengthy entry on Traquair House MacGibbon and Ross quote three verses from one of Sir Walter Scott's Scots ballads, 'Sang of the Outlaw Murray' (2: 446), when discussing the intricacies of the ownership history, and quote his opinion on the matter.

Sir Walter Scott drew upon the castellated architecture of Scotland to anchor his novels in the romantic landscape and as inspiration for his stories. Grandtully Castle is said to be the basis of 'Tully-Veolan' in the Waverley novels. Both Barholm and Carsluith castles lay claim to be the original model for Ellangowan in *Guy Mannering*, although neither fits the description in the novel accurately. The illustrations for various editions tend rather to resemble Caerlaverock Castle. Abbot's Tower was once occupied by Gilbert Broun, the last abbot of nearby Sweetheart Abbey.

A colourful character, Gilbert was famed for his vain attempts to turn the tide of the Reformation in Scotland. Sir Walter Scott romanticised the story by using Gilbert Broun as a model for the central character in his novel *The Abbot*. In their entry on Fast Castle in Berwickshire, which features in *The Bride of Lammermoor*, MacGibbon and Ross describe the lightning strike of 1871 which caused a great deal of damage to the castle. 'The fate which Sir Walter Scott pictured as happening to Wolf's Craig (of which Fast Castle was the prototype) has thus now been realised' (3: 223).

In 1834 the artist J.M.W. Turner, who had already painted a number of watercolours to be engraved as illustrations for Sir Walter Scott's *Collected Poetical Works*, provided illustrations for Scott's *Waverley* (see Plate 30). Scott's writing is so pictorial that it must have been a visual inspiration for Turner: 'While getting into order, they exhibited a changing, fluctuating, confused appearance of waving tartans and floating plumes, and of banners displaying the proud gathering-word of each clan. At length the mixed and wavering multitude arranged themselves into a narrow and dusky column of great length, stretching through the whole extent of the vale.'[17]

Scott was a magpie collector of antiquarian artefacts. The Threave Castle jougs[18] is fixed to a wall outside his home at Abbotsford, obtained from Joseph Train, a great collector of antiquities. 'He nearly herry't the haill country-side tae get things tae sen' tae Sir Walter Scott, an took the verra jougs aff Threave Castle an sent them.'[19]

Scott was a regular visitor to Darnick Tower in Roxburghshire and unsuccessfully begged John Heiton to sell it to him. 'Darnick has always been an inhabited house, and in the constant possession of the Heitons, an ancient Scottish family' (5: 260). Andrew Heiton, who was an architect, provided MacGibbon and Ross with the plans for the tower. He was a notable collector of antiquities, particu-

larly armour, weapons and furniture, and on inheriting the estate of Darnick turned the ancient tower house into a showplace for his collection. Darnick stayed in the Heiton family until the twenty-first century when it was inherited by a member of the Heiton family resident in New Zealand, who sold it. The new owner has carried out a great deal of renovation to bring the building up to modern standards; although the house was always occupied, it had been tenanted and not well looked after for many years.

In 1794 Scott applied to the factor of Glamis Castle, which was then uninhabited, for permission to spend the night in one of its rooms. 'After a very hospitable reception, I was conducted to my apartment in a distant part of the building. I must own that when I heard door after door shut, after my conductor had retired, I began to consider myself too far from the living and somewhat too near the dead.'[20] Perhaps the reason for his supernatural dread might be inferred from his anecdote about his activity before bedtime. In a note to *Waverley* he says:

> The Poculum Potatorium of the valiant Baron, his blessed Bear, has a prototype at the fine old castle of Glamis, so rich in memorials of ancient times. It is a massive beaker of silver, double gilt, molded into the shape of a lion and holding about an English pint of wine. The form alludes to the family name of Strathmore, which is Lyon, and when exhibited the cup must necessarily be emptied to the Earl's health. The author ought, perhaps, to be ashamed of recording that he has had the honor of swallowing the contents of the lion, and the recollection of the feat served to suggest the story of the 'Bear of Bradwardine'.[21]

Scott thought fondly of the inspiration he gained

from Bothwell Castle early in his career: 'I shall have a peep at Bothwell Castle if it is only for half an hour. It is a place of many recollections to me, for I cannot but think how changed I am from the same Walter Scott who was so passionately ambitious of fame when I wrote the song of Young Lochinvar at Bothwell.'[22]

Neidpath Castle was visited by William and Dorothy Wordsworth during their Scottish trip in 1803. Dorothy Wordsworth, in her journal of 18 September, noted that 'When we were with Mr. Scott [Sir Walter] he spoke of cheerful days he had spent in that castle not many years ago, when it was inhabited by Professor Ferguson [Adam Fergusson] and his family, whom the Duke of Queensberry, its churlish owner, forced to quit it.'[23] The 4th Duke was one of the wealthiest landlords, but did nothing to care for his lands or Neidpath itself. In 1795, he ruthlessly cut down all the trees and demolished the beautiful hanging gardens that sloped down to the Tweed. He was humiliated for doing this by William Wordsworth, in a sonnet written after the poet's visit in 1803:

Degenerate Douglass! thou unworthy Lord
Whom mere despite of heart could so far please,
And love of havoc (for with such disease
Fame taxes him) that he could send forth word
To level with the dust a noble horde,
A brotherhood of venerable trees,
Leaving an ancient Dome and Towers like these
Beggar'd and outraged! Many hearts deplored
The fate of those old trees; and oft with pain
The Traveller at this day will stop and gaze
On wrongs which Nature scarcely seems to heed;
For shelter'd places, bosoms, nooks, and bays,
And the pure mountains, and the gentle Tweed,
And the green silent pastures yet remain.

MacGibbon and Ross mention the fine terraced gardens constructed by the Earl of Tweeddale in 1654, 'a few remains of which are still visible' (1: 183). But there are no longer any gardens at Neidpath.

Other Castle Visitors

Craigcrook Castle in Edinburgh was known for its literary soirées; Sir Walter Scott was a frequent visitor. Among the guests during the nineteenth century were Charles Dickens, Hans Christian Andersen, George Eliot and Lord Tennyson. Boswell and Johnson visited Breachacha and Dunvegan castles in Skye, and Auchans Castle in Ayrshire: 'In 1773 Dr Johnson and Boswell spent a day here for the purpose of visiting the Dowager Countess of Eglinton, who died at Auchans in the year 1780, in her ninety-first year' (2: 179). Kellie Castle was home to a family of famous artists and great minds. James Lorimer, professor of public law, had restored the castle from dereliction after renting it in 1878. His son, Robert, became one of Scotland's most prolific and famous architects. Robert's older brother, John Henry Lorimer, was a genre and portrait painter. Their sister, Hannah, became a painter and sculptor and also worked on the moulded plaster ceilings of the Marquess of Bute. Robert's son, Hew, became a famous sculptor. Visitors to the NTS-owned castle can see the hand of the talented Lorimer family in almost every element of the property, in the furniture, the paintings and sculpture and the gardens. The stables feature an exhibition dedicated to Hew Lorimer.

Not long after the visit of MacGibbon and Ross, Charles Rennie Mackintosh sketched Baltersan and Maybole Castle in Ayrshire in 1895 and drew inspiration from their fine architectural details in his designs for the Glasgow School of Art, the Hill House and the Willow Tea Rooms.[24] Baltersan was far from a source of inspiration for Robert Louis Stevenson, however. In 1876, not long before the visit of MacGibbon and Ross, Stevenson set out on a walk through Carrick and Galloway. In his subsequent travel essay, he appeared somewhat curmudgeonly, when he dismissed Baltersan and Crossraguel Abbey as mere 'dilapidated castles and monasteries'.[25]

John Knox stayed in St Andrews Castle in 1547 when it was besieged by the French forces of Mary of Guise. He was then captured and forced to row in the French galleys as a slave. He is said to have hidden at Barholm Castle when on the run from Mary Queen of Scots, but the story, although repeated in various antiquarian texts, does not bear close scrutiny. At Calder House in Midlothian Knox is said to have celebrated his first Reformed Communion in Scotland.

In August 1787 Robert Burns paid his first visit to Stirling. Disturbed by the ruinous state of Stirling Castle, he is said to have scrawled on the window of his room in a Stirling inn, with a diamond pen he had recently acquired:

Here Stewarts once in triumph reigned,
And laws for Scotland's weal ordained;
But now unroofed their palace stands,
Their sceptre's swayed by other hands;
Fallen, indeed, and to the earth
Whence grovelling reptiles take their birth,
The injured Stewart line is gone.
A race outlandish fills their throne;
An idiot race, to honour lost;
Who knows them best despite them most.

Burns visited Stirling again, in company with Dr James M'Kittrick Adair, in October. Adair later recounted: 'At Stirling the prospects from the Castle strongly interested him; in a former visit to which, his national feelings had been powerfully excited by the ruinous and roofless state of the hall in which the Scottish parliaments had frequently been held. His indignation had vented itself in some imprudent, but not unpoetical lines, which had given much offence, and which he took this opportunity of erasing by breaking the pane of window at the inn in which they were written.'[26] Burns also visited Kenmure Castle with his friend John Syme. They stayed for three days in July 1793 as the guest of the laird, John Gordon, Viscount Kenmure.

Royal Castles

Royal connections seem to enhance the excitement of a castle visit for visitors; those that are tourist destinations capitalise on this appeal in their interpretation. Mary, Queen of Scots is a favourite, as is Bonnie Prince Charlie. MacGibbon and Ross tell a few royal tales in passing. In their entry on Fast Castle in Berwickshire they report: 'A cavern penetrates the rock beneath the keep, and it is supposed that there existed a staircase which communicated between the castle and the cave. Had the Gowrie conspiracy[27] prospered, this would probably have been the passage by which the king, James VI, would have passed to his prison in Logan's castle above' (3: 224).

MacGibbon and Ross detail the royal connections of Alloa Tower, first bemoaning the changes it had undergone: 'Unfortunately, the tower has been greatly altered and its original features destroyed, the interior having been entirely remodelled, and the exterior cut up with a number of large inserted windows, all arranged at equal intervals, and a good many of which are actually *mock* windows [italics as in original]' (1: 155). They go on: 'The original newel staircase in the south-west angle is still preserved, and the loopholes which light it are visible in the view from the west. Additions were made to the tower at a later date, when it was extended into the mansion where Queen Mary, James I and Prince Henry[28] spent much of their youthful time; but these additions were all destroyed by a great fire in 1800' (1: 156).

More than 50 Scottish castles can legitimately claim that Mary Queen of Scots slept there, or at least paid a visit. In less than seven years, from 1561 to 1568, the Queen made a series of royal tours of Scotland. Chris Tabraham estimates that she covered 4,000 miles in her six-year reign, sometimes travelling on the road for months at a time.[29] Although MacGibbon and Ross omitted many of Scotland's castles in their surveys, most of those visited by Mary are recorded by them and they make occasional passing reference to Queen Mary, as in the Lochleven Castle entry (1: 146). Mary first visited Lochleven Castle in 1565 as a guest of Sir William Douglas and in June 1567 was held there as his prisoner, until she escaped in disguise to England in May the following year. She never saw Scotland again. Whilst staying at Lochleven, Mary met with her arch-critic John Knox, suffered a miscarriage of twins and was compelled to abdicate the Scottish throne in favour of her son, James.

Most of the castles Mary visited are open for public access. Eleven are owned by the NTS and 35 are in the care of HES. The rest are owned privately or by trusts. In September 1565, Mary and her husband Darnley attended a banquet in Lochmaben Castle, before returning to Edinburgh, after the breathless episode known as the 'Chaseabout Raid', in which she and her troops went in pursuit of her half-brother the Earl of Moray. She was rowed in to Lochmaben, with fiddlers lining the route. Of Lochmaben she is reported to have said that it was 'the very home of beauty'. Over 300 years later, Queen Victoria visited Lochmaben in 1887, the year of her Golden Jubilee and the year that MacGibbon and Ross published their account of the castle. Prior to her visit, the canal in front of the stone castle was cleared out so that her barge could sail up to the castle in an echo of Mary's entrance. Victoria may have had a picnic there as indicated by the shelter

in the grounds (page 208) – since demolished – on which can be seen Victoria's crest. Victoria also visited Blair Castle in 1844 and Stirling Castle in 1849.

The great royal palaces and castles surveyed by MacGibbon and Ross are mainly written up in Volume 1, with the exception of Holyrood Palace. 'The Abbey at Holyrood was a frequent residence of the Stuart kings, and from at least the time of James III, it may be regarded as the principal palace of Scotland' (4: 130). It became the official Scottish residence of the British monarch in the 1920s, after George V had central heating and electric lights installed before his first visit in 1911 and improvements to kitchens and bathrooms were carried out after the First World War.

The royal palace at Stirling has had many royal connections. MacGibbon and Ross relate an anecdote about James IV: 'The courtyard . . . is known as the "Lion's Den", the tradition being that James IV, who was fond of wild animals, kept his lions there. The animals were kept by the King as an emblem of royal state and dignity' (1: 473). At Linlithgow Palace 'James V spared no pains to make the palace ready for the reception of his bride, Mary of Guise, who is said to have declared, when brought home to it, that she "had never seen a more princely palace"' (1: 479). Other royal residences include Lochmaben Castle, Dundonald Castle, Rothesay Castle – 'a favourite residence of Robert II and Robert III' (1: 80) – and Falkland Palace, 'a favourite retreat for the Scottish kings' (1: 501). At Dunfermline Palace, Malcolm Canmore was married in 1070. 'From Malcolm's time Dunfermline became a constant residence of the Scottish kings' (1: 514).

Movie Star Castles

From the mid twentieth century, increasing numbers of Scottish castles began to feature in

VICTORIA

OPPOSITE. Shelter at Lochmaben Castle in Dumfriesshire. Did Queen Victoria picnic there?

ABOVE. Midhope Castle Gateway, near Edinburgh, by MacGibbon and Ross: 'Lallybroch Castle' in the *Outlander* film series.

television programmes and movies. For some it has been a lucrative source of income and there are now specialist agencies which broker deals between castle owners and film studios. Midhope Castle, formerly an obscure and derelict ruin on the Hopetoun Estate, stars in the *Outlander* television series as 'Lallybroch Castle'. MacGibbon and Ross had been impressed by its romantic aspect: 'Midhope is beautifully situated in a picturesque dell near the old church of Abercorn. The house is quite concealed from view till one is almost in

call of it. We give a sketch of the first glimpse a visitor gets of the house, along a shaded avenue, with quaint gate pillars on either side, as he ascends from the bridge over the Midhope Burn' (2: 502).

Blackness Castle has been used as a filming location in several productions, including Franco Zeffirelli's *Hamlet* (1990) and *Doomsday* (2008). On television, Blackness has featured in the series *Ivanhoe* (1997) and *Outlander* (2014–20). The enormously popular television series *Outlander*, a historical fantasy first broadcast in 2014, has benefited

209

several castles used as locations and background sets – Doune, Aberdour, Blackness, Midhope, Balgonie, Linlithgow Palace, Drummond Castle gardens, Drumlanrig and Craigmillar. A tourist industry has sprung up around the locations, leading to a sharp rise in visitor numbers. Dundas Castle is not featured in the series, but it capitalised on the interest by advertising a 'luxury Outlander inspired experience' with prices starting from £5,930 per night for private hire of the castle and its 17 bedrooms. The castle has become a far cry from the semi-derelict distillery visited by MacGibbon and Ross. In contrast to the well-managed and popular visitor attractions that Edinburgh and Stirling castles have become, remote Morton Castle in the Southern Uplands, also in the care of HES, has had few visitors until a recent upturn due to its use as a location in *Outlander*. It is a splendid ruin in the landscape and can scarcely have changed since MacGibbon and Ross visited. 'The aspect of the grey but solid old ashlar walls, and the ruined towers still rearing their front in the midst of the wild and desolate moor, and above the chill waters of the tortuous lake, is most unlooked for and impressive' (1: 545–56).

Dunnottar was also used as a location for the 1991 version of *Hamlet,* Duart was the location for *Entrapment* (1999) and Doune was used to represent Camelot, Castle Anthrax and Swamp Castle in *Monty Python and the Holy Grail* (1975), leading to annual pilgrimages by Python fans. It was also used in the pilot for the television series *Game of Thrones.* Eilean Donan has starred in many films, including *Bonnie Prince Charlie* starring David Niven (1948), *The Master of Ballantree* starring Errol Flynn (1953), *The New Avengers* (1976), *Highlander* (1986) and the James Bond movie *The World is Not Enough* (1999). The romantic vision of the Scottish castle promoted in film and television has raised the profile of many buildings, become an income generator for the owners and a focus of pilgrimage for fans.

Conclusion

When MacGibbon and Ross carried out their surveys, relatively few castles were accessible to the general public. By calling for museums in MacLellan's and Edinburgh castles they signalled their support of the principle of public access. Kinnaird Tower in Perthshire was a museum when MacGibbon and Ross visited, and had recently been restored. 'The building is in a fine state of preservation, having been renovated a few years ago by the late Sir Patrick Murray Threipland, Bart. When it came in to his possession it was a roofless ruin; but appreciating its value, Sir Patrick had it repaired and converted into an interesting local museum, in which capacity we trust it will long remain a monument of his enlightened taste' (1: 270–71). It is now no longer a museum, but a private home, unlike the many castles that have formerly been private homes and later become museums. Haggs Castle in Glasgow is another that was once a museum and now is a private residence.

There has been a democratisation of castles since the second half of the twentieth century, partly because of an increase in leisure time coupled with a growing interest in heritage, and partly because more owners are opening to the public, either as tourist attractions or accommodation providers. The numbers of 'ordinary' people who have stayed in, or visited, a castle must have risen enormously throughout the decades since the Second World War. More and more citizens have had access to more and more castles that had formerly been completely private and closed to previous generations of the general public. The castles that open to visitors tend to be the grandest and best-known in Scotland. They have been visited by millions, and some of the more famous visitors – or guests – have been creatively inspired by their visits to write or paint, or they have inspired others, by the very fact of their visits.

9

The Future

———

That which is valued by a dominant culture or cultures in society is preserved and cared for; the rest can be mindlessly or purposefully destroyed, or just left to rot.

R. Bevan (2006) *The Destruction of Memory: Architecture at War*

The truth is that the architecture of a nation not only reflects the broad lines of its history, but also its changing habits and power of satisfying new needs. By these changes it advances and apart from them it cannot profitably be studied.

Sir John Stirling Maxwell (1938)
Shrines and Homes of Scotland

What would MacGibbon and Ross think of the state of Scotland's stock of castellated buildings 130 years after their survey, and of our attitudes towards them? They had a passion for castles – a passion that has been shared by millions. There is no other building form that has so consistently been associated with history, romance, war and adventure and that has provided so much fascinated interest. Castles are more popular than ever. In a visual world, we are assailed by images of the castle, in art, the Internet, computer games, movies and television. This survey, like that of MacGibbon and Ross, captures a mere moment in time. By next year, all may have changed, while we wait to try to grasp the impact of a global pandemic, an economic recession and a climate emergency upon the castellated architecture of Scotland.

Our attitudes to built heritage have changed since the late nineteenth century, in many ways for the better. There is at least legal protection now, where none existed in MacGibbon and Ross's time. Around 200 of the buildings that MacGibbon and Ross surveyed had been continuously inhabited when they visited and most of those are still lived in and well cared for. But 52 castles have disappeared and at least as many again are still at risk out of the 720 or so that they surveyed. It is clear that restoration is neither a failsafe solution nor always an appropriate one. Rebuilding can, even in recent times, be reversed and castles slide back into dereliction – e.g. Crosbie, Kenmure – and some projects, particularly those carried out in the mid twentieth century, were almost as destructive as they were restorative. But it is difficult to imagine the castles of Scotland which have been restored to a high standard returning to their previous vulnerable state. Unless something catastrophic happens, such as gutting by fire, flooding or the discovery of extensive dry rot or structural damage, they are valuable commodities that can be sold on as assets on the high-end housing market, if the need arises. What the future holds for the many castles still at risk of collapse can only be guessed. It would be comforting to think most could at least be secured from further degeneration through adaptive re-use, but that is only likely if they are in attractive and accessible locations, and are suitable for restoration, which in practice applies to a relatively small number.

Dozens more castles are accessible to the public now than when MacGibbon and Ross visited them. But public access can be a double-edged sword. Accessibility is a twenty-first-century mantra, yet an increased appetite and enthusiasm for visiting historic sites means that these visitors pose a threat to the buildings they most care about, including some of Scotland's most splendid examples of built heritage. HES and NTS depend on the income from visitors. For some castles there are simply too many visitors for comfort, safety and the conservation of the building itself. Edinburgh Castle's two million visitors in 2019 put a strain on the site and is not a sustainable number for the future; there is a constant tension between welcoming and conservation. Tourism as an economic driver has been in danger of killing the goose that lays its golden eggs. Across the world, thousands of sites including Venice, Machu Picchu, Dubrovnik, Angkor Wat, the Great Wall of China,

the Taj Mahal, Mount Everest and the Galapagos Islands have struggled to survive in the face of tsunamis of tourists, and for some the strain on a delicate infrastructure is exacerbated by global warming. The United Nations World Tourism Organization recorded 7% annual growth in international tourism in 2017, a rate that seemed to be set for the future. When Covid-19 took hold in 2020, however, at a stroke it deprived organisations of their visitor income, albeit temporarily. The precarious business model of the NTS, dependent on the driving up of revenue from ever-increasing numbers of visitors, was brutally exposed and its immediate response of mothballing most properties and making large numbers of staff redundant was sharply criticised. Charitable trusts such as the NTS sustain their property portfolio by generating income from visitors. Once the visitors disappear, the revenue is no longer sufficient for staffing and maintenance, although endowments and membership income should act as a cushion. The current series of global crises means a demoralising uncertainty about the future for heritage.

No country can consider its heritage in isolation, and in practice conservationists across the world are connected through international organisations and conferences, sharing best practice. In 1959 the International Centre for the Study of the Preservation and Restoration of Cultural Property (ICCROM) was founded in Rome, under the auspices of the Cultural Heritage Division of UNESCO. In the 1960s, three important international conservation NGOs were set up: Europa Nostra, a pan-European Federation for Cultural Heritage, was established in 1963; in 1965 the International Council on Monuments and Sites (ICOMOS) was set up, and in 1966 the International Council of Museums (ICOM) Committee for Conservation was set up in New York. All four of these organisations continue to campaign, research, formulate policy and disseminate information on matters of heritage and conservation at an international level and all have grown in size and influence since they were inaugurated. In October 1985, during the Second European Conference of Ministers responsible for the Architectural Heritage, the 'Monuments' Open Doors' initiative launched in France in 1984 was extended to a European level; in Scotland the Doors Open scheme is administered by the Scottish Civic Trust.

The World Monuments Fund is a private non-profit organisation founded in 1965. It sponsors an ongoing programme for the conservation of cultural heritage worldwide. There are 50 World Monuments Fund projects in the UK, mainly in England, but Castle Sinclair Girnigoe is the only one of MacGibbon and Ross's castles that is on their project list. In 2007 it received funding available for the immediate and long-term conservation of the castle. The work included the building of a bridge to facilitate construction and visitor access to the site, as well as emergency consolidation of the north-west and south-west corners of the complex.

The Zeitgeist

MacGibbon and Ross's pleas for the saving of Scotland's architectural heritage seem so unequivocally to have right on their side that it is difficult to take a step back and understand that their view was not – and, indeed, is not – a truth universally acknowledged. There were and are several players in the field of architectural heritage whose views do not chime with those of MacGibbon and Ross. From the mid 1980s, a reaction to the rise of heritage set in. Heritage was seen as having been appropriated by conservatism and the political forces of the Right, despite the New Right's rejection of sentimental views of the past, and came to represent, for some academics at least, pejorative and almost comic connotations. In 1979 Patrick Wright

returned to Britain from a five-year stay in North America and reported, 'I felt as if I had inadvertently stumbled into some sort of anthropological museum.'[1] He wrote his excoriating review of a country in decline because of its emphasis on heritage, *On Living in an Old Country*, published in 1985, which was followed in 1987 by the publication of Robert Hewison's *The Heritage Industry*.[2] Hewison argued that 'The growth of a heritage culture has led not only to a distortion of the past, but to a stifling of the culture of the present.'[3] Both books had a profound influence on academic political and social science, with their argument that heritage, as McCrone puts it, 'was used by the [Thatcher] regime to paper over some fundamental ideological and political cracks in the fabric of the state'.[4]

Postmodern debates over heritage in the past 25 years have been played out in the pages of Britain's broadsheet newspapers and literary and political magazines, distinguished by the witty ripostes and the sharp turn of phrase of a cast of male academics and cultural critics from the south of England. Many indulged a sneering anti-heritage polemic ('The British heritage industry is a loathsome collection of theme parks and dead values', claimed Tom Paulin in 1993[5]). Prince Charles had waded into the debate in 1984, in a speech at the 150th anniversary of the Royal Institute of British Architects. He launched a blistering attack on architects [who] 'have consistently ignored the feelings and wishes of the mass of ordinary people in this country'.[6] Although he was ridiculed by sections of the architectural community, his points about conservation and lack of consultation struck a chord with the public and the media. He was generally lauded by the media and went on to make a documentary film about architecture with the BBC, *A Vision of Britain*, in 1988. In 1989 an accompanying book was published,[7] in which he pointed the finger of blame for the destruction of the built heritage firmly at the architectural profession: 'The further I delve into the shadowy world of architecture, planning and property development the more I become aware of various interest groups . . . I believe it was the architectural establishment, or a powerful group within it, which made the running in the 50s and 60s. It was they who set the cultural agenda.'[8] The Prince represented the antithesis of everything that Mark Pawley, architectural critic, believed in. Writing in the *Architectural Review* in 1990 Pawley provocatively compared the impact of Prince Charles to that of Adolf Hitler: 'It can be seen that in both theory and practice there are strong parallels between the system of aesthetic and planning control in architecture that is evolving under Prince Charles' influence, and that which existed in the Third Reich.'[9]

At the start of the twenty-first century the debate was harnessed in a very public manner by three BBC *Restoration* programmes, broadcast in 2003, 2004 and 2006, which used a format where viewers could vote in a competition for the 'most deserving' historic building or village in need of restoration to receive the necessary finance. Each competing building was championed by a celebrity presenter. These programmes were enormously popular and resulted in spin-off books.[10] Patrick Wright, heritage historian, commented:

> There can be no doubt that *Restoration* has been a major success. The ratings show well over three million people watching most episodes. People have been phoning in their votes by the thousand. The programme website has been filled with animated debate, and the Restoration fund has pulled in fortunes. Destined to be restored with money from the BBC's hugely publicised appeal, the winning buildings can surely look forward to becoming the stars of a new kind of makeover show . . . which

concentrates on the historical building as a single endangered structure, and sees conservation as a wholly good cause: a secular version of church-going, which only a satanic monster would question.[11]

The debate rumbles on, though perhaps with less passion now, with King Charles still a keen building conservationist and activist, highlighting the mismatch between popular opinion and that of a sector of the architectural community. MacGibbon and Ross might not have been surprised. But they would probably have been surprised by the growth of community groups, such as the group that formed to save Portencross Castle in Ayrshire, from a private buyer. The group entered Portencross in the BBC Restoration competition. It did not win, but garnered enough publicity to help with funding and give an impetus to the goal of conserving the castle. Castle restoration is no longer confined to individuals; indeed, the repair grants given by HES now have a strong focus on community benefit as one of the main criteria for success. The Community Empowerment Act of 2015 means that local groups will potentially be able to request a transfer of the assets of some castles from HES or local authorities to groups who have developed ideas for the benefit of local communities, and it is not out of the question that some castles will be transferred out of HES's care in the future.

Protective Societies

Overtly political campaigning started before MacGibbon and Ross wrote *The Castellated and Domestic Architecture of Scotland,* when the Society for the Protection of Ancient Buildings (SPAB) was formed in 1877 by William Morris, and other members of the Pre-Raphaelite brotherhood, as a campaigning body. There is no evidence that either MacGibbon or Ross became members; at £1 annual subscription fee, equivalent to over £100 at today's rates, it was an expensive club to join and most of its activities were London-based. A Scottish branch was not formed until 1995. MacGibbon and Ross were enthusiastic Fellows of the Society of Antiquaries of Scotland and members of other local antiquarian societies and were committed supporters of these organisations. Both gave talks for antiquarian societies, led educational field trips and wrote scholarly articles for the journals. These were not campaigning organisations, however, although the antiquarian societies published occasional articles which highlighted castles at risk from neglect, vandalism and the weather, and *The Castellated and Domestic Architecture of Scotland* contains dozens of exhortations to protect specific buildings. In Edinburgh, the Cockburn Association was founded in 1875 to campaign for the improvement of Edinburgh and its neighbourhood. But it was not until the mid twentieth century that heritage protection societies began to proliferate in Scotland, with the specific aim of protecting the historic environment rather than simply recording it. The Architectural Heritage Society of Scotland was founded in 1956, the Scottish Civic Trust was founded in 1967 and dozens of offshoots, from Aberdeen Civic Society to the Water of Leith Conservation Trust, are now affiliated and campaign on local issues. The Scottish Castles Association, the Scottish Historic Buildings Trust and Historic Houses also campaign on historic building preservation issues. In recent years the internet, and social media in particular, has revolutionised the ways in which campaigning is carried out, with a potential reach of millions of users within hours of publication.

A New and Deadly Threat

MacGibbon and Ross could never have predicted the current global climate emergency. They did, however, understand that the elements can have a devastating impact on buildings. They describe the incursion of the sea upon St Andrews Castle: 'The rocks are of fine soft sandstone with seams of shale and limestone, the whole being of a rather friable nature, so that during the six centuries which have elapsed, since the first building was erected, their outline to the north and east has undergone great changes. Even in the century since Grose's time considerable alteration is apparent, the stretch of grass in the east shown in his sketch being now washed away except at the north corner' (3: 330). St Andrews Castle is still at risk from the sea, and from the changes in climate.

Ross, in his essay on Restoration (see Appendix) vividly describes the impact of rain and frost on historic buildings:

> Who can resist the glamour of light and shade seen amid the arches and pillars of the old Abbeys? But alas it is not always May. Visit the ruins on some day of furious rain and see the water streaming down both outside and inside the walls. Think what this means – every drop of rain is helping to eat out the substance of the wall – the sodden mass is laid hold of by frost and expansion moves it one way and the contraction which follows the thaw moves it the other way and thus blow after blow repeated with the constant changing of the weather will bring every unprotected building to the ground.

This century, Scotland's climate has become warmer and much wetter, with more frequent extreme weather events. Annual rainfall over Scotland has increased in recent decades to a level about 13% above the average for the early decades of the twentieth century. Flooding poses the greatest long-term risk to infrastructure from climate change, but the risks outlined by Ross have become a greater threat to unprotected buildings. There are also growing risks from heat, water scarcity, and slope instability caused by severe weather.

On 15 January 2018, the *Guardian* newspaper printed a report entitled 'Scotland's historic sites at high risk from climate change': 'Dozens of Scotland's most famous historic sites are at very high risk of being badly damaged by climate change and need urgent protection, an expert survey has found.' HES had just published its first ever *Climate Change Risk Assessment*, analysing the challenges faced by all of the properties in care. Nearly one-fifth of its sites face grave risks caused by floodwaters, rising tide and extreme weather events. 'Very high' levels of risk were recorded at Castle Sween, Dundonald Castle, Elcho Castle, Inchcolm Abbey, Kisimul Castle, Newark Castle, and Spynie Palace, all surveyed by MacGibbon and Ross. Also with very high inherent risk ratings (although mitigated by action and assessed as less likely) are Aberdour Castle, Blackness Castle, Broughty Castle, Castle Campbell, Doune Castle, Drumcoltran Tower, Dumbarton Castle, Dunstaffnage Castle, Edinburgh Castle, Huntingtower Castle, Kinnaird Head Castle Lighthouse and St Andrews Castle. Blackness Castle is somewhat protected by its own impressive curtain wall. However, the south-east corner of the site is at 'high' risk of coastal erosion and coastal flooding. To mitigate against these hazards a small retaining wall was constructed to protect the site. Island and coastal strongholds such as the castles of Kisimul and Newark and Inchcolm Abbey, situated on its tiny island in the Firth of Forth, and among the most picturesque sites in Scotland, may not survive for much longer.

A stark example of a castle directly impacted by recent severe weather is Abergeldie Castle, 'beautifully situated on the south bank of the Dee' (2: 54–55), the Highland residence of the Prince of Wales when MacGibbon and Ross visited. It was left hanging precipitously on the edge of the river after severe flooding washed away the supporting banking in January 2016 during Storm Frank. Over a period of five days and nights following the storm, tons of rock were deposited to shore up the banking and save the castle from being washed into the River Dee. Abergeldie is privately owned and resources were found to make the repairs needed. If the castle had been in state care, would the decision to expend resources in order to save the building have been the same?

The risk is urgent but resources to care for built heritage assets in care were already stretched prior to the climate change assessment. Difficult questions will have to be faced, priorities identified, and resources allocated according to the value we place on historic structures at risk. Many of the castles that are HES properties in care are in the collective ownership of the Scottish people, and currently supported by government funding, but they are in a minority. Privately owned buildings make up the majority of Scottish castles, many owned by wealthy landowners, but with a sizeable minority in the hands of embattled local authorities, small charitable trusts and private individuals without access to large resources.

Tomorrow's Heritage? The New Castle

The heyday of Scottish tower house building was from 1500 to 1600 and by the middle of the seventeenth century the tower house was beginning to fall out of fashion. By the middle of the eighteenth century, towers were being abandoned in droves for the much more convenient Adam-style mansions that were springing up. What MacGibbon and Ross called the Scottish style had come to an end. Or had it? Almost before fashion could declare the Scottish style outdated, Scots Baronial revivalism reared up, cheered on by Sir Walter Scott and made regally fashionable by Queen Victoria. Long before MacGibbon and Ross came

Satirical sketch of the 'Modern Castellated Mansion' by A. Welby Pugin, 1841.

along to survey the real thing, pastiche revivalism was already subjected to rude satire by A. Welby Pugin in a delightful sketch of 1841.

> What can be more absurd than houses built in what is termed the castellated style? Castellated architecture originated in the wants consequent on a certain state of society; of course the necessity of great strength, and the means of defence suited to the military tactics of the day, dictated to the builders of ancient castles the most appropriate style for their construction. Viewed as historical monuments, they are of surprising interest, but as models for our imitation they are worse than useless.[12]

A century later, the cartoonist Osbert Lancaster also lampooned Scots Baronial architecture. In every region in Scotland, buildings with flourishes of turrets and crenellations can be seen, from prisons to slurry towers.

Twentieth-century newbuild castles, whilst not common, have amongst their revivalist – and modernist – towers some architectural gems. Conservation architect Ian Begg, veteran restorer of ruined towers, designed himself a concrete tower house in Plockton, called Ravenscraig, in

Osbert Lancaster's fantasy Scottish castle.

1994: 'It's not old, of course. It's new. It's not a copy of an old building, but it does try to get the feel of one, because I'm very, very passionately interested in the tradition. The idea was to see if I could build something modern, meeting all building regulations, using modern materials, and yet get a feeling inside that this was a protecting structure, achieve that very strong sense of enclosure. I wanted it to look, or rather feel old inside.'[13]

Another contemporary tower house, Castle Dhu, is described by John Dunbar in the Buildings of Scotland series: 'An eye-catching tower house by Crichton Wood, 1998–2000. Strictly contemporary design, relying for its effect upon form and massing rather than replication of medieval detail. Three main storeys and a stepped L-plan, each element slightly dynamic . . . Rendered breeze block and brick, with gabled slate covered roofs.

The stair-turret rises to a glazed caphouse, and two of the salient angles of the main tower sprout metal-framed glass turrets to capture the magnificent views to S and E.'[14] Not far away, the young Basil Spence designed Broughton Place in the Borders in the 1930s as a baronial mansion for a wealthy doctor; it is now divided into apartments. Fortesk House in Forfar is an extraordinary and dramatic contemporary tower house of 1995, with two wings, four projecting turrets and a large conservatory built on the side.

Robert Lorimer's superb Arts and Crafts mansion in the Highlands, Ardkinglas, was completed for Sir Andrew Noble in 1907, 'a sensuous composition of "tumbling rhythms" that recalls late-sixteenth-century towerhouse and combines the spirit of vernacular building with concrete floors, a telephone exchange and hydro-electric power.'[15] More recently, a striking Modernist tower house, Corrour Lodge, was designed by Moshie Safdie and constructed in the Highlands from 1999 to 2003. Built of granite, steel and glass with pyramidal glass towers, it sits on the site of Sir John Stirling Maxwell's Edwardian lodge (burned out in 1942) on the bank of Loch Ossian and retains the alpine garden designed by him at the start of the twentieth century. The Royal Fine Arts Commission of Scotland noted that Corrour Lodge is 'destined to become one of the few examples of world-class 20th-century architecture in Scotland'.[16] It is rented out as holiday accommodation.

Conclusions

> There is no castle so strong that it cannot be overthrown by money.
>
> *Marcus Tullius Cicero*

None of us knows what the future holds for Scotland's castles; although we like to think that society can learn lessons from the past – surely the very raison d'etre of historical studies – the past is at best a very poor predictor of the future. It is clear that passion alone is not enough to save threatened buildings; it must be matched by economic resources. The next decades may not see such a positive future for ruined and derelict Scottish castles, particularly if recent economic changes mean a slow-down in financial markets and an ensuing atmosphere of austerity leads to changed priorities which negatively affect the care of historic buildings. There are so many competing demands on the public purse – the arts, health, education, care for the elderly, prisons, the justice system, the natural environment – that it is important that built heritage makes its case for funding cogently and persistently. Scotland is one of the world's richest nations in terms of the historic built environment; it is also one of the world's richest nations economically. We can surely marshal the resources and the imagination to cherish and protect the country's built heritage, given the political will.

We can summon up the spirit of MacGibbon and Ross quite readily, as they have left us so many clues as to their values. They cared deeply about the historic buildings of Scotland. They were pragmatists, willing to tolerate changes in historic buildings if this meant giving a building a future. They did not approve of wholesale change and especially not of the destruction of ancient aspects of a building in order to 'modernise' it, but they tolerated change and even contributed to it – e.g. at Inch Castle in Edinburgh, for which they drew up plans for intrusive extensions. Like most of us, they showed some evidence of internal contradictions, but as architectural historians they were steadfast, consistent and transparent in their beliefs and passionate in their commitment to saving threatened historic buildings. MacGibbon and Ross conclude Volume 5 with an essay on masters of work, master masons and architects:

In recent times many examples of this process might be cited; but perhaps no more striking illustration could be selected than the building of Abbotsford by Sir Walter Scott. No doubt Sir Walter conferred with Blore and other architects; but the story of the growth of the house, as narrated in the Life of the proprietor, shows that it owes all its characteristic and prominent features to Sir Walter himself, working in conjunction with his master mason from Darnick. (5: 569)

This is a rather humble admission from two architects, i.e. that total surrender to the will of the client is sometimes necessary, although there is a marked lack of admiration for the house itself, perhaps a damning with faint praise. Abbotsford has its detractors[17] and is certainly idiosyncratic in its style and expression, but the point MacGibbon and Ross make is that the individual can make a difference. They tell the stories of many individuals who made a difference by conserving and cherishing castles. They, too, are individuals who made a difference. Their legacy has underpinned our understanding and knowledge of Scottish castles and has been the springboard for research and interest, a source of reference and an inspiration for castle lovers and restorers for the past 130 years.

Postscript

At the time of going to press, HES has closed or partially closed 79 of its properties, many of which were surveyed by MacGibbon and Ross, while it surveys and assesses potentially dangerous high-level masonry at significant buildings such as St Andrews Castle and Jedburgh Abbey. The causes of the deterioration of the fabric of these historic buildings are a mixture of longstanding underinvestment in repairs and the ravages of severe weather, accelerated by climate change. The HES website states:

> We are taking proactive action now to assess the nature and scale of the immediate challenge, and to explore a range of solutions and options. It is inevitable our approach to protecting historic buildings will have to change – we need to reimagine how we manage these historic and much-loved places. A range of solutions is needed, including repairs, investment and new and innovative interventions. In some cases reduced physical access and accepting the natural process of decay will need to be considered.

Ian Baxter, Vice-chair of the Built Environment Forum Scotland, has provocatively suggested that we may need to enable 'a good death' for some properties,[18] and David Mitchell, HES Director of Conservation, has publicly stated 'I think the days of us just looking at these sites as historic in their own right, like museum pieces in the landscape, have gone . . . some sites are simply reaching the end of their lifespan.'[19] What is urgently needed is a national debate about the future for the historic built environment, with compelling arguments and practical solutions from those who do not accept the inevitability of such decline in a country that truly values its heritage. Surely MacGibbon and Ross would be among them.

Thomas Ross's Essay
on Restoration

————

The following essay by Thomas Ross is on the ecclesiastical and castellated buildings of Europe erected from the beginning of the twelfth century to the end of the fifteenth century (but mainly the ecclesiastical ones). It is from MS 694, the second last document, and is undated. It is signed Thomas Ross (in a different pen from other documents). The handwriting is firm, attractive and easy to read, whereas many of the documents in this manuscript box are in very shaky handwriting. It therefore seems safe to conclude that it was written before he was elderly.

The word Restoration as applied to these buildings is used with various shades of meaning. It is sometimes a term of contempt and sometimes a term of praise with various shades between depending very much on the temperament of the individual. These regard it as preservation of the building and those as the destruction of its interest and beauty. So sharp is this conflict of opinion that many prudent men eschew the word and speak of *preservation* and *repair* when their object is Restoration . . .

Then, as individuals, there are two classes of men: the Restorers and the anti-Restorers. In the former class there are those who are strictly conservative who would alter nothing of the old work which is in a condition to endure, and others who will take any liberty to cut and carve as they choose. It will probably be admitted that this latter kind of restoration is not so frequent as it once was. The creed of the anti-Restorer is to leave things very much as they are, cement the tops of the walls, and with the same material fill up all cracks, rents and joints. Both classes have wrought much evil which it is difficult to apportion justly between them . . .

Now the purpose of these two parties is so far the same – to transmit these matchless and unique buildings to posterity, and the question comes to be, how is this to be best done? To accomplish this end something must be done. To leave them alone is to ensure their fall, later or sooner.

Many a one wandering amid these ruins on a bright summer day when nature has clothed every vent and cranny with bright and cheerful colour and seems to have taken the venerable ruins into her special care, then has the writer seen men and especially women become intoxicated with the beauty of the scene and small wonder need be expressed thereat. Scenes such as this make the Anti-Restorer and confirm those who are so already. Who can resist the glamour of light and shade seen amid the arches and pillars of the old Abbeys? But alas it is not always May. Visit the ruins on some day of furious rain and see the water streaming down both outside and inside the walls. Think what this means – every drop of rain is helping to eat out the substance of the wall – the sodden mass is laid hold of by frost and expansion moves it one way and the contraction which follows the thaw moves it the other way and thus blow after blow repeated with the constant changing of the weather will bring very unprotected building to the ground. And for this there is only one effectual remedy – put a protecting roof over it. All other schemes are mere makeshifts. It is quite true that the roof is new, but what of that if it saves what is considered worthy of saving and restores an ancient Xane(?) to its original and sacred purpose? Surely this is a greater gain to man than to leave the walls to bide the bitter pelting of the storm. It is surely a curious triumph of the illusion of time that the restoration of the Temple destroyed yesterday begun today is approved of by all men – while the one destroyed many yester-

days ago is because its restoration has been delayed to remain hereafter untouched. Even Mr Ruskin who . . . writes of restoration 'The thing is lie from beginning to end', and even as something 'loathsome' seems to regard a roof as necessary for the preservation of a building and conveniently supposes one to exist in his imaginary restoration and he advises that it be kept in good order and so ensure the preservation of the building. But what if it has no roof? To deny it the advantage of a new one is to hand the building over to lingering decay.

The admiration of ruins as such is a new idea and would not have been understood two centuries ago. Sir Walter Scott gave it an impetus when he embellishes his landscape in the 'Lady of the Lake' with fancy towers and bowers and 'on yonder meadow far away the ruins of an Abbey grey'. This quickly bore fruit and the embellishing of ruins became an art, the professors of which trimmed up real ruins to make the picturesque and romantic, and even built new ones, and the present day veneration of ruins is the lingering remnant of this diseased state of mind. How much healthier is the mental condition displayed by Carlyle's hero Abbot Sampson [sic]. 'Many are the roofs' we are told, 'once thatched with reeds which he caused to be covered with tiles; or if they were Churches, probably with lead. For all ruinous incomplete things, buildings or other, were an eyesorrow to the man.'

Notes

Introduction to Part 1

1 The Ross Collection, National Library of Scotland MS 694, p. 1.
2 Miles Glendinning and Aonghus MacKechnie (2004) *Scottish Architecture*, Thames and Hudson, London, p. 160.
3 E.A. Horsman, ed. (1953) *The Diary of Alfred Domett 1872–1885*, Oxford University Press, London.
4 Queen Victoria, *Leaves from the Journal of our Lives in the Highlands 1848 to 1861*, entry for Saturday 3 September 1842.
5 Colin McWilliam (1978) *The Buildings of Scotland: Lothian*, Penguin, London, p. 301.
6 Stuart Eydmann, Richard Jaques and Charles McKean (2008) *West Lothian: An Illustrated Architectural Guide*, Rutland Press, London.
7 William Morris et al. (1877) *The SPAB Manifesto*, Society for the Protection of Ancient Buildings. Until recently, SPAB members were required to sign up to agreement with the manifesto.
8 See Appendix for the full text.
9 'William Burn', Dictionary of Scottish Architects. Available at http://www.scottisharchitects.org.uk/.
10 Thomas Ross Obituary, *The Scotsman*, 12 December 1930.
11 David Walker (1984) 'The Architecture of MacGibbon and Ross: The Background to the Books', in D.J. Breeze (ed.), *Studies in Scottish Antiquity*, John Donald, Edinburgh, p. 415.
12 Ibid., p. 431.
13 John Gifford, Colin McWilliam and David Walker (1984) *The Buildings of Scotland*, Penguin, London, p. 585. The entry on Inch House was written by John Gifford.
14 Walker, 'The Architecture of MacGibbon and Ross', p. 437.

Chapter 1

1 The Dean of Guild Court was a powerful body responsible for enforcing the burgh's building regulations.
2 Terence Reeves-Smyth and Richard Oram, eds (2003) *Avenues to the Past*, Ulster Architectural Heritage Society, p. 321.
3 'Proceedings of the Society of Arts for Scotland', *Edinburgh Philosophical Journal*, vol. 20 (1838), p. 400.
4 Jessie (1840), Charles (1842), Margaret (1844), James (1846), John (1848) and Agnes (1851).
5 William C.A. Ross (1934) *The Royal High School*, Oliver and Boyd, Edinburgh, p. 97.
6 Ibid., p. 59.
7 Robert D. Anderson (2003) *The University of Edinburgh: An Illustrated History*, Edinburgh University Press, Edinburgh, p. 111.
8 Ibid.
9 'John Lessels', Dictionary of Scottish Architects. Available at http://www.scottisharchitects.org.uk/.
10 Scott got to know Burn as the architect of the Edinburgh Tanfield Gas Works, of which Scott was a director. Scott secured the patronage of the Duke of Buccleuch for Burn, leading to the commission for major alterations at Drumlanrig Castle.
11 David MacGibbon's senior assistant colleagues in Burn's office were Burn's nephew John Macvicar Anderson (1835–1915), John Honeyman (1831–1914), John Wornham Penfold (1828–1909), Richard Norman Shaw (1831–1912) and William Eden Nesfield (1835–1888), all of whom became productive and distinguished architects in the second half of the nineteenth century, a cohort of great talent and influence.
12 Margaret H. Sanderson (1992) *Robert Adam and Scotland: Portrait of an Architect*, HMSO, Edinburgh, p. 37.

13 David Walker (1984) 'The Architecture of MacGibbon and Ross: The Background to the Books', in D.J. Breeze (ed.), *Studies in Scottish Antiquity*, John Donald, Edinburgh, p. 394.

14 Ibid., p. 401.

15 In the early 1780s, when the Adam brothers faced serious financial difficulties, 'They looked to speculative building and town planning schemes to revive their fortunes, materially and artistically' (Sanderson, *Robert Adam and Scotland*, p. 99).

16 Ibid., p. 415.

17 Richard Saville (1996) *Bank of Scotland, A History 1695–1995*, Edinburgh University Press, Edinburgh, p. 423.

18 Collecting the eggs and nests of wild birds, although illegal in the UK since 1954 and regarded with some revulsion nowadays, was in Victorian times a wholesome hobby for children. Doubtless it was felt that William Peter and Rachel were engaged in worthwhile nature study when they went off with a family servant to prop a ladder against a sandbank and search for nests. Their parents surely were unaware that, as *The Scotsman* reported further on in the report, a few years previously a girl came by her death in exactly the same place and under the same circumstances.

19 The five churches were: Sweetheart Abbey, Dundrennan Abbey, Glenluce Abbey, Lincluden College and Whithorn Priory. The frontispiece of *The Five Great Churches of Galloway*, which was published by the Ayrshire and Galloway Archaeological Association, attributes both David MacGibbon and Thomas Ross as authors. In the copy held at RIAS, Thomas Ross has added a typically self-deprecating handwritten note: 'For this book I wrote the description of Lincluden College and made all the drawings and nothing else. Thomas Ross.'

Chapter 2

1 MS 88, University of Dundee Archives.

2 Ibid.

3 Letter from Robert T. Skinner, mathematician and antiquarian, 'In Tribute to The Late Dr Thomas Ross', *The Scotsman*, 5 December 1930.

4 David Walker (1984) 'The Architecture of MacGibbon and Ross. The Background to the Books', in D.J. Breeze (ed.), *Studies in Scottish Antiquity*, John Donald, Edinburgh, p. 415 – from information told to him by Ronald Cant.

5 Ernest Ralph Vernon (1860) *A Narrative of the Royal Scottish Volunteer Review in Holyrood Park on the Seventh of August 1860 with a List of the Names of all the Volunteers who were Present on the Occasion*, Edinburgh.

6 Thomas Ross Obituary, *The Scotsman*, 12 December 1930.

7 The late Miss Elizabeth Hume Ross (1969) 'James McLaren, Schoolmaster', *The Book of the Old Edinburgh Club*, vol. 33 part 1, p. 30.

8 Personal communication from Ralph Sutherland, John Sutherland's great grandson, 25 December 2018.

9 Personal communication, David Walker, 13 January 2019.

10 For a full account of the politics involved, see Peter Savage (1980) *Lorimer and the Edinburgh Craft Designers*, Steve Savage, Glasgow, pp. 84–85.

11 *The Scotsman*, 15 September 1915.

12 'Description of the Plans by Thomas Ross', *Proceedings of the Society of Antiquaries of Scotland*, vol. 36 (1901), p. 203.

13 The Ross Collection, National Library of Scotland MS 694.

14 Thomas Ross Obituary, *Proceedings of the Society of Antiquaries of Scotland*, vol. 66 (1931–32), p. 8.

15 *The Scotsman*, 7 December 1930.

Chapter 3

1 Charles McKean (2001) *The Scottish Chateau: The Country House of Renaissance Scotland*, Sutton, Stroud.

2 We are fortunate in the twenty-first century in having online access to the National Library of Scotland (NLS) maps collection in digitised form, which makes it possible to zoom in and check details of the symbols of towers and castles surveyed by Pont, to a degree of magnified clarity almost impossible for the naked eye – even aided by good spectacles – to match. It is a source of wonder that Pont was able to put such detail into his minute drawings.

3 Current scholarship places Gordon as an editor and embellisher of Pont's original notes, along with material from other sources. This was done for the publisher Blaeu in the 1640s (information from the National Library of Scotland website).

4 In 1628 Lithgow was entertained for some days at Brodick Castle in Arran by the Marquess of Hamilton, and afterwards he journeyed through Galloway and Dumfriesshire, and thence northward to Caithness and Kirkwall in Orkney, gathering material for a work called 'Lithgowes Surueigh of Scotland', which was never published.

5 'The cornice and parapet, with the angle bartizans shown in the general view (Fig. 407) are partly suggested restorations; but for these the data are obtained from Slezer's views, which show that the gables had crow-steps and angle bartizans, and that the eastern staircase turret had a conical roof in his time (1693)' (1: 470).

6 James Crawford, Lesley Ferguson and Kristina Watson (2010) *Victorian Scotland*, RCAHMS, Edinburgh, p. 116.

7 Thomas Ross recorded, in his history of the Architectural Institute of Scotland, that 'Mr Billings made a proposal to the Institute to aid him in raising a sum of £1500 to be placed to his credit, unfettered in any way except for the accomplishment of the stated object, viz. the further illustration of the *Ecclesiastical and Baronial Antiquities of Scotland*. As is well known nothing came out of this, so that his four previously published splendid volumes remain as his sole contribution on this subject.' NLS MS 694, pp. 222–23.

8 R.W. Billings (1901) *Baronial and Ecclesiastical Antiquities of Scotland*, Introduction by Rowand Anderson.

9 Ibid.

10 Sam McKinstrey (1991) *Rowand Anderson: The Premier Architect of Scotland*, Edinburgh University Press, Edinburgh, p. 23.

11 McKean, *The Scottish Chateau*, p. 35.

12 Billings, *Baronial and Ecclesiastical Antiquities of Scotland*, vol. 1, p. 43.

13 Billings sometimes incorporated artistic greenery to hide areas of the buildings obscured by later additions which he had left out.

14 Quoted in Christopher Woodward (2002) *In Ruins*, Vintage, London, p. 13.

Chapter 4

1 Audrey Dakin, Miles Glendinning and Aonghus MacKechnie, eds (2011) *Scotland's Castle Culture*, John Donald, Edinburgh, p. xxiii.

2 Janet Brennan-Inglis (2014) 'The Castles of Dumfries and Galloway Described by MacGibbon and Ross: What Has Become of Them Since?', *Transactions of the Dumfriesshire and Galloway Natural History and Antiquarian Society*, vol. 88, pp. 57–78.

3 Geoffrey Stell (2011) 'Foundations of a Castle Culture: Pre-1603', in Dakin et al., *Scotland's Castle Culture*, p. 9.

4 A copy of this was lent to them by a Mrs Edith Robertson from Cleveland, Ohio, who had written an article in *The Century Magazine* in 1890 about the artist, 'Archibald Robertson, an Aberdeenshire artist, who went to New York in 1791, and, remaining there, became one of the "pioneers of American art"' (5: 329).

5 They carried bicycles with them on some trips, but the 'safety bicycle', which replaced the high-wheeled penny farthing design, was not invented until 1885 and pneumatic tyres not until 1888, so that it was around 1890 before an easy and comfortable two-wheeled ride was in widespread use.

6 The Ordnance Survey 6-inch maps of Scotland were published between 1843 and 1882.

7 From Robert Burns (1789) 'On the Late Captain Grose's Peregrinations through Scotland: Collecting the Antiquities of that Kingdom'.

8 'David MacGibbon', Dictionary of Scottish Architects. Available at: http://www.scottisharchitects.org.uk/.

9 Riccarton Junction, in the county of Roxburghshire, was a railway village and station. In its heyday it had 118 residents and its own school, post office and grocery store. The station was an interchange between the Border Counties Railway branch to Hexham and the North British Railway's Border Union Railway. It opened on 2 July 1862 and closed on 6 January 1969.

10 Charles McKean (2001) *The Scottish Chateau: The Country House of Renaissance Scotland*, Sutton, Stroud, p. 4.

11 I am grateful to Richard Agnew for pointing out that MacGibbon and Ross 'invented' an extra house at Auchinleck (3: 497) and that they missed the fact that Sanquhar Tolbooth was designed by William Adam.

12 Anna Ritchie (2012) 'From Colonsay to Whithorn: The Work of a 19th-century Antiquary, William Galloway', *Proceedings of the Society of Antiquaries of Scotland*, vol. 142, pp. 435–65.

13 Only one woman is acknowledged in the text, in the entries for the castles of Dunyveg and Lochgorme on Islay: 'we have to thank Mrs Forbes Irvine of Drum for the use of the sketches from which our illustrations of these castles are made' (5: 296).

14 Obituary of Thomas Ross, *The Scotsman*, 12 December 1930.

15 A popular set of volumes celebrating architecture was Walter Hutchinson's *Britain Beautiful*, published by Hazell, Watson and Viney in 1924–26. These are lavishly illustrated with maps and colour plates of places of interest. In his Introduction Hutchinson wrote: 'Wood blocks and engraving have become prehistoric and the Publishers feel that the transformation of photography as a science into photography as an art deserves commemoration by the appearance of a work . . . in a really worthy form' (pp. 1–2). The two-tone photographs look rather bizarre to modern eyes, featuring abbeys in a lurid shade of green, castles tinted blue and numerous ancient monuments in sepia. However, the watercolour artist is still recognised as having a contribution to make, with a dozen full colour plates in each volume, specially commissioned for the series.

16 Nigel Tranter (1970) *The Fortified House in Scotland*, vol. 5, Mercat Press, Edinburgh, p. 7.

17 Ian Grimble (1984) *Castles of Scotland*, BBC, London, Introduction.

18 McKean, *The Scottish Chateau*, p. 5.

19 Charles McKean (2006) 'A Scottish Problem with Castles', *Historical Research*, vol. 79, no. 204, p. 168.

20 Schomberg Scott (1976) 'Castles and Country Houses' in R. Prentice (ed.), *The National Trust for Scotland Guide*, W.W. Norton, Edinburgh, p. 37. Schomberg Scott himself lived in a tower house, Northfield at Prestonpans.

21 Nicholas Fairbairn (1987) *A Life Is Too Short: Autobiography,* vol. 1, Quartet Books, London, p. 184.

22 Lesley Astaire, Roderick Martine and Fritz Von der Schulenberg (1987) *Living in Scotland*, Thames and Hudson, London, p. 110.

23 Stewart Cruden (1960) *The Scottish Castle*, Thomas Nelson, Edinburgh, p. vii.

24 McKean, *The Scottish Chateau,* pl. 4.

25 David Walker (2000) 'The Adaptation and Restoration of Tower Houses: An Historical Review from the Reign of Charles II to the Present', in Robert Clow (ed.), *Restoring Scotland's Castles*, John Smith and Son, Glasgow, p. 1.

26 Charles Wemyss (2014) *The Noble Houses of Scotland*, Prestel, London.

27 Joachim Zeune (1992) *The Last Scottish Castles,* Marie L.Leidorf, Buch am Erlbach, p. 21.

28 Richard Oram (2008) 'Castles, Concepts and Contexts: Castle Studies in Scotland in Retrospect and Prospect', *Château Gaillard*, vol. 23, p. 349.

29 McKean, *The Scottish Chateau*, p. 1.

30 Stell, 'Foundations of a Castle Culture', pp. 4–5.

31 Ibid., p. 5.

32 Sir John Stirling Maxwell (1938) *Shrines and Homes of Scotland*, Alexander MacLehose and Co., London p. 3.

33 Nigel Tranter (1965) *The Fortified House in Scotland*, vol. 1, Mercat Press, Edinburgh, preface.

34 Nigel Tranter (1970) *The Fortified House in Scotland*, vol. 5, Mercat Press, Edinburgh, p. 6.

35 Nigel Tranter (1966) *The Fortified House in Scotland*, vol. 2, Mercat Press, Edinburgh, p. 6.

36 Mike Salter (1993–95) *The Castles of Scotland Series* (5 vols).

37 Alastair M.T. Maxwell-Irving (2000) *The Border Towers of Scotland: The West March,* Alastair M.T. Maxwell-Irving, Blairlogie.

38 Nikolaus Pevsner, 24 November 1959; see 'A Brief History of Pevsner's Buildings of Scotland Series', 20 October 2016. Available at: https://yalebooksblog.co.uk/2016/10/ 20/a-brief-history-of-pevsners-buildings-of-scotland-series/.

Introduction to Part 3

1 Catherine Maxwell-Stuart (2005) 'Making it Pay – the Challenge of Conserving and Profiting from the Family Home', paper presented at the HHA/HS conference in the Scottish Parliament, 25 November 2005

Chapter 5

1 H. Gordon Slade (1972) 'Balbithan House, Aberdeenshire', *Proceedings of the Society of Antiquaries of Scotland*, vol. 104, pp. 257–67.

2 Up until 1890, there were 34 County Councils, some of whose areas had evolved rather chaotically over the centuries from the stewartries and sheriffdoms of mediaeval Scotland. In 1890, these were reorganised from 34 into 33 County Councils, removing the worst of the irregularities. This system remained in place until 1975, when a dramatic re-structuring took place; 12 Scottish Regions were created, with those on the mainland sub-divided into between 3 and 19 Districts. In 1996, the system of counties was reintroduced, replacing the 12 regions with 32 Council areas – some reflect the 1890 counties, while others were based on the 1975 Regions or Districts.

3 Throughout this chapter, MacGibbon and Ross's terms and spellings are used – for example, Midlothianshire instead of Midlothian, Drumcoltern instead of Drumcoltran, Dumbartonshire instead of Dunbartonshire.

4 The statistics given are those that relate *only* to the castles that MacGibbon and Ross surveyed; these represent about half of the castles currently extant in Scotland.

5 Sir Walter Scott popularised the term, in *Tales of a Grandfather*, to describe the last major conflict between England and Scotland 1543–51.

6 Sir Herbert Maxwell (1909) *The Story of the Tweed*, London.

7 It is not clear whether Buckholm Tower was roofed or not. MacGibbon and Ross say it was, but they had their information second hand from Mr W. Anderson. There is a sketch of 1893 on Canmore from J.D. Finlayson's Sketchbook showing it roofless, but also an Edwardian postcard showing it roofed. It was said to be 'recently ruined' in 1933.

8 Alastair Maxwell-Irving (2014) *The Border Towers of Scotland*, Vol. 2, Alastair Maxwell-Irving, Blairlogie, p. 146.

9 Crosbie Towers entry on the Buildings at Risk Register website: buildingsatrisk.org.uk.

10 Or it could be Magdalens House (2: 545), also opposite Northfield House.

11 David MacGibbon had been apprenticed to John Lessels from 1849 to 1851.

12 David W. Walker and Matthew Woodworth (2015) *Aberdeenshire: North and Moray*, Yale University Press, London, p. 1.

13 Maurice Lindsay (1986) *The Castles of Scotland*, Constable, London, p. 394.

14 George Watson (1998) 'A Second Glance at Brims Castle', *Caithness Field Bulletin*, April edition.

Chapter 6

1 Despite his destructive career, Charles Brand lived to a great age – he died just short of his 99th year.

2 Marcus Binney et al. (1980) *Lost Houses of Scotland,* Save Britain's Heritage, London, p. 10.

3 George Scott-Moncrieff (1939) *The Lowlands of Scotland*, B.T. Batsford, London, p. 66.

4 Ian Gow (2006) *Scotland's Lost Houses*, Aurum Press, London, list in Appendix. Houses gutted or only partially demolished have not been counted among the 280; these were all lost entirely.

5 Earlier in the entry they say, 'It was probably built after the English invasion in 1544, when Hertford landed his troops at Granton, and carried destruction far and near' (2: 185).

6 'How Granton Lost its Castle', *Edinburgh Life,* May/June 2016, pp. 16–18.

7 Quoted in the Canmore entry on Gladney House. Available at: https://canmore.org.uk/site/52903/kirkcaldy-bute-wynd-gladney-house.

8 The Ross Collection, NLS MS 717/66.

9 Sir Herbert Maxwell (1909) *The Story of the Tweed*, James Nisbet and Co., London.

10 James Crawford, Lesley Ferguson and Kristina Watson (2010) *Victorian Scotland*, RCAHMS, Edinburgh, p. 118.

11 Gow, *Scotland's Lost Houses*, p. 181.

12 George Birkbeck Hill (1890) *Footsteps of Dr. Johnson*, Samson Low, London, p. 301.

13 Gow, *Scotland's Lost Houses*, p. 13.

14 BBC broadcast interview 'Edinburgh Castle, Scotland: The One O'Clock Gun', with Nicki Scott of HES, 11 November 2014. Available at: https://www.bbc.co.uk/sounds/play/po2blp3c.

15 HES Statement of Significance, *Blackness Castle* (2013).

16 HES Statement of Significance, *Inchcolm Abbey* (2011).

17 Marcus Dean and Mary Miers (1990) *Scotland's Endangered Houses*, Save Britain's Heritage, London, p. 5.

18 J. Gerrard (1998) 'The Scottish Civic Trust', in Lesley Borley (ed.), *Dear Maurice: Culture and Identity in Late 20th-Century Scotland,* Tuckwell Press, East Linton, p. 161.

19 The story as told by the architect L. Rolland in November 1977 is reprinted in 'Rossend Castle'. Available at: http://www.brand-dd.com/burntisland/rossend2.html.

20 Nigel Tranter (1965) *The Fortified House in Scotland,* Vol. 1, Mercat Press, Edinburgh, p. 7.

21 Eric Jamieson (2005) 'Cramond Tower', *SCA Newsletter*, February 2005.

22 Marcus Binney and Marianne Watson-Smyth (1991) *SAVE Britain's Heritage Action Guide*, Collins and Brown, London, p. 54.

23 Hugh MacDonald (1860) *Rambles Round Glasgow*, Robert Lindsay, Glasgow.

24 John Coyne (2000) 'The restoration of Tilquhillie Castle', in Clow, *Restoring Scotland's Castles*, p. 71.

25 Thomas Ross, September 1878 Notes on Balvaird Castle. FC/CS/7/3/6/15 Fife Archives.

26 James Charles Roy (2003) *The Fields of Athenry*, Westview Press, Oxford, p. 6.

27 The farmers who purchased Wigg Farm a few years ago told me that shortly after they moved in, their young son came running inside, shouting, 'Come and see what I've found!' The family were amazed to find a ruined mansion near the farmyard, which had not been listed in the sale particulars, and which they had not previously spotted through the high undergrowth.

28 From the Derelict Places website. Available at: .

29 John Gifford (2007) *The Buildings of Scotland: Perth and Kinross*, Yale University Press, London, p. 394.

30 John Dickson (1894) *The Ruined Castles of Midlothian*, R.R. Sutherland, Edinburgh, pp. 223–24.

31 K.L.S. Murdoch (1991) 'Methven Castle', *Journal of the Perthshire Society of Natural Science*, vol. 16, pp. 6–13.

32 Helen Brown (2008) 'Wanted: Laird to Take on the Ultimate Doer-upper', *The Independent*, 5 March 2008.

33 A friend of Ian Fleming and supposedly the model for James Bond.

34 Gerald Warner (2004) 'High Time to Demolish the Ruin that is Historic Scotland', *The Scotsman*, 22 August 2004.

35 Minute of Historic Scotland Board meeting to discuss Castle Tioram, August 2006.

36 Available at: http://data.historic-scotland.gov.uk/pls/htmldb/f?p=2920:15:0::NO::CASTLE:3417.

37 Alastair Maxwell-Irving (2014) *The Border Towers of Scotland*, Vol. 2, Alastair Maxwell-Irving, Blairlogie, p. 259.

Chapter 7

1 John Ruskin (1889) *The Seven Lamps of Architecture*, George Allen, London, p. 196.

2 John Gifford (1988) *The Buildings of Scotland: Fife*, Pevsner Architectural Guides, Yale University Press, London, p. 199.

3 Ranald MacInnes (1996) '"Rubblemania": Ethic and Aesthetic in Scottish Architecture', *Journal of Design History*, vol. 9, no. 3.

4 Lorna Martin (2002) 'Father, Daughter Hunted by Heritage Watchdog', *The Herald,* 10 August 2002.

5 See appendix for full text.

6 Brown 'Wanted: Laird to Take on the Ultimate Doer-upper'.

7 Maurice Lindsay (1986) *The Castles of Scotland*, Constable, London, p. 102.

8 For an extensive and fascinating history of Broughty Castle, see Sir Francis Mudie, David Walker and Iain MacIvor (1970), *Broughty Castle*, Abertay Historical Society.

9 'Kirkhill House' entry, Canmore website. Available at: https://canmore.org.uk/site/61989/kirkhill-house.

10 Lindsay, *The Castles of Scotland*, p. 268.

11 John Gifford, Colin McWilliam and David Walker
   (1984) *The Buildings of Scotland,* Penguin Books,
   Edinburgh, p. 497.
12 Ibid., p. 498.
13 Gerard Laing (1974) *Kinkell: The Reconstruction of a
   Scottish Castle,* Ardulllie House, Dingwall, p. 129.
14 Ibid., p. 129.
15 Ibid., p. 80.
16 Stuart Eydmann, Richard Jaques and Charles McKean
   (2008) *West Lothian: An Illustrated Architectural Guide,*
   Rutland Press, Edinburgh.
17 Anna Keay and Caroline Stanford (2015) *Landmark:
   A History of Britain in 50 Buildings,* Frances Lincoln,
   London, p. 9.
18 Alastair M.T. Maxwell-Irving (2000) *The Border Towers
   of Scotland: The West March,* Alastair M.T. Maxwell-
   Irving, Blairlogie, p. 191.
19 Oliver Hilson (1927) 'Fatlips Castle in Roxburghshire',
   Border Magazine, vol. 32, October 1927.
20 Graham Carson (2000) 'Rusco Tower', in Clow,
   Restoring Scotland's Castles, p. 165.
21 Marilyn Brown (2015) *Scotland's Lost Gardens,*
   RCAHMS, Edinburgh, gives a comprehensive
   overview of the major historic gardens of Scotland
   that have disappeared.
22 Theodore Ziolkowski (1998), *The View from the Tower:
   Origins of an Antimodernist Image,* Princeton University
   Press, Princeton, NJ, p. 9.
23 Ibid., p. 49.
24 *Birmingham Magazine,* September 1997.
25 Laing, *Kinkell,* p. 169.
26 Ibid., p. 150.
27 Peter Savage (1980) *Lorimer and the Edinburgh Craft
   Designers,* Steve Savage, Edinburgh, pp. 2–3.
28 Susan Cromarty (1999) 'Castle of Dreams', *SCOTS
   Magazine,* February 1999.

Chapter 8

1 As at early 2020, before the Covid pandemic.
2 *Scotland's Ancient Heritage* (1934) Special Summer
   Number of *The SMT Magazine,* Foreword.
3 Patrick Cormack (1978) *Heritage in Danger,* Quartet
   Books, London, p. 17.
4 Statements of Significance for all HES properties in
   care are available online.
5 John Gifford, Colin McWilliam and David Walker
   (1984) *The Buildings of Scotland,* Penguin Books,
   Edinburgh, p. 88.
6 HES (2012) Statement of Significance, Edinburgh
   Castle, The Great Hall.
7 HES (2017) Statement of Significance, Threave Castle.
8 Notes Describing Balvaird Castle by Thomas Ross
   FC/CS/7/3/6/15 Fife Archives.
9 HES (2018) Statement of Significance, Aberdour
   Castle, p. 2.

10 Ross's notes on Balvaird, p. 27.
11 Douglas Bremner (2001) *For the Benefit of the Nation,*
   NTS, Edinburgh, p. 298.
12 HES looks after Threave Castle and Crookston Castle,
   both scheduled monuments and consolidated ruins,
   on behalf of the NTS.
13 Bremner, *For the Benefit of the Nation,* p. 1.
14 Response to a question submitted by a members'
   Group in an NTS virtual question and answer session
   June 2020.
15 Michael Davis (1996) *Scots Baronial,* Spindrift,
   Ardrishaig, p. 57.
16 Gifford et al., *The Buildings of Scotland: Edinburgh,*
   p. 585.
17 Sir Walter Scott (1814) *Waverley,* Chapter 12 'The
   March'. The Tate Gallery website has a great deal of
   information on the association between Scott and
   Turner.
18 The jougs is an iron collar chained to a wall, used in
   mediaeval Scotland as an instrument of punishment
   to shame offenders publicly.
19 Bruce de Trotter (1901) *Galloway Gossip,* Courier and
   Herald Printers, p. 115.
20 Lady Glamis (1900) *Glamis Castle.* Available at:
   https://electricscotland.com/historic/castles/glamis.
   htm.
21 'Glamis Castle, Relic of Dark Ages', *San Francisco Call,*
   vol. 87, 27 May 1901, p. 178.
22 Letter to Lord Montagu, 28 June 1825, quoted in
   Sir Walter Scott (1890) *The Journal of Sir Walter Scott,*
   David Douglas, Edinburgh, preface.
23 Dorothy Wordsworth, *Recollections of a Tour Made
   in Scotland 1803,* entry for 18 September, in E.
   De Selincourt (1952), *Journals of Dorothy Wordsworth,*
   2 vols, Macmillan, London, Vol. 2, 1952,
24 James Brown (2007) 'Mackintosh's Ayrshire
   Connections, Architectural and Familial', *Charles
   Rennie Mackintosh Society Journal,* vol. 92,
   pp. 12–13.
25 Robert Louis Stevenson (1905) 'A Winter's Walk in
   Carrick and Galloway – a Fragment', in *Essays of
   Travel,* Chatto and Windus, London, p. 134.
26 Maurice Lindsay (1959) *The Burns Encyclopedia,*
   Hutchinson, London, p. 248.
27 An unsuccessful attempt by John Ruthven,
   3rd Earl of Gowrie, and his brother Alexander to
   kidnap James VI; 'Logan's Castle' is a reference to
   Logan of Restalrig, who owned Fast Castle from
   1580.
28 Prince Henry was Prince of Wales, eldest son of
   James VI and I, born in Stirling Castle.
29 Chris Tabraham, 'Mary Slept Here: On the Road
   with the Queen of Scots', National Museums
   Scotland blog, 19 August 2013.
   Available at: https://blog.nms.ac.uk/
   2013/08/19/mary-slept-here-on-the-road-with-the-
   queen-of-scots.

Chapter 9

1 Patrick Wright (1985) *On Living in an Old Country: The National Past in Contemporary Britain*, Verso, London, p. 12.
2 Robert Hewison (1987) *The Heritage Industry: Britain in a Climate of Decline*, Methuen, London.
3 Ibid., p. 10.
4 David McCrone, Angela Morris and Richard Kiely (1995) *Scotland – The Brand*, Edinburgh University Press, Edinburgh, p. 21.
5 Quoted in T. Hunt, 'Monumental Mistakes; Heritage Wonks have Colonized the Past for Profit, Replacing Understanding with Kitsch', *New Statesman*, 2 December 2002.
6 The full text of the speech is available on the Prince of Wales's website.
7 Charles, Prince of Wales (1989) *A Vision of Britain: A Personal View of Architecture*, Doubleday, London.
8 Ibid., p. 9.
9 Obituary of Martin Pawley, *The Independent*, 12 April 2008.
10 Philip Wilkinson (2003) *Restoration: Discovering Britain's Hidden Architectural Treasures*, Headline, London; Philip Wilkinson (2004) *Restoration: The Story Continues*, English Heritage, Swindon; Philip Wilkinson (2006) *Restoration Village*, English Heritage, Swindon.
11 P. Wright, 'Restoration Tragedy', *The Guardian*, 13 September 2003.
12 A. Welby Pugin (1841) *True Principles of Pointed or Christian Architecture*, John Weale, London, p. 58.
13 *The Scotsman*, 11 April 1994.
14 Kitty Cruft, John Dunbar and Richard Fawcett (2006) *The Buildings of Scotland: Borders*, Yale University Press, London, p. 511.
15 Mary Miers (2017) *Highland Retreats*, Rizzoli, New York, p. 187.
16 Quoted in the Glasgow Architecture website. Available at: http://www.glasgowarchitecture. co.uk/moshe_ safdie_corrour.htm.
17 George Scott-Moncrieff (1939) *The Lowlands of Scotland*, B.T. Batsford, London, pp. 32–33, paints a very unkind picture of Abbotsford: 'the extraordinary lack of judgment of a man who could rear Abbotsford must have condemned many to "improvements" in the Scottish baronial style to the point of obliteration: as if an El Greco were to have its corners clipped, fresh detail painted in, and the whole incorporated in a vast Victorian canvas.'
18 Ian Baxter (2022) 'A Good Death for Scotland's Heritage?' Built Environment Forum Scotland. Available at https://www.befs.org.uk/latest/good-death-for-scotlands-heritage/ .
19 Sandra Dick (2022) 'What Price Heritage? Scotland's Ancient Buildings to be Left to the Elements', Herald Scotland, 30 January.

Select Bibliography

Anderson, Robert D. (2003) *The University of Edinburgh: An Illustrated History*, Edinburgh University Press, Edinburgh

Bevan, Robert (2006) *The Destruction of Memory: Architecture at War*, Reaktion Books Ltd, London

Billings, R.W. (1901) *Baronial and Ecclesiastical Antiquities of Scotland*, Oliver and Boyd, Edinburgh

Binney, Marcus (1984) *Our Vanishing Heritage*, Arlington Books, London

Binney, Marcus, Harris, John and Winnington, Emma (1980) *Lost Houses of Scotland*, SAVE Britain's Heritage, London

Borley, Lesley, ed. (1998) *Dear Maurice: Culture and Identity in 20th Century Scotland*, Tuckwell Press, East Linton

Brennan-Inglis, Janet (2014) *Scotland's Castles: Rescued, Rebuilt and Reoccupied*, History Press, Stroud

Cormack, Patrick (1978) *Heritage in Danger*, Quartet Books, London

Crawford, James et al. (2010) *Victorian Scotland*, RCAHMS, Edinburgh

Cruden, Stewart (1960) *The Scottish Castle*, Thomas Nelson and Sons, Edinburgh

Dakin, Audrey, Glendinning, Miles and MacKechnie, Aonghus (2011) *Scotland's Castle Culture*, Birlinn, Edinburgh

Davis, Michael (1996) Scots Baronial. *Mansions and Castle Restorations in the West of Scotland*, Spindrift, Ardrishaig

Dean, Marcus and Miers, Mary (1990) *Scotland's Endangered Houses*, SAVE Britain's Heritage, London

Fairbairn, Nicholas (1987) *A Life Is Too Short: Autobiography*, Vol. 1, Quartet Books, London

Fawcett, Richard (2001) *The Conservation of Architectural Ancient Monuments in Scotland: Guidance on Principles*, Historic Scotland, Edinburgh

Fleming, John (1954) *Scottish Country Houses and Gardens Open to the Public*, Country Life Books, London

Gifford, John, McWilliam, Colin and Walker, David (1984) *The Buildings of Scotland*, Penguin, London

Glendinning, Miles, MacInnes, Ranald and MacKechnie, Aonghus (1996) *A History of Scottish Architecture from the Renaissance to the Present Day*, Edinburgh University Press, Edinburgh

Glendinning, Miles and MacKechnie, Aonghus (2004) *Scottish Architecture*, Thames and Hudson, London

Glendinning, Miles and MacKechnie, Aonghus (2019) *Scotch Baronial: Architecture and National Identity in Scotland*, Bloomsbury Visual Arts, London

Gow, Ian (1997) *Scottish Houses and Gardens from the Archives of Country Life*, Aurum Press, London

Gow, Ian (2006) *Scotland's Lost Houses*, Aurum Press, London

Grimble, Ian (1984) *Castles of Scotland*, BBC, London

Hewison, Robert (1987) *The Heritage Industry: Britain in a Climate of Decline*, Methuen, London

Hill, Oliver (1953) *Scottish Castles of the Sixteenth and Seventeenth Centuries*, Country Life Books, London

Horsman, E.A., ed. (1953) *The Diary of Alfred Domett 1872–1885*, Oxford University Press, London

Jokilehto, Jukka (1999) *A History of Architectural Conservation*, Elsevier, Oxford

Kelsall, Moultrie R. and Harris, Stuart (1961) *A Future for the Past*, Oliver and Boyd, Edinburgh

Liddiard, Robert (2005) *Castles in Context: Power, Symbolism and Landscape, 1066 to 1500*, Central Books, London

Lowenthal, David (1998) *The Heritage Crusade and the Spoils of History*, Cambridge University Press, Cambridge

Macaulay, Rose (1953) *Pleasure of Ruins*, Walker & Co., New York

MacGibbon, David and Ross, Thomas (1887–92), *The Castellated and Domestic Architecture of Scotland*, 5 vols, Thomas and Archibald Constable

Maxwell-Irving, Alastair M.T. (2000) *The Border Towers of Scotland: The West March*, Alastair M.T. Maxwell-Irving, Blairlogie

Maxwell-Irving, Alastair M.T. (2014) *The Border Towers of Scotland 2: Their Evolution and Architecture*, Alastair M.T. Maxwell-Irving, Blairlogie

McCrone, David, Morris, Angela and Kiely, Richard (1995) *Scotland – The Brand*, Edinburgh University Press, Edinburgh

McKean, Charles (2001) *The Scottish Chateau: The Country House of Renaissance Scotland*, Sutton, Stroud

McKean, Charles (2006) 'A Scottish Problem with Castles', *Historical Research*, vol. 79, no. 204, pp. 166–69

Miers, Mary 'To Restore or Not to Restore?', *Country Life*, 22 September 2005

Morris, William (1877) Manifesto of the Society for the Protection of Ancient Buildings (SPAB). Available at: http://www.marxists.org/archive/morris/works/1877/spabman.htm

Oram, Richard (2008) 'Castles, Concepts and Contexts: Castle Studies in Scotland in Retrospect and Prospect', *Château Gaillard*, vol. 23, pp. 349–59

Oram, Richard (2010) 'Medieval Scottish castles: some insights, images and perceptions from archaeological and historical investigation', *Château Gaillard*, vol. 24, pp. 213–22

Peacock, Alan, ed. (1998) *Does the Past Have a Future? The Political Economy of Heritage*, Institute of Economic Affairs, London

Pendlebury, John (2009) *Conservation in the Age of Consensus*, Routledge, Abingdon

HMSO (1950) *Report of the Gowers Committee on Houses of Outstanding Historic or Architectural Interest*, HMSO, Edinburgh

The late Miss Elizabeth Hume Ross (1969) 'James McLaren, Schoolmaster', *The Book of the Old Edinburgh Club*, vol. 33, part 1

Ross, William C.A. (1934) *The Royal High School*, Oliver and Boyd, Edinburgh

Ruskin, John (1889) *The Seven Lamps of Architecture*, Sunnyside, London

Salter, Mike (1993–95) *The Castles of Scotland* (5 vols), Folly Publications, Malvern

Sanderson, Margaret H. (1992) *Robert Adam and Scotland: Portait of an Architect*, HMSO, Edinburgh

Saville, Richard (1996) *Bank of Scotland, A History 1695–1995*, Edinburgh University Press, Edinburgh

Schomberg, Scott (1976) 'Castles and Country Houses', in R. Prentice (ed.), *The National Trust for Scotland Guide*, Jonathan Cape, London

Scotland's Ancient Heritage (1934) *The Special Summer Number of the S.M.T. Magazine*

Scott-Moncrieff, George (1939) *The Lowlands of Scotland*, B.T. Batsford, London

Simpson, George, and Towers, J.F. (2014) *Towers and Castles of East Lothian: A Collection of Photographs Comparing East Lothian's Castles of Today with the Survey Carried Out by David MacGibbon and Thomas Ross in 1887–1892*, Gullane & Dirleton History Society

Simpson, James (1998) *British Standard Guide to the Principles of the Conservation of Historic Buildings* [BS7913], BSI, London

Stamp, Gavin (2004) 'When an Owner Gives Up', *Apollo*, July 2004

Stell, Geoffrey, Shaw, John and Storrier, Susan, eds (2003) *Scotland's Buildings*, Scottish Life and Society series, Vol. 3, Tuckwell Press, East Lothian

Stirling Maxwell, Sir John (1938) *Shrines and Homes of Scotland*, Alexander, MacLehose and Co., London

Strong, Roy, Binney, Marcus and Harris, John (1974) *The Destruction of the Country House*, Thames and Hudson, London

Tabraham, Christopher (1988) 'The Scottish Medieval Towerhouse as Lordly Residence in the Light of Recent Excavation', *Proceedings of the Society of Antiquaries of Scotland*, vol. 118, pp. 267–76

Tranter, Nigel (1962–70) *The Fortified House in Scotland* (5 vols), Mercat Press, Edinburgh

Victoria, Queen (1861) *Leaves from the Journal of our Lives in the Highlands 1848 to 1861*, Smith, Elder & Co., London, 1868

Wales, Charles, Prince of (1989) *A Vision of Britain: A Personal View of Architecture*, Doubleday, London

Walker, David (1984) 'The Architecture of MacGibbon and Ross: The Background to the Books', in D.J. Breeze (ed.), *Studies in Scottish Antiquity*, John Donald, Edinburgh

Walker, David (2000) 'The Adaptation and Restoration of Tower Houses: An Historical Review from the Reign of Charles II to the Present', in Robert Clow (ed.), *Restoring Scotland's Castles*, John Smith and Son, Glasgow

Wemyss, Charles (2014) *The Noble Houses of Scotland*, Prestel, London

Wilkinson, Philip (2003) *Restoration: Discovering Britain's Hidden Architectural Treasures*, Headline, London

Wilkinson, Philip (2004) *Restoration: The Story Continues*, English Heritage, London

Woodward, Christopher (2002) *In Ruins*, Vintage, London

Wright, Patrick (1985) *On Living in an Old Country: The National Past in Contemporary Britain*, Verso, London

Zeune, Joachim (1992) *The Last Scottish Castles*, Marie L. Leidorf, Buch am Erlbach

Ziolkowski, Theodore (1998) *The View from the Tower: Origins of an Antimodernist Image*, Princeton University Press, Princeton, NJ

Index of Castles and Other Buildings

General Index